AF334157

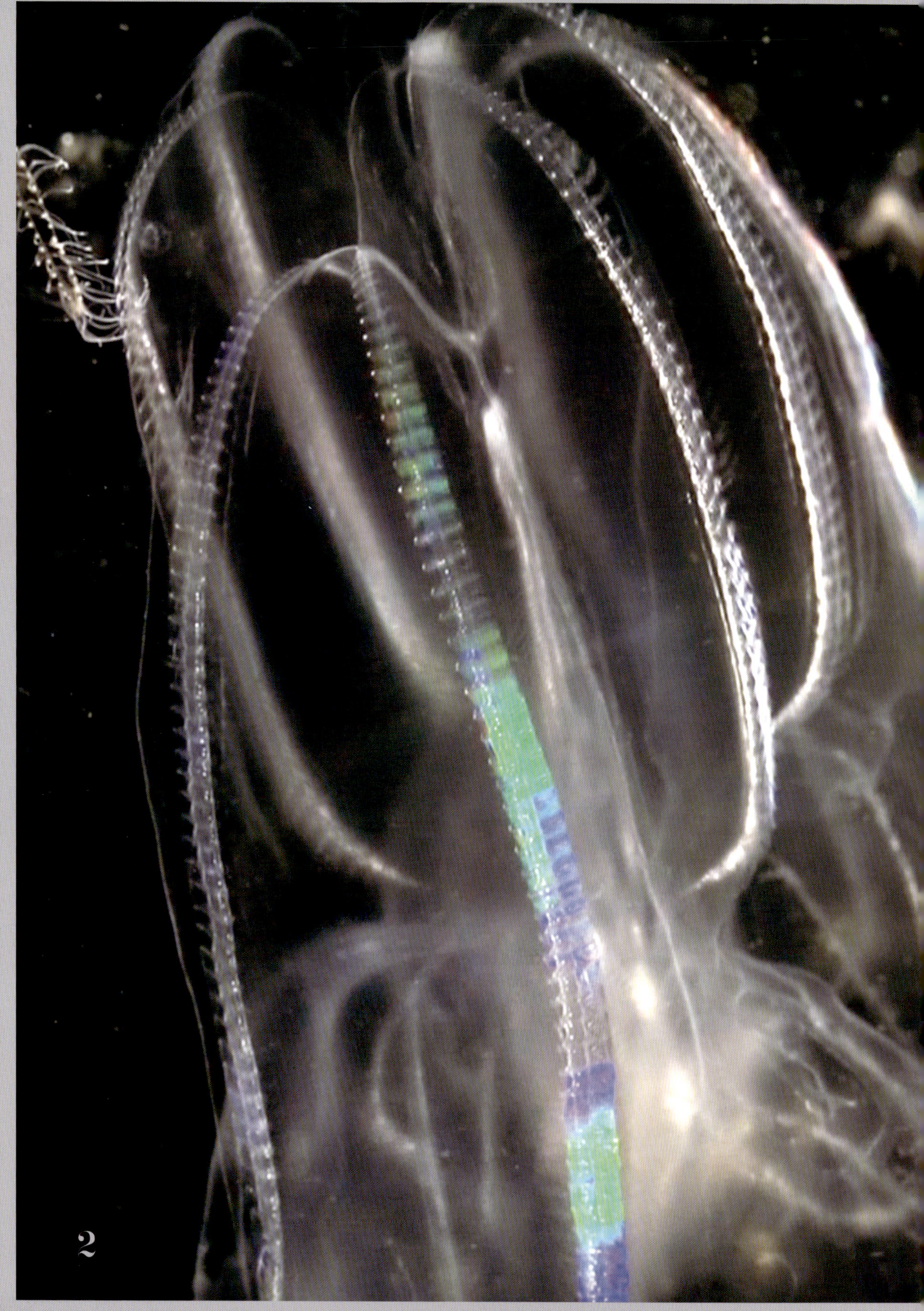

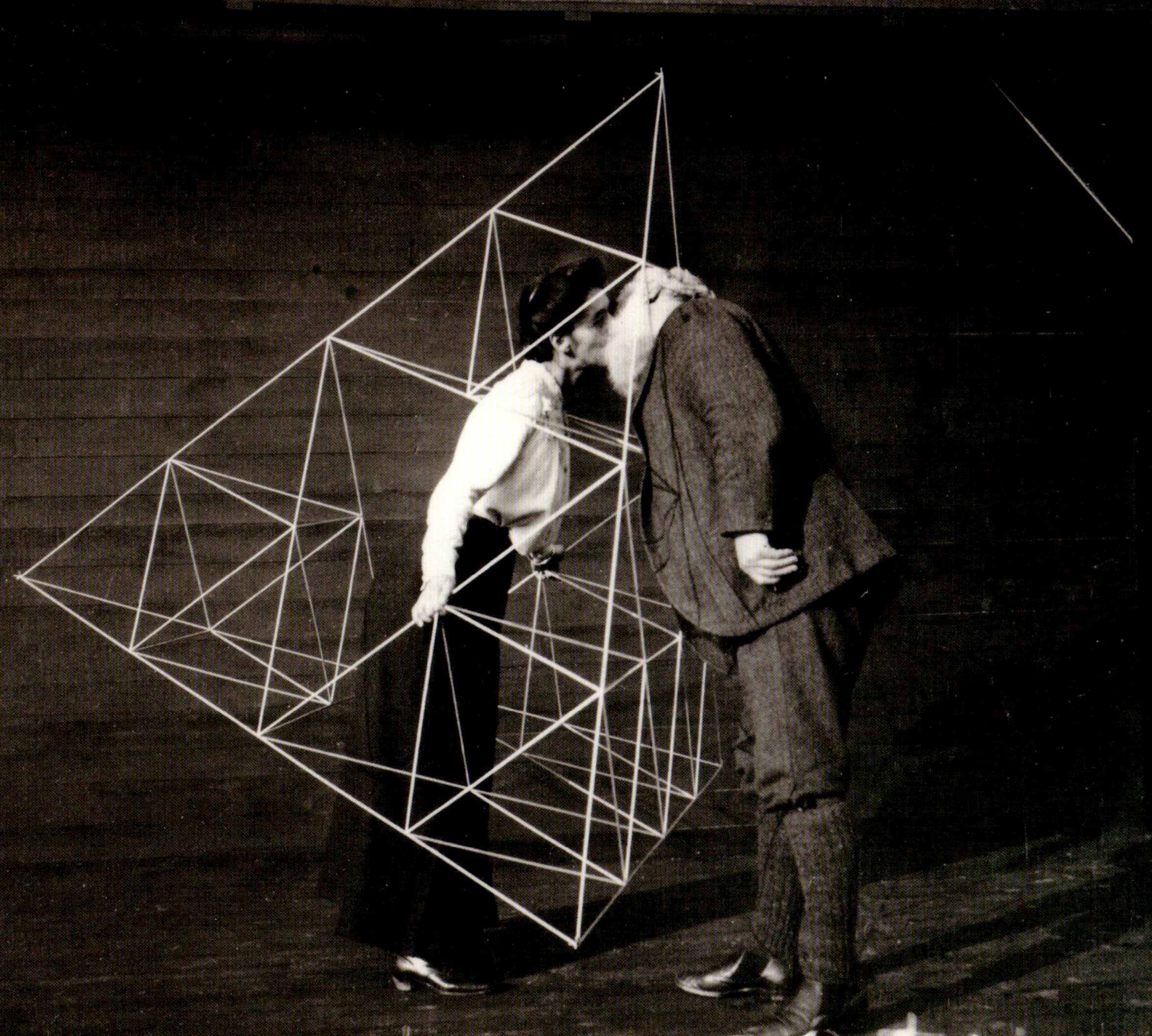

3

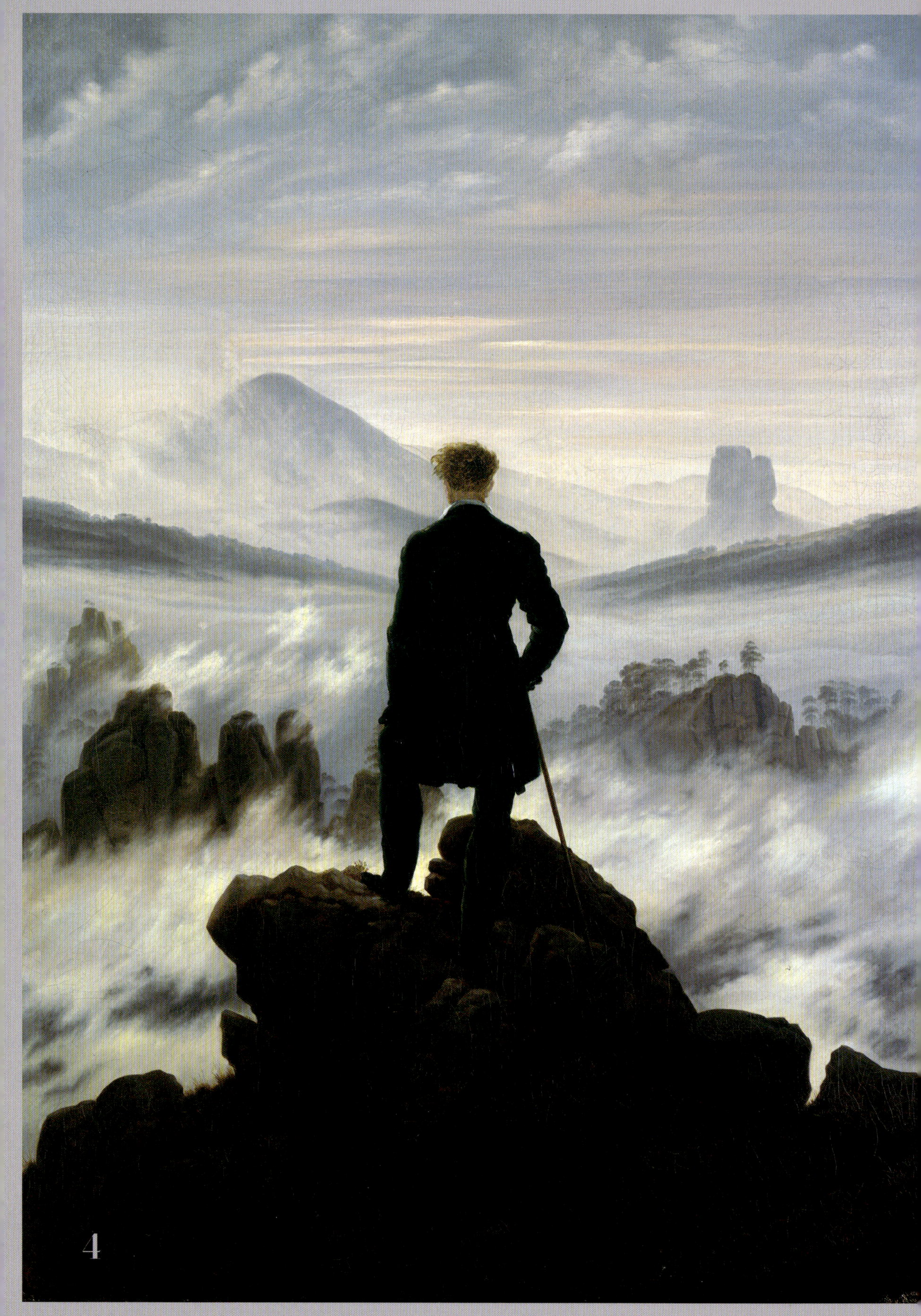

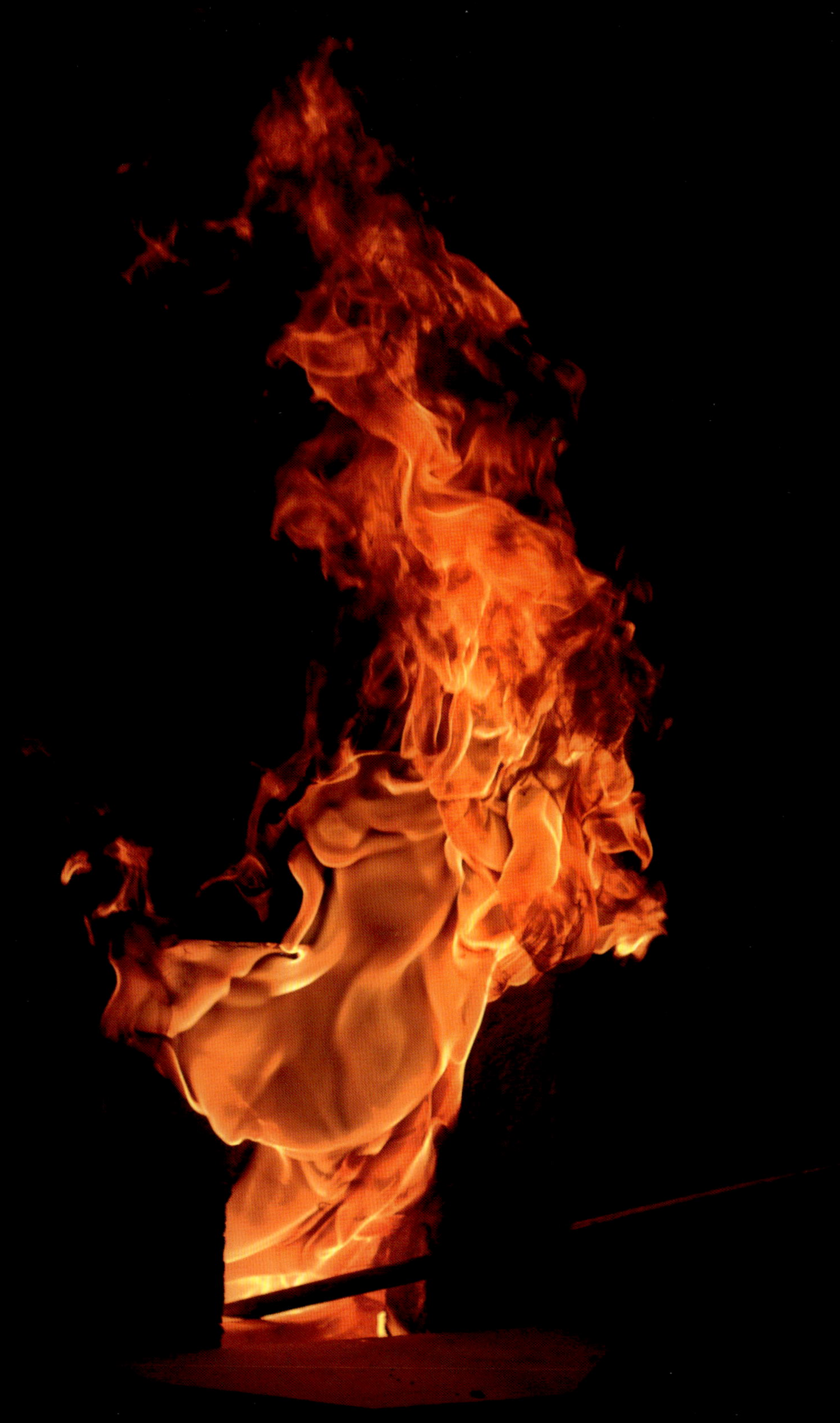

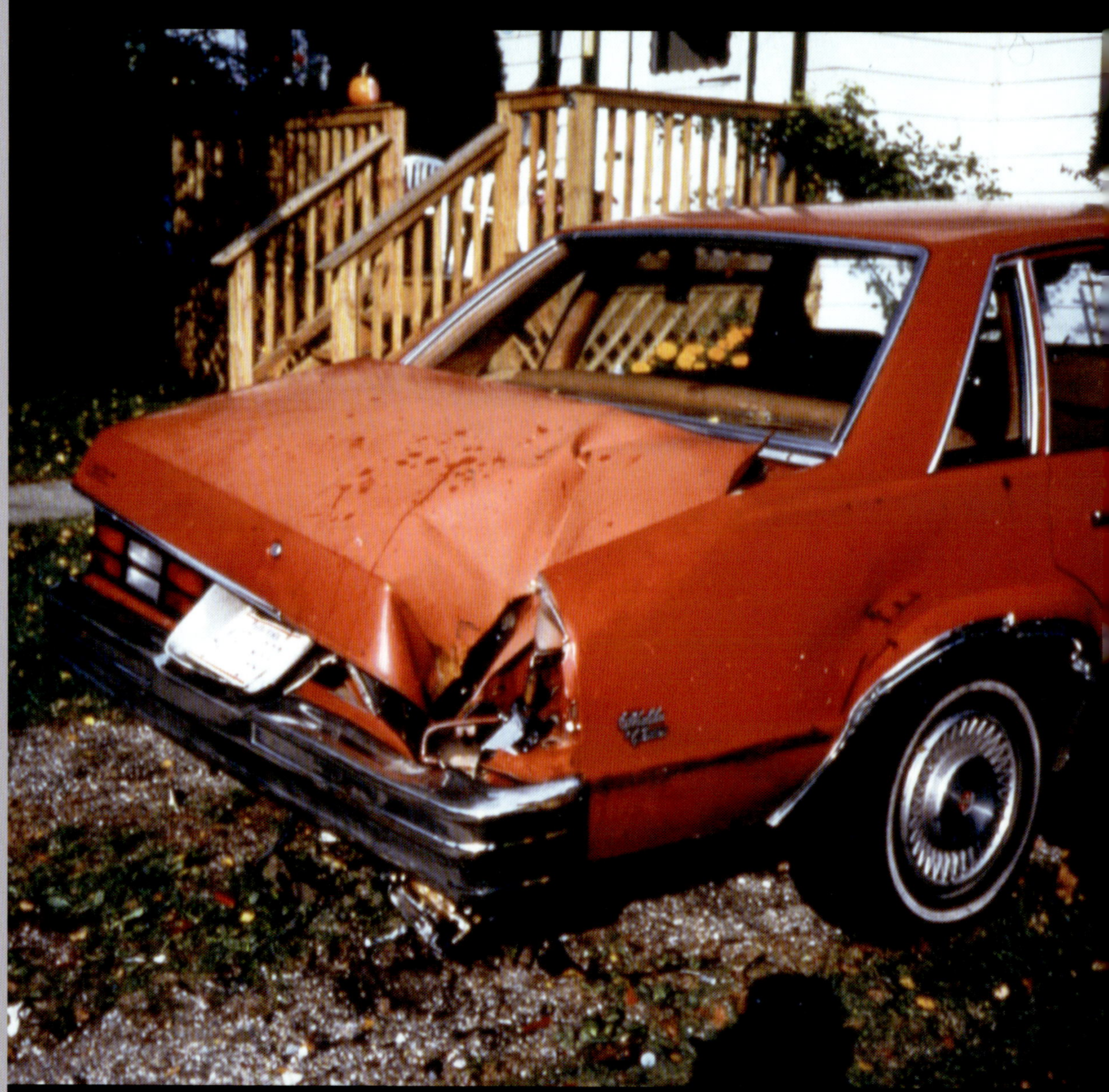

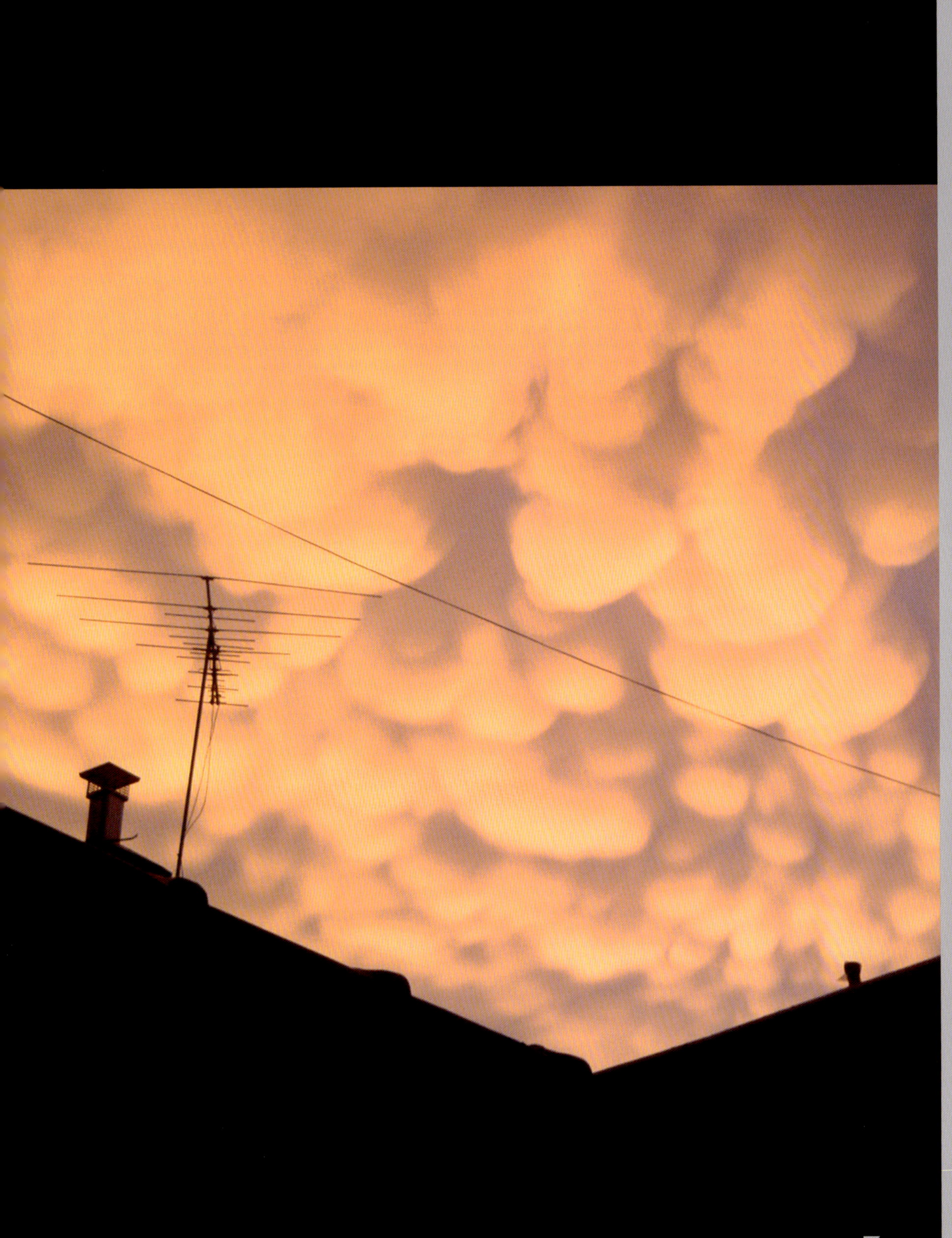

Joules of the Universe

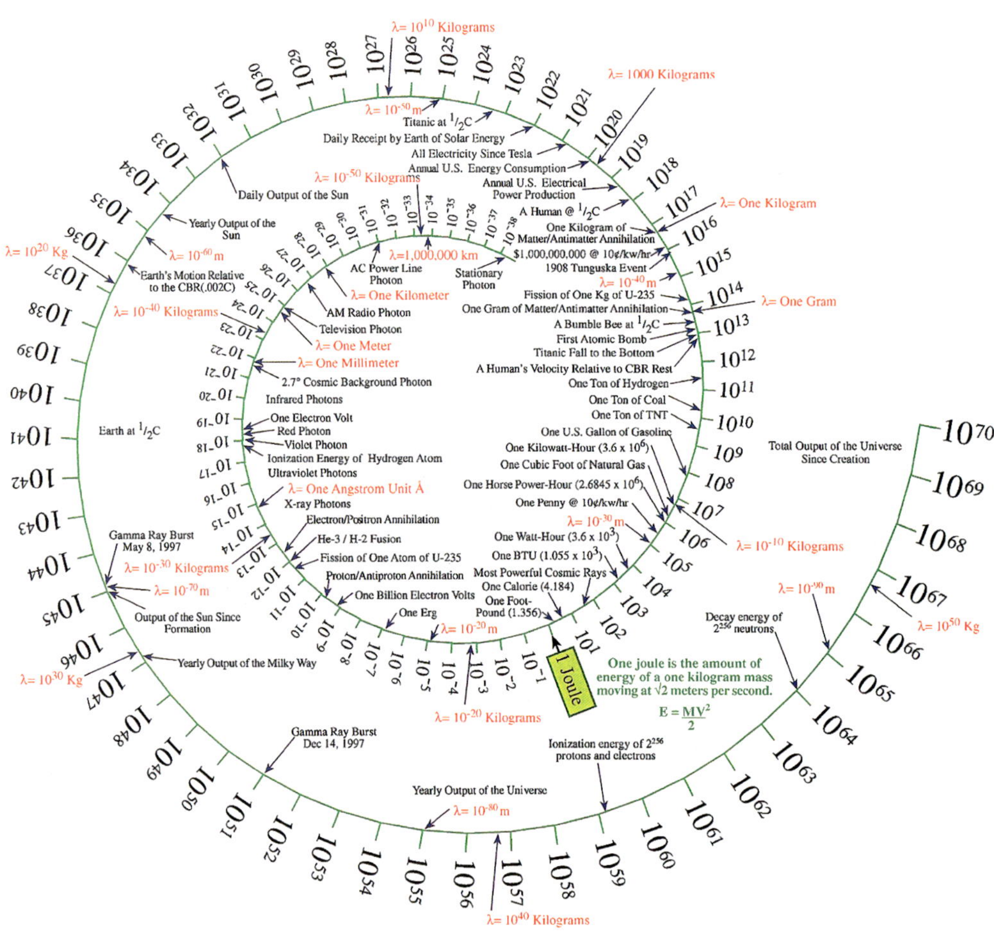

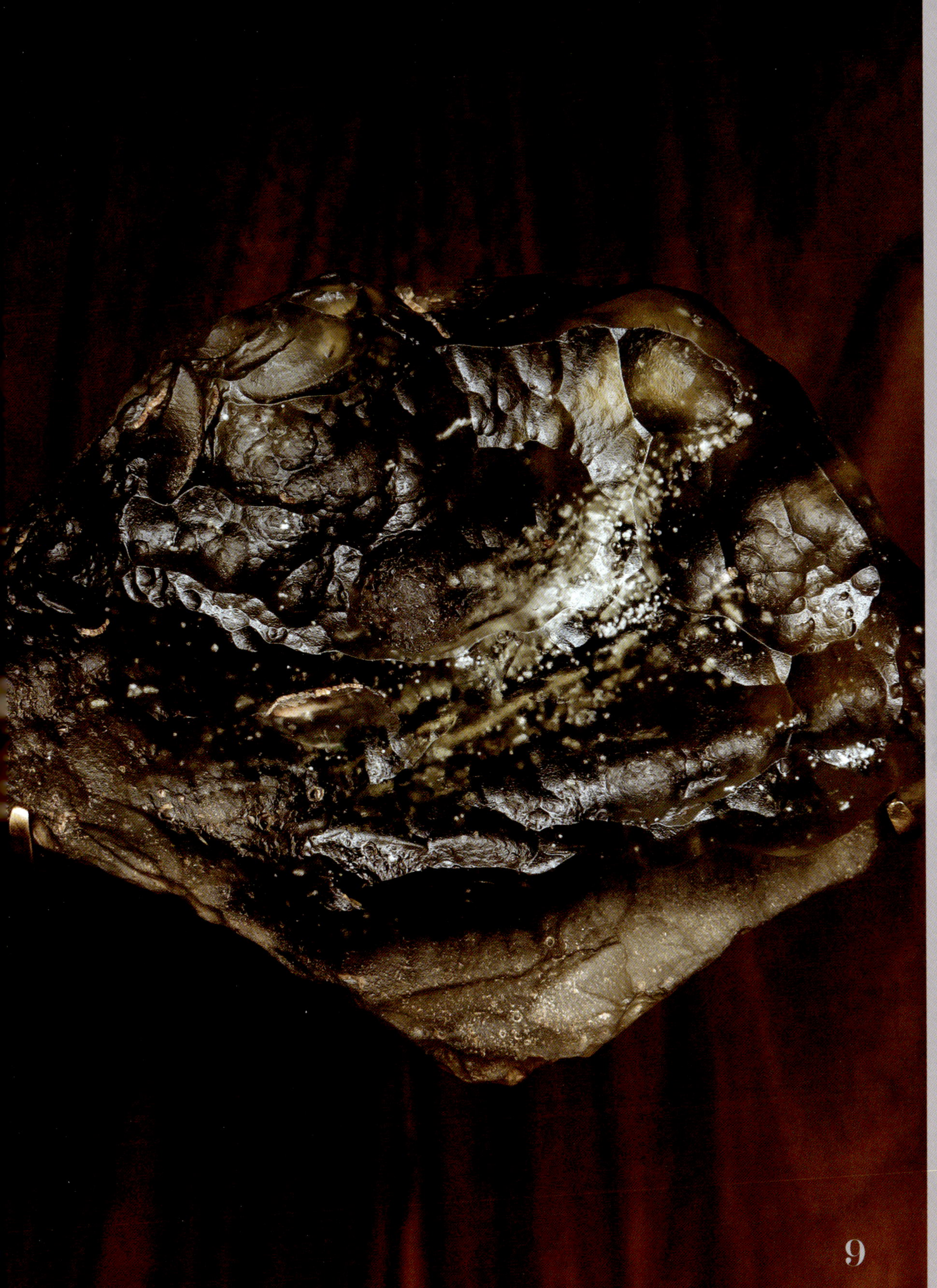

"You remain in inner child by every day. You about the futu worry about t just explode.

1. From Sam Weller, *Listen to the Echoes: The Ray Bradbury Interviews* (Chicago: Stop Smiling Book, 2010). Originally recorded at Comic-Con 2010 by Jeff Goldsmith, maker of the free storytelling app Backstory.

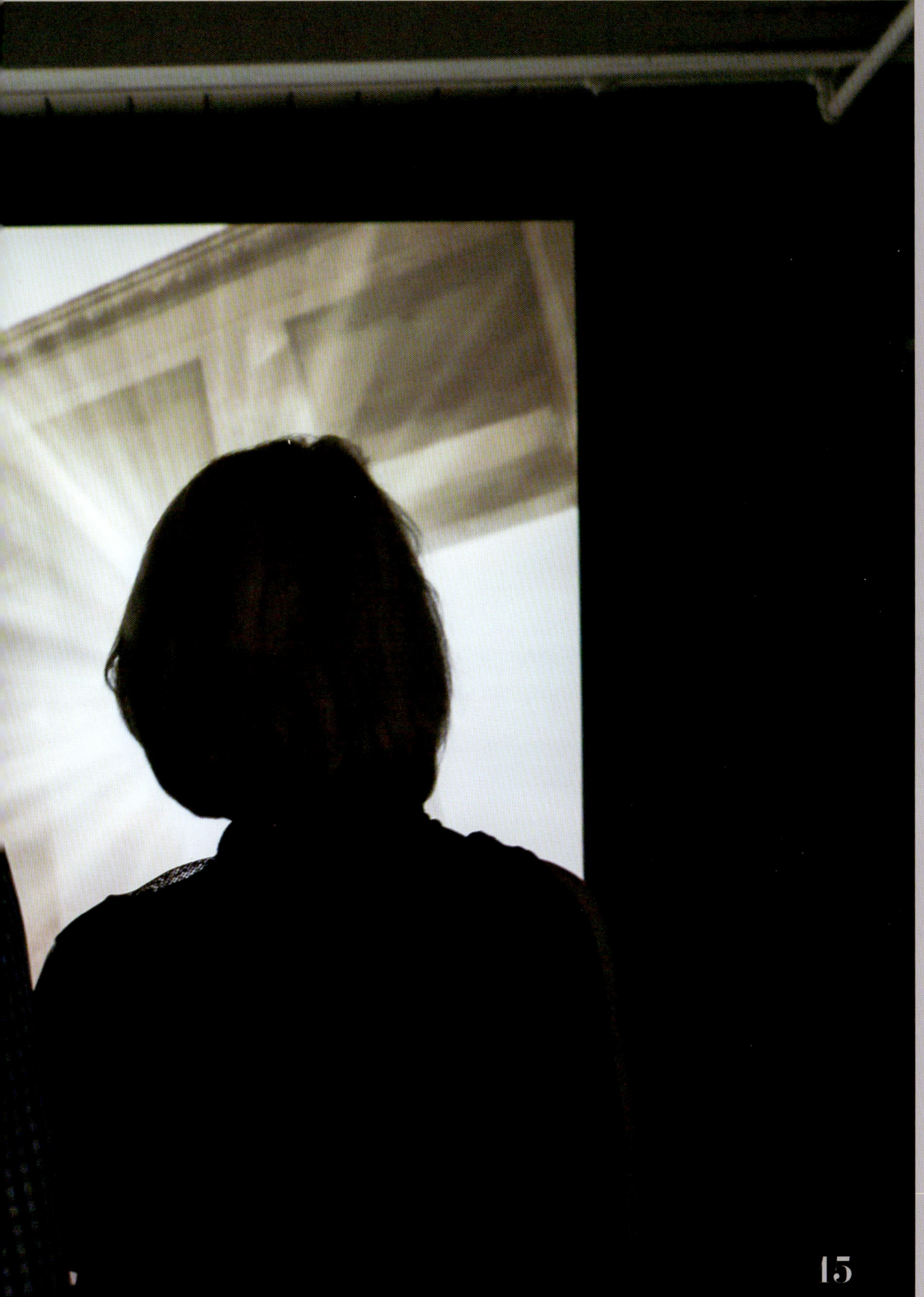

Foreword
by Joseph C. Thompson, Director, MASS MoCA

The state of wonder has fragile borders, as described in this insightful publication
replete with wide-eyed contributors. True wonder—soft-gasping, slack-jawed, eye-
riveting wonder—doesn't come easily to most adults in these days of distraction.
Museums—along with places like the Grand Canyon—are often viewed as locations
where wonder just might make a rare appearance in our lives. But often, museums
fail to deliver, or rather deliver in different ways, behind a juggernaut of didactics,
educational programs, and interpretive tools—all things that make viewing art more
understandable, more informed and comprehensible, but also somehow less full of
wonder. To fall under the charms of wonderment, you have to be willing to get a bit
lost, to become temporarily disoriented, to disintermediate. If you are a museum,
that means you have to provide the opportunities for your patrons (and artists) to
disappear into the rabbit hole, agape, untethered to things our eyes and minds may
think we already know. We like to think that's possible here at MASS MoCA, at least
for the curious and the brave.

   With its labyrinthine layout of nineteenth-century mill buildings—some vast and
light filled, others dark and narrow, most meeting at odd angles, walls askew and
floors a-tilt—our visitors certainly do have to be a bit more intrepid, more open to
unexpected pathways, than in many custom-built museums of modern and more
logical design. To my knowledge, we've not yet lost any patrons permanently, though
we have discovered more than a few in—let's just say—unlikely spots, fixated on

unlikely things: a spacecraft that has seemingly just crashed-landed onsite or a copse of sky-yearning trees, root-side up.

There is something about the gymnasium-like floors, the rough-hewn finishes, and the raw, convoluted quality of the architecture at MASS MoCA that invites exploration; a kind of primitive imperative that draws our visitors athletically across the site, searching, looking closely. Artists, too, take the opportunity to explore: intervening in our site in surprising ways, unearthing histories, further inciting visitors to seek out the wonder around them. For example, for this exhibition Julianne Swartz's <u>In Harmonicity, The Tonal Walkway</u>—a new sound installation in the long industrial walkway between our lobby and the <u>Sol LeWitt Wall Drawing Retrospective</u>—fills what would normally be seen as an interstitial space with an unexpected and haunting choir of voices, including those of Roomful of Teeth, the marvelous all-voice ensemble that annually makes MASS MoCA its rehearsal and production lab. Megan and Murray McMillan's installation, <u>In What Distant Sky</u>, started as a rather terrifying piece of filmmaking, with fabricated coal boulders dangled within a vast coal bin in our quasi-abandoned Boiler House in a manner that would make even Michael Heizer gasp. The charred result somehow channels the sublime nature of late-stage industrial decay, even as it brings visitors into an utterly new relationship with our gallery spaces. Jason de Haan's gold ring, placed on a branch of the blaze maple tree that marks MASS MoCA's front door, will gradually be consumed into the grain of the wood. Among the other wondrous things you might find if you look hard in the dark corners and crevices are the <u>Pholcidae</u>; this squad of cellar spiders offers traces of the fauna-art propagated and liberated here for the summer of 2016 by Pierre Huyghe. Who knows how long they will be with us....

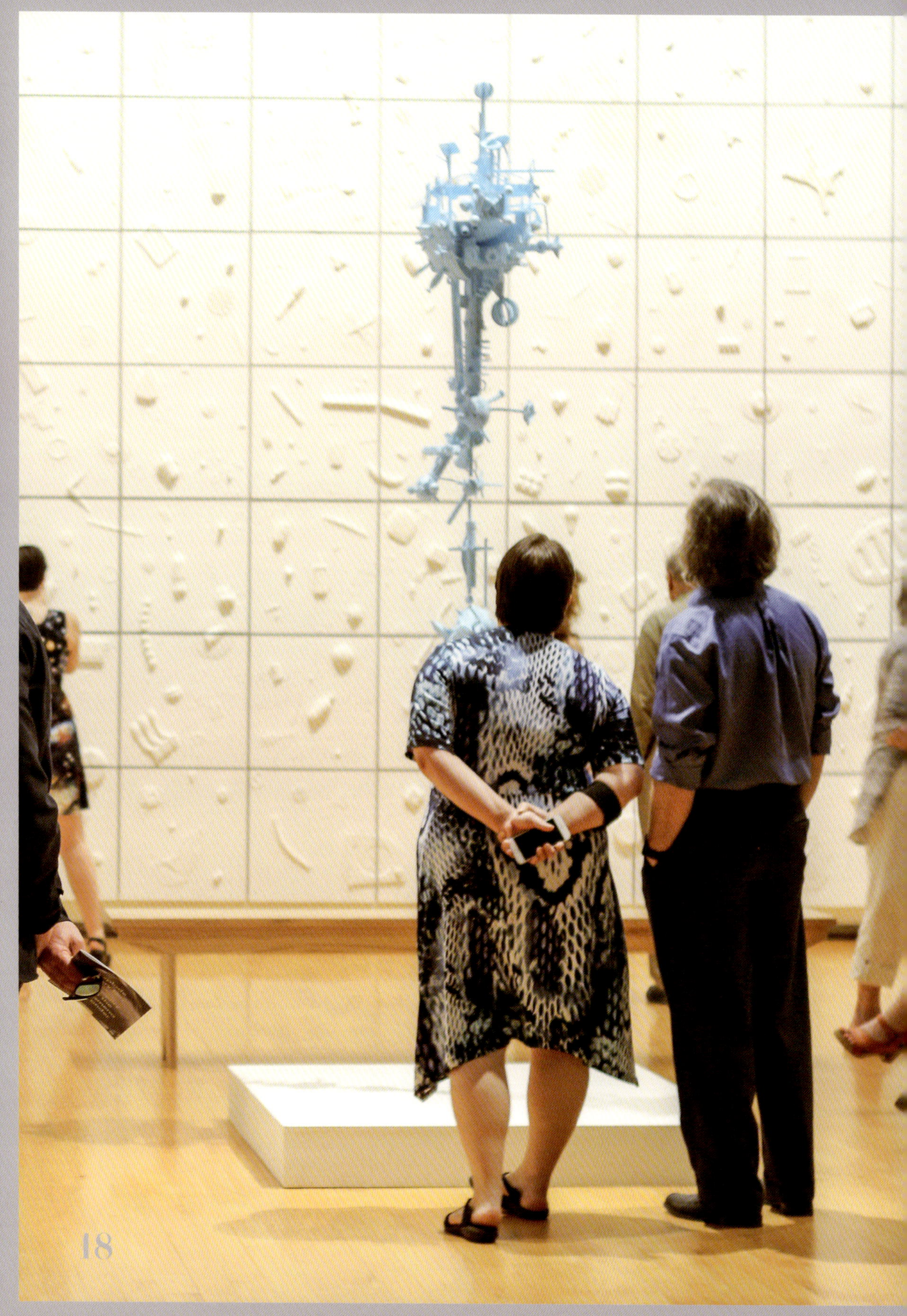

To accomplish this it was crucial to set the stage, to provide prompts through the visual and experiential. We started visiting artists' studios and asking questions such as: "What is your earliest childhood memory of wonder?" and "How does wonder present itself to you in the studio?" We heard extraordinary stories and aha moments, leading us to realize that what we were looking for was a group of artists who are attuned to wonder in their work, who explode every day. The conversations were the impetus for the questionnaires that run through this book, answered by every artist in the exhibition. In them, you will find artists talking about wonder through their own experience of it, often vulnerably sharing these moments for the first time. In addition to these texts, each artist was asked to submit a "wonder image" so that you, the reader, can be surprised by the moments of awe that have inspired this group—from art historical images and personal photos to images of clouds and the cosmos.

In addition to the artists, it was important to Sean and me that we bring in a variety of voices to write about the different facets of wonder; we see this as a guidebook, picking up where Descartes left off in 1649 and bringing wonder into the now, exploring it through art, philosophy, science, psychology, humor, religion, literature, and most importantly, humanity. To that end, we have writers like filmmaker Sam Green, graphic designer Stefan Sagmeister, and astronomer Jill Tarter next to art historian Barbara Maria Stafford, writer Lawrence Weschler, curator and theologian Steven Holmes, and behavioral psychologist Kay Redfield Jamison; we have also added blogger Maria Popova, poet Mary Ruefle, and comedian Robin Ince for good measure. Rather than a traditional ordering of artists and texts, we see the structure of both the book and exhibition functioning like a constellation—a nebulous form in which different nodes can connect to create thoughts, images, and cohesion in a variety of ways. We want our audience to treat this as an experience.

At a time when more and more information is available to us in the blink of an eye, when more and more is known, this exhibition and publication proffer a radical call to knowing less, to allowing ourselves to exist in the liminality of wonder, in a space between knowing and not knowing. Perhaps, since we started with Einstein's theory, it is best to end with his words: "The fairest thing we can experience is the mysterious.... He who knows it not and can no longer wonder, no longer feel amazement, is as good as dead. A snuffed-out candle."[3] We hope this exhibition and publication will keep your candle alit with an explosion every day.

...

1. Lawrence M. Krauss, "Finding Beauty in the Darkness," *The New York Times*, February 11, 2016. nytimes.com/2016/02/14/opinion/sunday/finding-beauty-in-the-darkness.html?smid=fb-share&_r=2

2. Krauss, "Finding Beauty."

3. Krista Tippett, *Einstein's God: Conversations About Science and the Human Spirit* (New York: Penguin Books, 2010), p. 23. This quote comes from Einstein's text *The World as I See It* (1956).

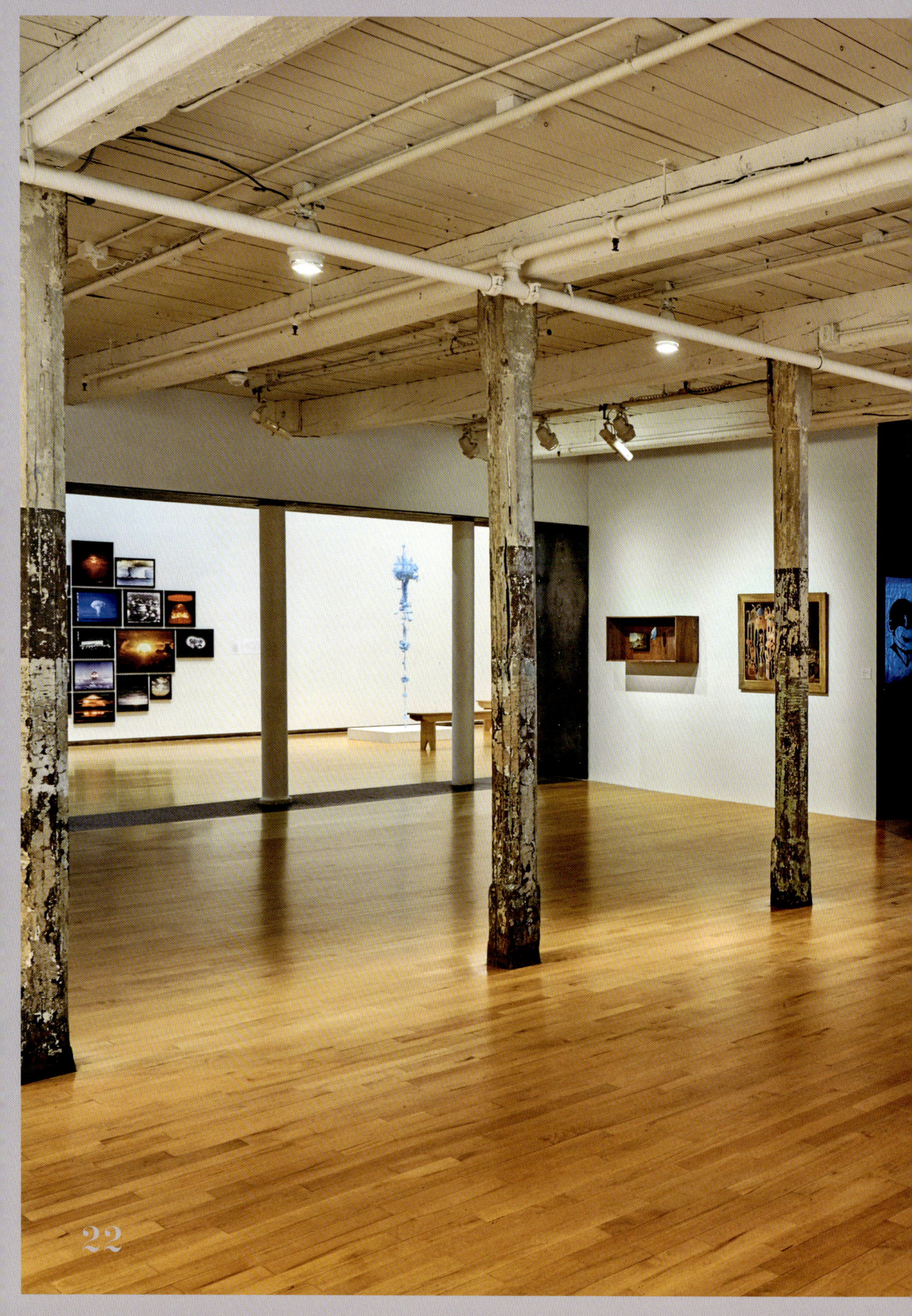

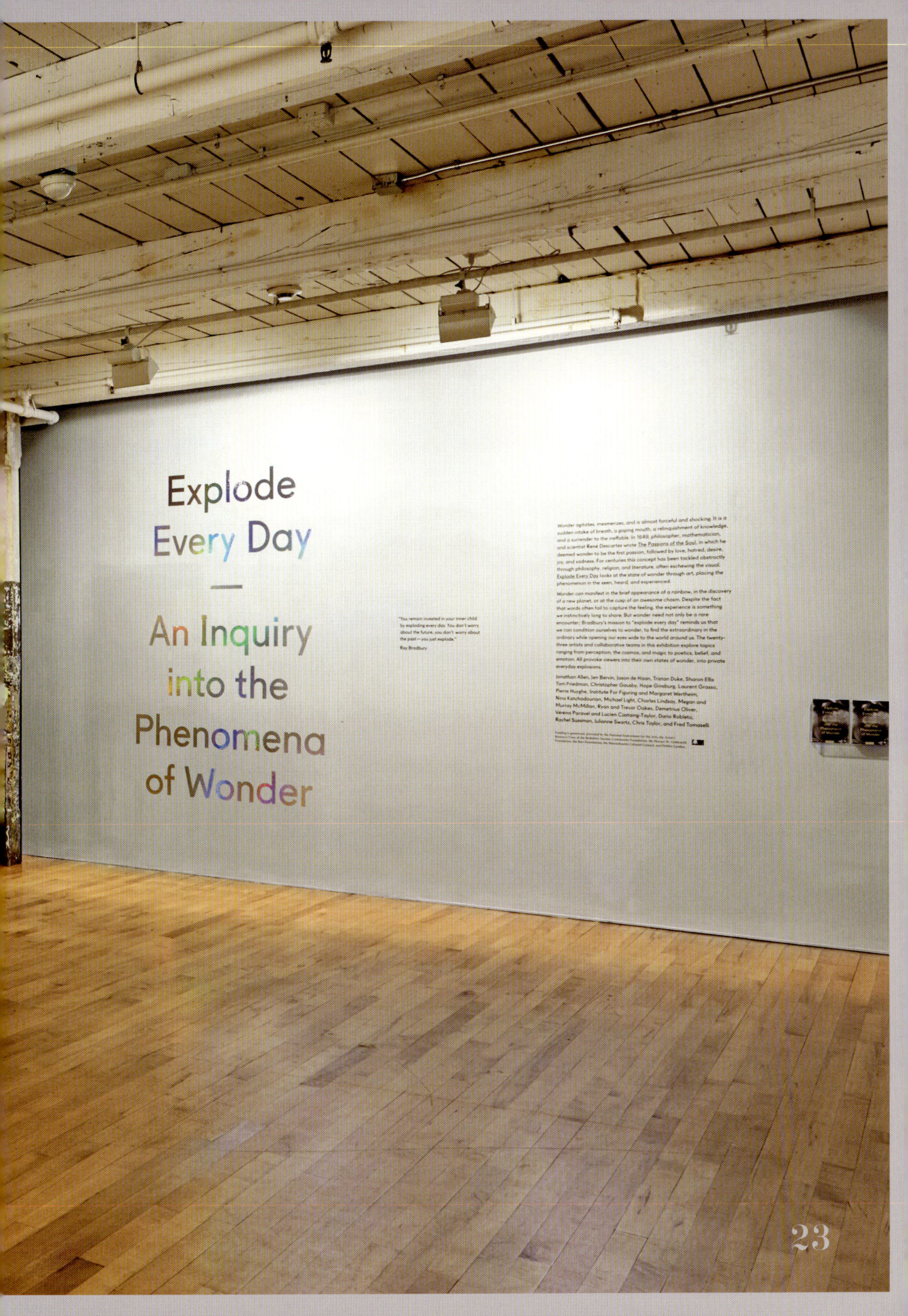

Explode
Every Day
—
An Inquiry
into the
Phenomena
of Wonder

"You remain invested in your inner child
by exploding every day. You don't worry
about the future, you don't worry about
the past — you just explode."

Ray Bradbury

Wonder agitates, mesmerizes, and is almost forceful and shocking. It is a
sudden intake of breath, a gaping mouth, a relinquishment of knowledge,
and a surrender to the ineffable. In 1649, philosopher, mathematician,
and scientist René Descartes wrote The Passions of the Soul, in which he
deemed wonder to be the first passion, followed by love, hatred, desire,
joy, and sadness. For centuries this concept has been tackled abstractly
through philosophy, religion, and literature, often eschewing the visual.
Explode Every Day looks at the state of wonder through art, placing the
phenomenon in the seen, heard, and experienced.

Wonder can manifest in the brief appearance of a rainbow, in the discovery
of a new planet, or at the cusp of an awesome chasm. Despite the fact
that words often fail to capture the feeling, the experience is something
we instinctively long to share. But wonder need not only be a rare
encounter; Bradbury's mission to "explode every day" reminds us that
we can condition ourselves to wonder, to find the extraordinary in the
ordinary while opening our eyes wide to the world around us. The twenty-
three artists and collaborative teams in this exhibition explore topics
ranging from perception, the cosmos, and magic to poetics, belief, and
emotion. All provoke viewers into their own states of wonder, into private
everyday explosions.

Jonathan Allen, Jen Bervin, Jason de Haan, Tristan Duke, Sharon Ellis
Tom Friedman, Christopher Gausby, Hope Ginsburg, Laurent Grasso,
Pierre Huyghe, Institute For Figuring and Margaret Wertheim,
Nina Katchadourian, Michael Light, Charles Lindsay, Megan and
Murray McMillan, Ryan and Trevor Oakes, Demetrius Oliver,
Verena Paravel and Lucien Castaing-Taylor, Dario Robleto,
Rachel Sussman, Julianne Swartz, Chris Taylor, and Fred Tomaselli

Funding is generously provided by the National Endowment for the Arts, the Artist's
Resource Trust of the Berkshire Taconic Community Foundation, the Horace W. Goldsmith
Foundation, the Barr Foundation, the Massachusetts Cultural Council, and Debbie Landau

Unknown Unknowns: An Inquiry into Wonder, the Rainbow, and the Aesthetics of Every Day Experiences

by Denise Markonish

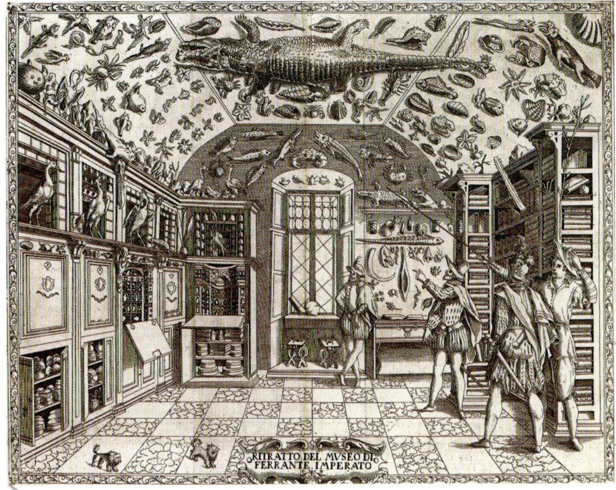

Wunderkammer, copper etching of the Natural History Collection of the Neapolitan Apothecary Ferrante Imperato, the earliest known depiction of a Nature Cabinet; frontispiece of Imperato, Ferrante, Dell'Historia Naturale, Naples, 1599 (here, as the title plate of the second edition, Venice 1672)

our ability to see all sides of a thing, which again is dangerous.[19] Now, we can't be arrested all the time, but Descartes is so cautious that he seems to want us to acknowledge rather than experience wonder.

The difference between naming and experiencing is at the heart of the dichotomous relationship between wonder and curiosity, a relationship of binaries like intent vs. surprise, yearning vs. satisfaction, or passivity vs. action. But it is not so simple, for wonder and curiosity are entwined rather than merely oppositional, they can lead to each other, moving in both directions. This comingling became evident in the Renaissance "Cabinet of Curiosity" or "Wunderkammer," nomenclature that further confuses the terms. In their book <u>Wonders and the Order of Nature</u>, Lorraine J. Daston and Katharine Park note that "Wunderkammern contained precious materials, exotica and antiquities, specimens of exquisite workmanship, and natural and artificial oddities—all crammed together in order to dazzle the onlooker. If each object by itself elicited wonder, all of them densely arrayed floor to ceiling or drawer upon drawer could only amplify the visitor's gasp of mingled astonishment and admiration."[20] They go on to state that "each object taken by itself could qualify as a 'curiosity' in at least one of three senses … meticulous workmanship … lack of function … a curiosity might excite a desire to know about the object in all its odd particularity."[21] So here again, while the individual object is curious, the experience of many of them, the excess of them, becomes wonder.

While wonder and curiosity are bedfellows, there are real differences between the two, particularly the state of not knowing and the ineffable.

Wonder alone resides in this space; once we move to knowing, to seeking out explanation, we are in the realm of curiosity. Curiosity is not dangerous; it can't stop us or overtake us. Curiosity is in the mind. Wonder is in the body. That may be why Johann Wolfgang von Goethe really had it right when in <u>Faust</u> (1790) he writes, "'In the beginning was the Word.' / Already I am stopped. It seems absurd. / The Word does not deserve the highest prize, I must translate it otherwise / If I am well inspired and not blind. / It says: In the beginning was the Mind. / Ponder that first line, wait and see, / Lest you should write too hastily. / Is mind the all-creating source? It ought to say: In the beginning there was Force. / Yet something warns me as I grasp the pen / That my translation must be changed again. / The spirit helps me. Now it is exact. / I write: In the beginning was the Act."[22] Though Goethe is not speaking of wonder in particular, he gets at the activeness of the state, for he throws out "Word" and "Mind" before moving on to "Force" and "Act," reaffirming that it is poetry and art that should be the seat of wonder.

Merging the poetic and philosophical, Christopher Gausby would have felt at home with Descartes and even more so in the Middle Ages, the height of the illuminated manuscript. The term manuscript comes from the Latin for "handwritten," fitting since these illuminated books, dating as far back as 400 to 600 AD and continuing through the invention of the Gutenberg press in the fifteenth century, were painstakingly rendered by hand, lavishly illustrated and gold leafed. It is somewhat curious that, in the 1970s, Gausby would start to make his own illuminated manuscripts. Inspired by Thomas Merton's <u>Contemplation in a World of Action</u> (1965), a text marrying philosophy and theology, and Edward Johnston's calligraphic manuscript <u>Writing</u> & <u>Illuminating</u> & <u>Lettering</u> (1906), he taught himself the necessary techniques: calligraphy, paint production, gold leafing, and burnishing, etc. Gausby started with writings from his <u>Philosophic Journal</u> (1979–92), a collection of short texts and musings on religion, life, and art, including, "The goal of my own art is the 'literal' expression of Word made flesh, the creation of a graphically incarnated metaphysics through the calligraphic and collagic transcription and illumination of my own and other's writing and ideas…"[23] His first foray, <u>Notebook I</u> (1982), took fourteen years, but he would go on to make additional notebooks, placing his own writing alongside philosophic texts, passages in Latin, personal correspondences, and art historical references. In <u>Notebook IV</u> (1990–91), he quotes Vincent van Gogh: "We must work as much and with as few pretensions as a peasant, if we want to last."[24] <u>Notebook V</u> (1993) contains a homage to Joseph Cornell, with a collage of Cornell's image and objects the artist has dimensionally in space, yet we can see the flat surface of the plane on which they exist. Another way of looking at a hologram is akin to recording music: with audio recording, invisible sound waves are captured so that they can be replayed, just as light is "replayed" for us in holography. Although they are usually created with lasers, there is a simpler way of making holograms. In 1995, research engineer and scientific hobbyist William J. Beaty published a paper about "abrasion holography" or hand-drawn holograms,[35] requiring only a compass and plastic. The aha moment for Beaty came as he walked through a parking lot; he noticed that the sunlight hitting a car hood produced a holographic image of a hand hovering above the car's surface. He realized that someone using a hand mitt had abraded the surface of the car when polishing it and that the angles of the scratches combined with direct sunlight to create a hologram. Duke, already involved in making laser holograms, had been asking himself, Photography is to drawing as holography is to what? This line of questioning led to Beaty's work and the realization that the answer lay in scratch holograms, both because of their link back to drawing and how they offer a more tangible, or human, way to understand holography. To that end, Duke began to further investigate and extrapolate upon Beaty's simple technique, diving deep into research to refine scratch holography, figuring out how to better isolate line, color, and brightness, and even create further innovations that would allow these to be placed onto actual vinyl records.[36] In the <u>above/below</u> series (2016), Duke represents the Platonic solids, the most elemental forms, scratching them onto nickel-plated copper disks: tetrahedron (four sides), cube (six sides), octahedron (eight sides), dodecahedron (twelve sides), and icosahedron (twenty sides). Duke's plates sit on pedestals equipped with motors (the plate attaches to the motor through a center pin, much like a record player), under focused overhead light. The slowly turning plates hover just above the pedestal surface, and then the holographic shapes float further above the plate, turning so that we can see every side of their structure. The mystery here is that there is no mystery; looking at the plates reveals their scratches and the hand of the artist. This sense of the hand in the midst of the magic, along with Duke's steadfast pursuit of innovation and investigation into holography, is what makes the simple shapes that float before our eyes all the more wondrous to behold.

     In 1413, painter Filippo Brunelleschi demonstrated the geometrical method of perspective by painting the outlines of buildings onto a mirror. When he completed his tracing, he realized that all the lines converged on the horizon. Twin brothers Ryan and Trevor Oakes have taken up this cause in

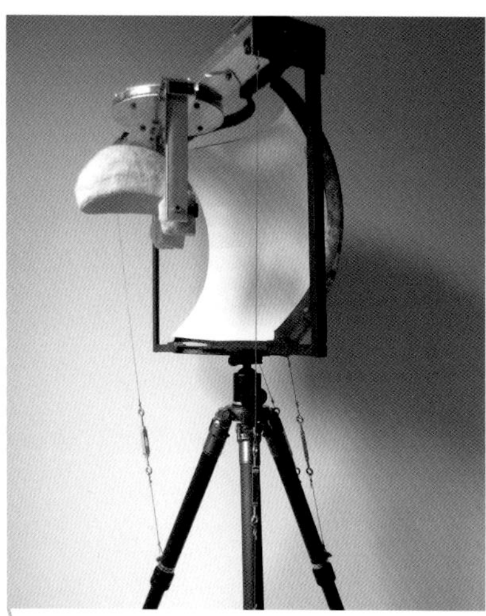
Ryan and Trevor Oakes, *Concave Easel*, 2004 (modified 2008); steel, aluminum, plaster

the twenty-first century. Unsatisfied with how traditional perspective doesn't take into account the shape of our eye or the refraction and reflection of light, the Oakeses developed a new system for illustrating how binocular vision interacts with the world. Eyes are curved, unlike Brunelleschi's flat plane, and our own features define their field of vision: browline, nose, and cheeks. For example: "Closing your right eye, gaze to the right with your left. Notice how your nose, looming huge, blocks a good part of the view in that direction ... now, with both eyes open, gaze right, and notice how your nose pretty much disappears from your visual field, even though your left eye is in fact clearly taking it in ... your brain, your visual cortex, suppresses the things it doesn't need to see."[37] With this in mind, Ryan discovered how to decouple his vision, or focus his eyes at two different lengths. When holding a pad of paper parallel to the ground, gazing out at the leaves, he noticed that if he focused his right eye on the leaves and his left on the paper he would see a doubled image of the leaves on the paper and could trace them. This led to the development of a curved easel, mimicking the eye, twenty inches wide and ten inches deep, representing most of the field of vision. On this, the brothers place strips of curved paper on which to render the scene in front of them, "a bookmark's worth" at a time. The early results were tracings; however, they soon developed new techniques for rendering light and adding color. First, they drew everything as a series of meandering coils, which would produce variations of shading and thus light. Then they realized that light exhibits "spherical behavior at multiple instances as it ricochets about the air" and that as "direct light burst from its source in a sphere (of electromagnetic waves, to be precise) … many other neighboring atoms composing the illuminated surfaces each scatter their own semispherical ambient bursts, all of which overlap in the air, co-occupying the same air volume."[38] This led them to draw light as concentric circles, mimicking the pooling effect of these particles (which they call "light foam"). This is evident in their two drawings of the Gardens at the Getty Museum, in Los Angeles, the first using meandering coils and the second concentric rings. In the first, shading and depth are evident, but, with the rings, the detail is astounding, and upon close inspection becomes almost photographic.[39] In the end, these works take on all components of seeing—the exterior viewing of the world, how the eye works in concert with the brain, how light is perceived—and bring them together, making us more aware, not just of the world around us, but of the inner workings of ourselves.

Turning vision inward shows that science and faith need not be as drastically separated as Martin Luther cautioned in response to Copernicus's discovery of our heliocentric planet: "People gave ear to an upstart astrologer who strove to show that the earth revolves, not the heavens or the firmament, the sun and the moon…. This fool wishes to reverse the entire science of astronomy; but sacred Scripture tells us [Joshua 10:13] that Joshua commanded the sun to stand still, and not the earth."[40] Instead it can be more as theoretical physicist Freeman Dyson says, "The world is full of mysteries, and I love mysteries. Of course, science is full of mysteries. Every time we discover something, we find two more questions to ask, and so there's no end of mysteries in science. That's what it's all about. And the same's true of religion."[41] So when science and faith threaten to dismantle wonder, we must, once again, rely on poetics. Protestant Reform may have taken away Catholicism's miracles, and the Wunderkammer may have been turned into knick-knacks, but outside Europe, in New England in the 1820s and 1830s, writers such as Henry David Thoreau and Ralph Waldo Emerson would shift focus to the purity of the individual and the faith of self-reliance— a trinity between God, man, and nature.

The Transcendentalists believed in intuition over empiricism; evolving out of and parallel to Unitarianism, they emphasized free conscience and intellectual reason. The Transcendentalists also believed in the power of the individual communing with the natural world as a form of spirituality, as exemplified in Emerson's Nature (1836) and Thoreau's Walden (1854). In Nature, Emerson states: "We return to reason and faith. There I feel that nothing can befall me in life,—no disgrace, no calamity, (leaving me my eyes,) which nature

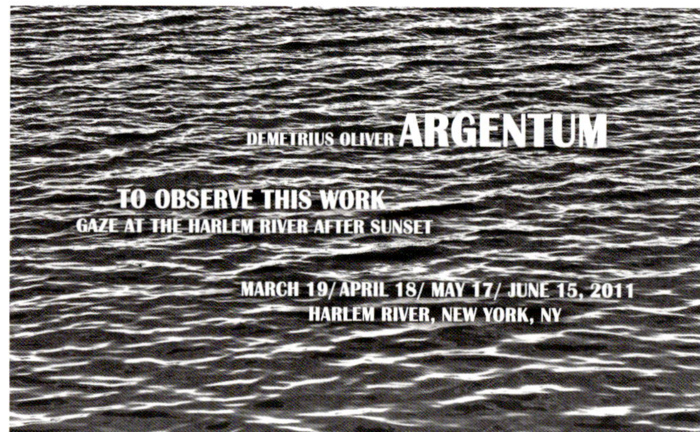

Demetrius Oliver, *Argentum*, 2011; postcard published by the Studio Museum in Harlem, NY

cannot repair. Standing on the bare ground,—my head bathed by the blithe air, and uplifted into infinite space,—all mean egotism vanishes. I become a transparent eye-ball; I am nothing; I see all; the currents of the Universal Being circulate through me; I am part or particle of God."[42] This connectivity is a sentiment that the poet Lucretius would cite in the first century BC; speaking of the fact that we and everything around us are made up of the same molecules, he states: "In expounding our philosophy I often call these elements 'matter' or 'generative particles of things' or 'seeds of things,' and, since they are the ultimate constituents of all things, another term I often use is 'ultimate particles."[43] Of these "ultimate particles," or what Carl Sagan would reference when stating that "we are all made of star stuff," Lucretius goes on to write, "nothing ever springs miraculously out of nothing."[44] These concepts of how we exist within the universe, our transparent eyeball and ultimate particles, are inherent in the works of Demetrius Oliver and Jason de Haan.

Demetrius Oliver channels the Transcendentalist awe of the natural world, combined with connectivity to the unknown. In 2011, he created Argentum (meaning silver), a postcard inviting its recipients to an "exhibition." The postcard read: "To observe this work gaze at the Harlem River after sunset. March 19/ April 18/ May 17/ June 15." No specific location, only the dates when the Moon would be full. One can imagine that, on those four nights, people on the eight-mile stretch of river would appear and gaze at the Moon, a kind of choreographed communion. This action, a social exhibition of the celestial variety, gets at the subtlety of Oliver's propositions. He doesn't give us all the information, but instead prompts us to have our own experience. To do this, Oliver often relies on the stuff of everyday life to show how the quotidian

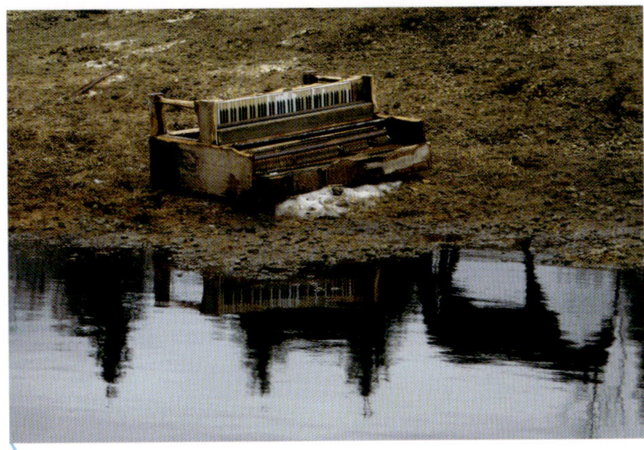

Jason de Haan, *Pie Powder*, 2010;
piano gnawed by horses for 763 days

can collide with the universe: umbrellas, tea kettles, light bulbs, and lumps of coal transcend their ordinariness and become harbingers of some celestial happening. In the photograph <u>Aerolite</u> (2016), scale is confounding, as a large rock, which seems to have crash-landed in a huge crater, dominates the frame. But step back and you see an aerial view of a building and realize that this isn't just a large rock … it's colossal. You think, Didn't rocks like that kill the dinosaurs? Once you realize you can't be looking at an actual scenario, your mind starts to bend and you wonder just what it is you are seeing. What Oliver did here was to place a hand-sized piece of coal atop an image of a meteor crater, re-photograph the pairing, and append a title that means meteorite. It serves as both an omen for the future and reminder of the past. This shift in scale is also evident in <u>Bolide II, III, IV</u> (2016), three small glass orbs whose title means "an extremely bright meteor." Oliver placed a metal whistle in the center of each orb, and as the glass and metal heated and cooled at different rates, the whistle bubbled and broke apart. In some spots you can see the original object, but in others the bubbles look like swirling galaxies, as if the whistle is expelling its last breath. We can hold these miniature universes, made of ultimate particles, in our hands, just like the coal/meteor. Thus, Oliver brings the universe to a human scale, allowing us to consider the vast in ways we never thought possible.

Like Oliver, Jason de Haan works with the subtleties of the natural world: what we see or don't see, and what we imagine to be potential. This notion of potentiality is the crux of de Haan's work, whether he is placing an upright piano in a field of horses for 763 days to see if horse-aided entropy and piano music would merge (<u>Pie Powder</u>, 2010); or hanging a haunted mirror across from a regular mirror, allowing a ghost to see itself (<u>Spirits Looking

<u>at Themselves</u>, 2014). In de Haan's work there is a sense of faith—faith in his viewers to believe that the ghost is there, and faith that his materials will act upon our imaginations, to tell stories, to take Cusa's leap and believe in the unknowable. De Haan's work requires the patience of geological time—fossilization, crystallization, growth, and erosion. For instance, in <u>Future Age</u> (2009–ongoing), de Haan placed a plaque on a tree at the entrance to MASS MoCA bearing the words "This Maple wears a rose gold ring." Is "rose" a reference to the redness of the maple, or is there an actual rose gold ring slipped over one of the tree's branches? The answer to both is yes, and one day the tree will wear the ring on the inside as the branch grows around it. This ring is a companion to <u>Swallow All the Brain</u> (2016), in which de Haan places humidifiers on concrete pedestals. The air in the space immediately feels different; there is moisture, but also an earthiness due to the fact that atop each stream of humid mist de Haan has placed fossils, which are slowly eroding. The fossils represent methodical time, and will eventually be undone by technology, but, as this occurs, their every particle will impregnate the air that we breathe. Lastly, in <u>Proposed Mt. Greylock Blowhole</u> (2016), de Haan begins with Herman Melville's <u>Moby-Dick</u> (1851), a book that has long been important to him.[45] Just beyond the windows of MASS MoCA sits the hump of the whale: Mount Greylock, the highest peak in Massachusetts and part of Melville's inspiration for <u>Moby-Dick</u>. De Haan proposes a blowhole in the mountain, taking a core sample from its top. The sample, placed in the gallery, reveals the geologic history of the mountain, but also opens a void in the bulk of its unknowable space. In the end, all of these works attune visitors to the small things around them; they breathe in deep history and create a spout in a mountain, almost as if "the great flood-gates of the wonder-world swung open."[46]

Wonder as a New Belief System

Descartes states: "The cause of wonder is wholly located in the brain, but the cause of these other five [remaining passions] is located also in the heart, the spleen, the liver, and any other parts of the body that contribute to the production of the blood and hence of the spirits."[47] But it seems wrong to place wonder in the head. Wonder must instead reside in the body; for only there can it function as a new belief system—a religion without doctrine or edicts, but with open mindfulness. Perhaps the problem resides in the difference between passions and emotions. Descartes lists wonder as the first passion, leading the charge alongside love, hatred, desire, joy, and sadness. He also believed that these passions must be sublimated to make way for true wisdom. Rather than suffer

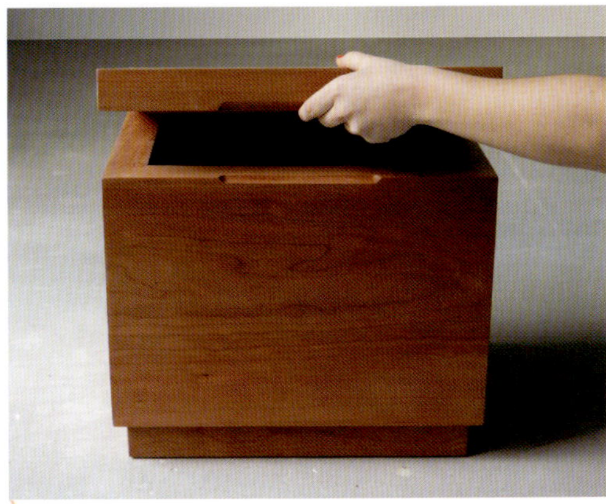

Julianne Swartz, *Open*, 2009; hardwood, electronics, soundtrack, hardware

modulated wonder, by beginning to think of this state as an emotion rather than a passion, we can see it as instinctive, felt, and put out into the world. Emotions exist in two categories: primary, or those existing at birth (fear, anger, sadness, amazement) and secondary or learned emotions (desire, love, grief). It is curious then, as Robert C. Fuller notes, that "not one major Western theorist in the past hundred years has explicitly listed wonder as one of the primary or secondary emotions."[48] Does this go back to Descartes's suspected fear that an excess of wonder leads to an arrest of reason? What is so bad about having reason arrested occasionally? Fuller goes on to state: "What distinguishes the experience of wonder from most other emotional experiences is that even though it occurs while the association cortex is active, it does not usher in immediate, goal-oriented behavior. Wonder, instead, is associated with a recognition and contemplation of the intrinsic significance of the stimuli at hand ... wonder is typically characterized by a strong sense of the fullness of the present, which has an effect of 'dethroning ordinary plans, purposes, and motivations.'"[49] This shift from an inward and controlled passion to an outward emotion may signal why we so often desire to share our wonder moments, and why they are intrinsically linked to the body.

Julianne Swartz's work is rooted in emotion, vulnerability, and the provocation to recognize and connect to one another as feeling human beings. There is empathy in this work and tenderness. For example, in Terrain (2008) Swartz recorded participants humming, breathing, and whispering, while simultaneously giving them prompts such as "Whisper 'I love you' for about one minute until the words start to sound like gibberish and lose their meaning" and "Imagine you are whispering into someone's ear."[50] The result is a chorus of compassion, much like her work Open (2009), in which the participant—for one is never just a viewer or listener with Swartz's work—approaches a non-descript wooden box humbly resting on the floor. Those who choose to open the box are met with whispers of "I love you," but the longer the box is held open, the louder and more aggressive the chorus becomes. This vacillation between comfort and discomfort is evident in <u>Lean</u> (2012), a slim metal rod, one end delicately touching the ground, and the other end curving up the wall. But look closer, and notice that the upper end is hovering just away from the wall, making its tenuous hold on the floor even more vulnerable. This precariousness is also palpable as we approach the <u>Bone Scores</u> (2016), a series of sculptures made of wood, ceramic, wire, and paper. These constructions serve as speakers, through which Swartz has placed coils and magnets. As sound is played through the sculptures, the coils excite the magnets, and the materials begin to vibrate. The objects tremble before us, as if sound has suddenly brought them to life. The audio includes recordings of electrical currents, heartbeats, chanting, lullabies, humming, pop songs, flocks of birds, and even a Kepler star signal. These quivering sculptures seem animate. There is a synesthesia in this work—we hear the sound, but also feel it—as if our body is excited by its own magnet. In the end, Swartz creates a somatic rather than aural experience, reminding us once again that wonder, when emotional, is felt in the body.

This poetics of the body is imprinted into the tissue of Jen Bervin's <u>The Silk Poems</u> (2012–16), which the artist describes as "an experimental poem that takes this ancient textile as its subject and form, exploring the cultural, scientific, and linguistic complexities of silk, mending, and the body through text and images nanoimprinted on silk film."[51] At Tufts University, Fiorenzo Omenetto is pioneering biomedical uses for liquefied silk, creating nanopatterned bioactive silk sensors that can be imprinted and embedded in the body (silk is universally biocompatible), allowing doctors to less invasively monitor long-term medical conditions. When Bervin, an artist and poet who works with text and textiles, visited Omenetto's lab, she was struck by the new possibilities inherent in this five-thousand-year-old material. Bervin researched the history and nature (both culturally and physically) of silk internationally—visiting laboratories, weaving studios, silkworm farms, archives, and museums. In Suzhou, China, she even encountered a reversible silk poem with thousands of possible readings written by a Chinese woman in the fourth century.[52] In the end, <u>The Silk Poems</u> is just that, a poem about silk made of silk. Bervin worked with Omenetto's lab to create a film onto which her poem is nanoprinted in the form of a sinuous six-character strand. If you were to x-ray an actual silk cocoon, you would find that the worm builds it by expelling silk while wriggling in a figure-eight pattern,

Denise Markonish

琴清流楚激弦商秦曲发声悲摧藏音和咏思惟空堂心忧增慕怀惨伤仁
芳廊东步阶西游王姿淑窈窕伯邵南周风兴自后妃荒经离所怀叹嗟智
兰休桃林阴翳桑怀归思广河女卫郑楚樊厉节中闹淫遐旷路伤中情怀
凋翔飞燕巢双鸠土迤逶路遐志咏歌长叹不能奋飞妄清帏房君无家德
茂流泉清水激扬眷顾其人硕兴齐商双发歌我衮衣想华饰容朗镜明圣
熙长君思悲好仇旧蕤葳桀翠荣曜流华观冶容为谁感英曜珠光纷葩虞
阳愁叹发容摧伤乡悲情我感伤情徵宫羽同声相追所多思感谁为荣唐
春方殊离仁君荣身苦惟艰生患多殷忧缠情将如何钦苍穹誓终笃志贞
墙禽心滨均深身加怀忧是婴藻文繁虎龙宁自感思岑形荧城荣明庭妙
面伯改汉物日我兼思何漫漫荣曜华雕旌孜孜伤情幽未犹倾苟难闹显
殊在者之品润乎愁苦艰是丁丽壮观饰容侧君在时岩在炎在不受乱华
意诚惑步育浸集悴我生何冤充颜曜绣衣梦想劳形峻慎盛戒义消作重
感故昵飘施愁殃少章时桑诗端无终始诗仁颜贞寒嵯深兴后姬源人荣
故遗亲飘生思愁精徽盛医风比平始璇情贤丧物岁峨虑渐孽班祸谗章
新旧闻离天罪辜神恨昭盛兴作苏心玑明别改知识深微至嬖女因奸臣
霜废远微地积何遐微业孟鹿丽氏诗图显行华终凋渊察大赵婕所佞贤
水故离隔德怨因幽元倾宣鸣辞理兴义怨士容始松重远伐氏好恃凶惟
齐君殊乔贵其备旷悼思伤怀日往感年衰念是旧愁涯祸用飞辞恣害圣
杰子我木平根当远叹水感悲思忧远劳情谁为独居经在昭燕辇极我配
志惟同谁均难苦离戚戚情哀慕岁殊叹时贱女怀欢网防青实汉骄忠英
清新裒阴匀寻辛凤知我者谁世异浮寄倾鄙贱何如罗萌青生成盈贞皇
纯贞志一专所当麟沙流颓逝异浮沉华英翳曜潜阳林西昭景薄榆桑伦
望微精感通明神龙驰若然倏逝惟时年殊白日西移光滋愚谗漫顽凶匹
谁云浮寄身轻飞昭亏不盈无倏必盛有衰无日不陂流蒙谦退休孝慈离
思辉光饬桀殊文德离忠体一达心意志殊愤激何施电疑危远家和雍飘
想群离散妾孤遗怀仪容仰俯荣华丽饰身将无谁为逝容节敦贞淑思浮
怀悲哀声殊乖分圣赏何情忧感惟哀志节上通神祇推持所贞记自恭江
所春伤应翔雁归皇辞成者作体下遗莳菲采者无差生从是敬孝为基湘
亲刚柔有女为贱人房幽处己悯微身长路悲旷感生民梁山殊塞隔河津

Jen Bervin, digital version of Su Hui's poem "Xuanji Tu"

weaving its own home, inscribed with its motion, from its body. This pattern resembles how silk DNA organizes into beta sheets, the building block of silk, and a form Bervin aligns to a weft thread in weaving (the horizontal threads looped through the vertical warp to create fabric). The beta sheet is often compared to the literary form Bervin uses for her poem, called a "boustrophedon," which means literally "as the ox turns," because the line reverses, as a plow turns, in alternating directions—incidentally, the same pattern that the silkworm uses to weave its cocoon."[53] Bervin's poem recounts this, her cocoon speaks to us: "i write it side to side/ in infinity loops / figure 8 spins ... i slow it down / concentrate on the line / elongate the loop / modulate it / trying to think of the words / i want to spend time with."[54] In the end, the silkworm will always have the last word: "it is so hard to let go / of contextualization / to separate your right brain / from your left, and build back up / to remove specific outcomes and / truly create something new."[55] This letting go, this relinquishing of the body to the motions of infinity, to the touch of silk, to it being embedded beneath our skin, is both physical and emotional. And we are left to witness the silkworm spinning in wonder.

At this moment, contemplate breathing, remembering that silkworms breathe through tubes that run down both sides of their bodies. The Greeks, too, were fans of this kind of full body breath. "The chest is regarded by the Greeks

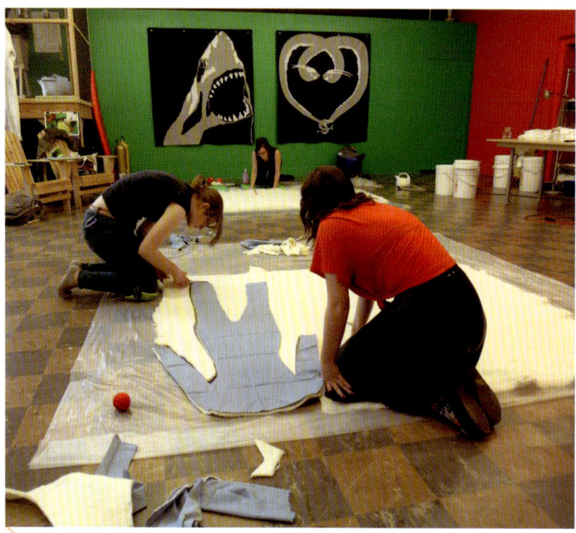

Hope Ginsburg, *Sponge HQ*, working on "Thirst" for Proteus Gowanus, 2014; participants, left to right: Jasmine Calvert, Lindsay Clements, Jessica Carey

as a receptacle of sense impressions and a vehicle for each of the five senses; even vision for, in seeing, something may be breathed from the object seen and received through the eyes of the seer."[56] This holistic approach, the placement of seeing and experiencing in the whole body, points to the fact that wonder is a mindful practice. Mindfulness need not always be about traditional meditation, but instead it is about awareness. Once again, Robert C. Fuller reminds us that "wonder prompts us to consider life from new perspectives. It helps us get in touch with the unitary and relational aspects of reality. In this way wonder gives us a version of our relatedness to the world, to other human beings, and to the ultimate source from which existence emerges."[57]

Hope Ginsburg's work has always been relational and collaborative. Her Sponge HQ (2010–15) was an interdisciplinary lab, workshop, classroom, and project space at Virginia Commonwealth University. At the Sponge, artists, beekeepers, felt makers, musicians, marine biologists, and students came together and practiced models of collectivity.[58] In 2013, while in Guánica, Puerto Rico, Ginsburg was scuba diving[59] and had a moment of feeling in sync with the seascape around her, which reminded her of a similar state achieved through meditation; she also realized that the respirator made her feel more aware of and connected to her own breathing. Then, in 2014, when Ginsburg was at the Robert Rauschenberg Residency in Captiva, Florida, she realized she wanted to bring together these notions of healing, diving, breathing, and meditation, but this time on land. Ginsburg assembled a "Land Dive" team of fellow residents,

Denise Markonish

all in full scuba gear, meditating on dry land, concentrating on every breath.
Ginsburg describes this collective action as follows: "The mild, if not moderate
discomfort of the equipment (its weight, warmth, constraints) keep the wearer
in mind of his or her physical presence, and the experience of a group of people
breathing in chorus is an unusual and amplified soundscape."[60] Conscious
of choosing sites where water is or may be an issue, Ginsburg assembled a
dive team at the Bay of Fundy in New Brunswick, Canada, a 170-mile Atlantic
coastal bay and home to the highest vertical tidal range in the world, ranging
from 47.5 to 53.5 feet, or approximately 160 billion tons of water a day. There
is a sublime majesty to the force, amount, and speed of the water in this region.
For Ginsburg, the challenge was not just breathing on land, but breathing
and meditating as the water came in and took over the team. The resulting
video features four divers sitting in the lotus position on the rocky shore; their
rhythmic breathing lulls us as it is modulated through their respirators, making
the sound more akin to hearing our own breathing echoing in our heads.
The water starts to come in and, before we know it, the dive team is being
submerged, and the breathing becomes the gurgling sound of water. There is
a fierce determination—or is it a radical calm and oneness with the body?—
evident in each diver's eyes. Finally, they disappear under the water. But we still
see the bubbles of their breath rising to the surface, reminding us to breathe
along with them and to be mindful of the wonders of nature that our bodies,
minds, and eyes breathe in.

Breathing is perhaps the most everyday thing that we experience, but if
you actually think about it, you realize just how extraordinary the ordinary is.
Many theories around wonder do not take into account the everyday. Philip
Fisher blatantly denies that you can experience both surprise and the ordinary
at the same time, stating "The ordinary can not or does not turn itself into
experiences. The ordinary is what is there when there are no experiences going
on."[61] However, we must remember the rainbow, which is an ordinary wonder.
In her essay <u>On the Value of Not Knowing</u>, Rachel Jones instead channels Luce
Irigaray, who "calls on us to cultivate the sense of wonder that can inhabit
<u>all</u> our encounters, even the most 'everyday' ..."[62] Here, wonder is not passive,
we don't just wait for it to surprise us; instead, we cultivate it—treat it like a
practice. In this way, it becomes possible to find wonder in the small moments,
the everyday, the quotidian, and to let ourselves unknow the known.

Tom Friedman's work exists in this space of unknown knowns; he takes
ordinary objects—a bar of soap and a misplaced hair, toilet paper, a sheet
of paper, or a seemingly empty pedestal—and he enacts upon them in ways

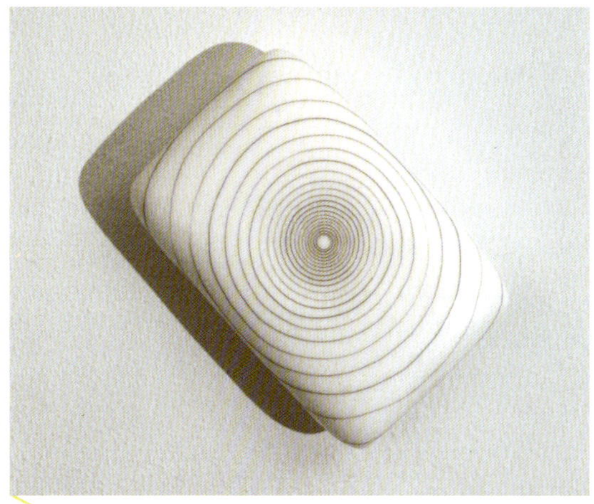

Tom Friedman, *Untitled*, 1990; hair and soap (Ivory)

that induce wonder. The soap has one long pubic hair incised into it in a neat spiral; the toilet paper is re-rolled without its cardboard insert (both Untitled, 1990); the paper is accompanied by the title 1,000 Hours of Staring (1992–97) and the pedestal's title is Untitled (A Curse) (1992), evidence of a curse the artist had placed on a 28 centimeter space above the pedestal. There is an absurdity to Friedman's practice, but also a sense of firm belief, a trust in both the staring and the curse. Friedman believes that wonder is a necessity in life, alongside water, food, shelter etc.; without it, he claims we "cannot look outside of ourselves."[63] He also once said that he enjoyed the label "infinitesimal minimalist."[64] This does not necessarily mean that all his work is small (though sometimes it is as tiny as a fly made from his own hair), but that his gestures are small; they are minimal with a slow-building sense of wonder. For his recent work, The Wall (2016), Friedman took over a three-story wall whose surface looks poorly treated, with drips and bulges, as if the museum needs to hire a new painter. But closer inspection reveals that Friedman built a new wall out of plaster panels with ordinary objects inside: a ball, a crumpled piece of paper, false teeth, a rolling pin, toys, etc. He then covered it all in plaster and Gesso. There is presence here, a sense of entombment and potentiality, and a sense of something in the wall breathing. This work is combined with a video projection, just as subtle. In Flashlight on Wall (UFO) (2016), the image of a slow loop of light is projected. As it moves across the wall, it becomes flatter and flatter as it dims, as if the light is breathing with the wall next to it. For as the Greeks said, we breathe in images; but with wonder as emotion, we exhale those images as well, sending them out to the next set of eyes.

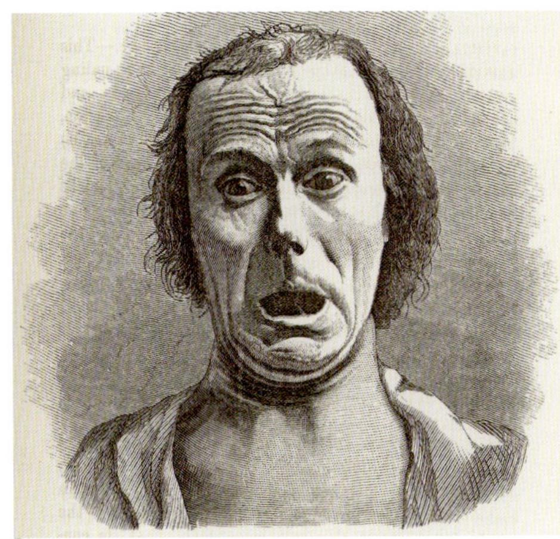

Illustration of terror from Chapter XII (Surprise, Astonishment, Fear, Honour) of Charles Darwin's *The Expression of the Emotions in Man and Animals*, 1872, by Guillaume-Benjamin-Armand Duchenne

Uncertain Wonder

While wonder is frequently accompanied by a beautiful and pleasant awe, uncertainty is also evident when dealing with such an arresting emotion. Wonder, like its sibling, the sublime, is associated with a feeling of terror, a feeling of caught breath and agitation at the lack of knowing. Emotions are uncomfortable; this is what makes them ineffable. Charles Darwin's <u>The Expression of the Emotions in Man and Animals</u> (1872) "equated wonder with raised eyebrows, opened and protruding lips, and a hand held up, palm out, with fingers open, reactions that, Darwin argued, increased the animal's chances of survival by making it see and breathe better in a crisis."[65] We all recognize this as both wonder and terror—eyes wide open, mouth agape, heart beating palpably. In <u>Metaphysics</u> (c. 1260) Albertus Magnus describes wonder as "shocked surprise [<u>agoniam</u>] and a suspension of the heart in amazement [<u>stupor</u>] before the sensible appearance of a great prodigy, so that the heart experiences systole. This wonder is somewhat similar to fear in the motion of the heart."[66] This type of wonder is historically seen in things like trembling before God or other divine entities, seeing spirits, or experiencing the vast sublime of the landscape—all things that seem outside of and far bigger than ourselves.

Jonathan Allen's work is rooted in the uncertainties of wonder, illusion, bewilderment, politics, and religion. Allen is a master illusionist and is careful to point out that magic has a complicated reception in the world, writing: "The construction of the conditions of wonderment can, however, be undertaken for both benign and nefarious ends. Herein lies another clue to our fascination: our concern over the distinction between temporary illusion (from <u>illudare</u>, to

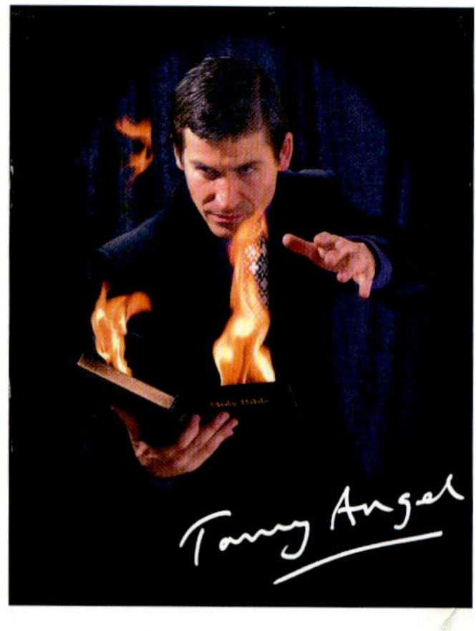

Jonathan Allen, *Tommy Angel #1C*, 2007

play) and permanent deception (from <u>decipere</u>, to ensnare or trap)."[67] Allen's
use of the term "fascination" is key to this notion of uncertain wonder and
bewilderment, and the drive to place ourselves into the path of the unknown.
From 2004 to 2006, Allen performed under the alter ego Tommy Angel, a gospel
magician whose illusions played with the theatricalization of power. Aligning
the magician with the evangelical preacher or campaigning politician, Allen
shows us perceived miracles through his own sleight of hand. Dressed in a slick
suit, he enchants his audience—rather than a wand, Angel has a cross; he
makes the Bible burn before our eyes, and conjures magicians' silks bearing
the image of Christ or proclaiming "Faith." Tommy Angel's polish makes his
motives even more uncertain, exemplifying that through the politicization of
magic, wonder becomes more unknowable, and also more enchanting. Allen's
most recent work, <u>Twenty-First-Century Silks</u> (2016), begins with the long history
of the empty-handed magician suddenly pulling flag after flag from his body.
These flags were often nationalistic, making the magician's body the center
of "the spontaneous production and choreography of diversified nationhood,
all accompanied from the orchestra pit with appropriate patriotic anthems."[68]
Preacher, politician, magician ... it gets harder to draw lines between the three.
Of particular interest to Allen is the British performer Kardoma, who during
World War II would "fill the stage with flags." This celebration of nationhood was
highly political and part of the United Kingdom's WWII propaganda campaigns.
At the end of the war, Kardoma, no longer wanting to play into nationalism,
began filling his stage with flowers (made of feathers), perhaps the most political

of his moves. Allen uses this concept to create a two-channel video. In the
work, two screens abut one another in the corner, and from the inky black
background Allen's hands appear and he unfurls a series of silks: War, Glory,
and God, etc. Rather than erasing the fact that we seem to be in a continual
state of war (heavily based in religion), Allen allows us to confront the illusions
of politicians and preachers, and to instead believe the magician, who, by
creating juxtapositions between faith and politics, is really telling us the truth.
Flowers cannot erase the atrocities of war, a true example of uncertain wonder.

When pondering the arresting wonder of atrocities, it is hard not
to think of the aboveground nuclear testing that took place in the United
States from 1945 to 1962. Artist Michael Light says of the atomic bomb: "In
a hundred-millionth of a second, the temperature at its core builds to several
hundred million degrees, many times the temperature of the center of the Sun,
and pressures reach a hundred million atmospheres, creating initial expansion
speeds of about five million miles an hour."[69] Upon witnessing the first atomic
test, theoretical physicist Robert Oppenheimer, clearly fighting back tears, said,
"We knew the world would not be the same. A few people laughed, a few people
cried, most people were silent. I remembered the line from the Hindu scripture,
the Bhagavad Gita. Vishnu is trying to persuade the Prince that he should do
his duty and to impress him takes on his multi-armed form and says, 'Now, I am
become Death, the destroyer of worlds.' I suppose we all thought that one way
or another."[70] It is chilling to watch Oppenheimer utter these words, but it is also
astounding that after such a human sentiment the testing continued. Light's 100
Suns (2003)[71] photographs were culled from archives at Los Alamos National
Laboratory and the US National Archives. What is striking about these images is
that they are truly beautiful, like tropical beach sunsets and thunderclouds, and
it is only in the realization of their content that they become uncertain wonders.
Most chilling are the images with people in them, bearing witness to the blasts,
eyes wide open and mouths agape, just as Darwin described. Light also spent
time on Bikini Atoll in the Marshall Islands, home to the fifteen-megaton Bravo
Test (1954). This test would change the island forever, sickening test personnel
and rendering the landscape uninhabitable. In 2003 and 2007, Light went scuba
diving at Bikini, taking both underwater and aerial photographs. It is hard to
tell above from below, and, as Light solarizes the images, he make us more
aware that it is impossible to see the effects of nuclear testing deep inside this
place. These ghostly images show a ship sunk by the test overgrown with kelp
and in pieces on the ocean floor, or a bunker facing the 200-foot deep crater
the bomb produced. A video taken while diving is perhaps the most surreal, for

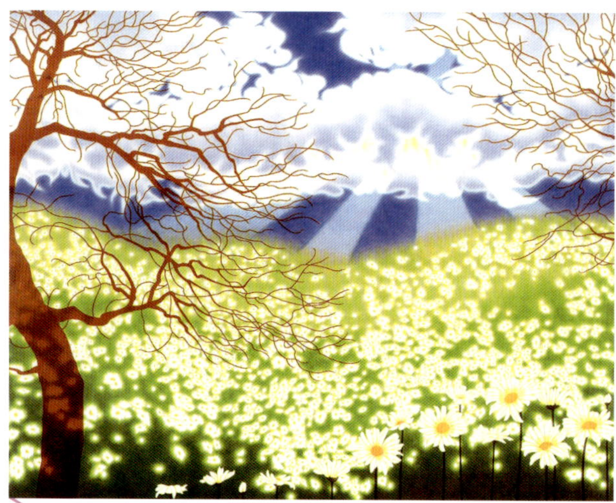

Sharon Ellis, *Reminiscence,* 2007; alkyd on canvas

the very act of seeing these small bodies in the vastness of the ocean, an ocean littered with atomic detritus, is a wonder and terror simultaneously.

Sharon Ellis's paintings show us nature untamed, one that is both out in the world but also in our mind's eye. Luminously painted, Ellis's works have a fairytale quality to them—they oscillate between serene transcendental beauty and dark foreboding woods. In the foreground of <u>Reminiscence</u> (2007), Ellis places wide-open daisies, the flowers and the dappled tree to their right almost bleached out by the blinding crepuscular rays of sunlight piercing through the background clouds. It's hard not to be reminded of the field of poppies in <u>The Wizard of Oz</u>, with sunlight forceful enough to make us feel drowsy from its warmth. But just as we are lulled into a sense of serenity, Ellis's paintings take a turn, showing the sublimity of nature. She paints her landscapes from memory, sometimes referring to specific places or events and other times referencing a feeling the landscape evokes in us: a wonder at its vastness and intricacies. Because of this, Ellis's paintings feel like dreams: their colors are vibrant, they are flat and warp space in kaleidoscopic swirls—these are as much about the wonder of the outdoors as they are about the ways in which our mind can transform these experiences. In <u>After the Fire</u> (2010), Ellis shows us the beauty of the regrowth that occurs post forest fire. She paints a snarl of blackened branches, but rather than the bare limbs of many of her paintings, Ellis remembered seeing "the delicate spring-green tendrils of bindweed, with their glowing white flowers"[72] growing up through the charred branches. It is remarkable to see how the terrifying and unruly nature of fire results in a

Denise Markonish

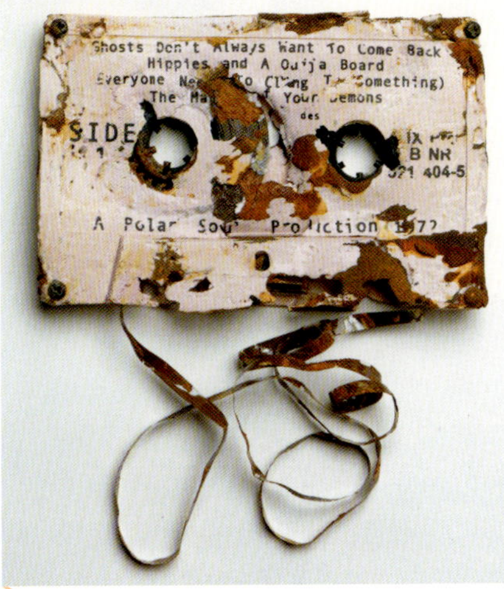

Dario Robleto, *At War With The Entropy Of Nature / Ghost Don't Always Want To Come Back*, 2002; cassette: carved bone and bone dust from every bone in the body, trinitite, (glass produced during the first atomic test explosion, circa 1945 from Trinity test site, when heat from blast melted surrounding sand), metal screws, rust, typeset; audio tape: an original composition of military drum marches, various weapon fire and soldiers' voices from battlefields of various wars made from E.V.P. recordings (Electronic Voice Phenomena: voices and sounds of the dead or past, detected through magnetic audiotape)

able to see and hear it, and understand what Earth was like. Voyager 1 was confirmed to have exited the solar bubble in 2013, making Druyan's recordings the first heart and mind in love to leave our solar system. This one sound, labeled only "life signs," would change Robleto, leading to a long-term investigation into the recorded history of the human heartbeat.

Robleto's work tackles deep humanity: love, loss, memory, longing, spirituality. He is an alchemist of sorts, transforming materials into talismans of emotion; melting his vinyl Billie Holiday records and casting them into shirt buttons (<u>Sometimes Billie is All That Holds Me Together</u>, 1998) or casting a cassette tape from bone dust of every bone in the body and Trinitite, the glass made when the sand melted at the 1945 Trinity Atomic explosion (<u>At War With The Entropy Of Nature / Ghosts Don't Always Want To Come Back</u>, 2002). His labels read like liner notes, so that we understand the depth and resonance of his materials as much as the ways in which he has transformed them. Robleto asks many questions through his work; <u>The Pulse Armed With a Pen (An Unknown History of the Human Heartbeat)</u> (2014) queried: "What does one gift to the only woman whose heart has left the Solar System?" The tentative answer: a boxed set of twenty-eight or more recordings tracing the three-century quest to record the human heartbeat.

To date, the project contains seven examples: Earliest Human Pulse (One Partner Seeing The Other's) 1854; Earliest-Born Human Pulse Ever Recorded (Born 1783, Recorded 1854); Earliest Human Heartbeat (As Sound Wave), 1865; Human Cerebral Pulse (Reflecting on Love), 1882; Earliest Fetal

Heartbeat (Registered by a Soap Bubble), 1908; First Human Heartbeats and Brainwaves Exiting the Solar System (in Love), 1977; and First Recording of a Continuous Flow "Beatless" Artificial Heart, 2014. The stories Robleto tells in his liner notes are extraordinary. The 1854 recording derives from German physiologist Karl Vierordt, who used a sphygmograph (like a blood pressure machine) to record the pulse via a stylus. The machine was so sensitive, the only stylus that would work was a strand of his hair. One of Vierordt's test subjects, his wife, had her pulse delicately drawn, with his hair, onto a sheet of candle-soot-covered paper. For the 1908 recording of the first fetal pulse, Otto Weiss used a phonoscope. He "placed a silvered glass thread, thinner than a single hair, at a right angle inside the bubble with one end of the glass thread attached to a holder to keep it in position.... As the soap film's membrane absorbed the sound waves and beat in unison with the heartbeat, it transferred its movements to the glass thread, and like a pebble tossed into a pond, the thread absorbed the ripples into its form."[82] The last recording, following Druyan's, is of a device created by Houston cardiologists Dr. O. H. 'Bud' Frazier and Dr. Billy Cohn—a continuous flow heart which functions like a turbine with a rotor blade constantly circulating blood, removing the heart's physiological need to pulse. The device was first implanted in Craig Lewis in 2011, and Robleto's recording was obtained from a second patient with the device. The sound is a haunting whirring, one Frazier describes as "a barren wind-swept landscape."[83] Technologically, this invention could change the face of medicine, but what does it do emotionally? There are feelings we associate with the heart—an increased pulse in the face of fear or excitement. With this recording, Robleto asks, "What does it mean to live with a heart that doesn't beat?" But as you listen more closely to the recording, you hear an even fainter, more organic beat. Robleto explains that this is the patient's actual heart, resting and healing while the artificial version does its work. Here, Robleto preserves these beats for us, so that their memories shall be kept alive and beat on.

      Wonder, like the heart, like love, will always remain mysterious, yet deeply known. No matter how often we try to name it, explain it, describe it, we will always fall short of just feeling it. So we should sit back and enjoy the ride; we should bask in the emotion of wonder and gaze at the rainbow. For all the known knowns, known unknowns, and unknown unknowns—the ultimate particles that comprise wonder—are forever carried in our hearts (in my heart); as they hurtle into the vast firmament of space, they explode fiercely like a string of firecrackers,[84] with a love powerful enough to move the Sun and all the other stars.[85] And the beat goes on....

1. Paul Beatty, *Slumberland* (New York: Bloomsbury, 2009), p. 36.

2. Originating from Rumsfeld's response to a question about the links between the government of Iraq with terrorism and weapons of mass destruction at a US Department of Defense briefing when he was Secretary of State, February 12, 2002. Rumsfeld cites NASA administrator William Graham for coining the term "unknown unknowns."

3. E.E. Cummings, "[i carry your heart with me (i carry it in]" from *Complete Poems: 1904–1962*, edited by George J. Firmage. Copyright 1952, © 1980, 1991 by the Trustees for the E. E. Cummings Trust. poetryfoundation.org/poetrymagazine/poem/179622

4. Nicholas of Cusa, *De docta ignorantia* [On Learned Ignorance], 1440, Book 1, Chapter 3: The Precise Truth is Incomprehensible. jasper-hopkins.info/DI-I-12-2000.pdf

5. Lawrence Weschler, "Places Where Creation Does a Little Work on Itself: Art and Science as Parallel and Divergent Ways of Knowing," 2011. exploratorium.edu/knowing/pdfs/Weschler.pdf

6. Philip Fisher, *Wonder, the Rainbow, and the Aesthetics of Rare Experiences* (Cambridge: Harvard University Press, 1998), p. 18.

7. William Wordsworth, "My Heart Leaps Up When I Behold," 1802. "My heart leaps up when I behold / A rainbow in the sky: / So was it when my life began; / So is it now I am a man; / Or let me die! / The Child is the father of the Man; /And I could wish my days to be / Bound each to each by natural piety." poets.org/poetsorg/poem/my-heart-leaps

8. *Fred Tomaselli: Early Work or How I Became a Painter* (New York: Grand Central Press, 2015), p. 43.

9. Carl Sagan, from *Pale Blue Dot: A Vision of the Human Figure in Space* (New York: Ballantine Books, 1994), quoted in Rachel Sussman, *The Oldest Living Things in the World* (Chicago: University of Chicago Press, 2014).

10. Sussman, p. xiii.

11. Sussman is currently developing *Loop*, an aboveground timeline/walking path tracing CERN's Large Hadron Collider. *Loop* will be seventeen miles long, span two countries, and cover 13.8 billion years.

12. Lyall Watson, *Supernature* (Anchor Press, 1973), p. xi.

13. A joke even more biting when you learn that Lindsay is poking fun at himself and his photojournalistic past life, when he published the acclaimed book *Lost Balls: Great Holes, Tough Shots, and Bad Lies* (2005), all about golf.

14. Watson, *Supernature*, p. xi.

15. This phrase, also known as the Socratic paradox, comes from Plato's account of Socrates. It has never been directly attributed to Socrates.

16. Aristotle, *Metaphysics*, Book 1, Section 982b in *Aristotle in 23 Volumes*, Vols. 17, 18, trans. Hugh Tredennick, (Cambridge: Harvard University Press; London, William Heinemann Ltd. 1933, 1989).

17. René Descartes, *The Passions of the Soul*, Part II: The Number and Order of the Passions and Explanation of the Six Basic Passions, Section 53: Wonder. earlymoderntexts.com/assets/pdfs/descartes1649part2.pdf

18. Descartes, *The Passions of the Soul*, Part II, Section 76: How Wonder Can Be Harmful, and How to Fix Things if There is Too Little or Too Much of It.

19. "Astonishment is an excess of wonder, and it is always bad because the body's immobility means that the person can perceive only one side of the wondered at object … If he weren't outright *astonished* he could turn the object over, walk around it, or the like, thus learning more about it." Descartes, Section 73: What Astonishment Is.

20. Lorraine J. Daston and Katharine Park, *Wonders and the Order of Nature* (New York: Zone Books, 1998), p. 260.

21. Daston and Park, pp. 273–76.

22. Johann Wolfgang von Goethe, *Faust*, trans. Walter Kaufmann (NY: Anchor, 1990), p. 153, Part 1, Scene III.

23. Christopher Gausby, *Philosophic Journal*, 1972–92, No. 200 (unpublished text by the artist).

24. Gausby, *Notebook IV*, 1990–91, p. 4, collection of the New York Public Library, Spencer Collection.

25. Gausby, *Notebook V*, 1992, p. 10, collection of the Newberry Library, Chicago. Cornell is also an apt reference, due to both artists' use of New York City as source material, inspiration, and a place of solitude.

26. Gausby's title is a nod to Thomas Aquinas's *Summa Theologica*, a fifteenth-century philosophic tome about God.

27. Joshua P. Waterman, "Miraculous Signs from Antiquity to the Renaissance," in *The Book of Miracles* (Cologne: Taschen, 2014), pp. 7–8.

28. In the early 1980s, scientists discovered that mass extinctions fall into a cyclical pattern around 27 million years, suggesting that a red dwarf star, named Nemesis, 1.5 light years away could be responsible. This theory is unproven. "Nemesis Star Theory: The Sun's 'Death Star' Companion," space.com/22538-nemesis-star.html.

29. Discovered in 2011, and 200 light years away, Kepler-16b is popularly called the first real Tatooine after the fictional home of Luke Skywalker in the *Star Wars* films; a scene of Skywalker watching a double sunset is one of the iconic images of the series. space.com/14203-alien-planets-2-suns-tatooine-star-wars-aas219.html

30. Quoted in Robert C. Fuller, *Wonder From Emotion to Spirituality* (Chapel Hill: University of North Carolina Press, 2006), p. 54.

31. Margaret Wertheim, *A Field Guide to Hyperbolic Space* (Los Angeles: Institute For Figuring Press, 2005).

32. Margaret Wertheim and Christine Wertheim, *Crochet Coral Reef* (Los Angeles: Institute For Figuring Press, 2015).

33. theiff.org/oexhibits/menger01.html

34. Margaret Wertheim, "Many Hands Make Fractals Tactile," *New York Times*, Science Section, January 21, 2013. The original fractal was named by Austrian mathematician Karl Menger (1902–1985) for its resemblance to a sea sponge. Wertheim writes: "Imagine a cube riddled with hundreds of square-shaped holes—it is the three-dimensional analogue of an important mathematical object known as the Cantor Set. After she had modeled the Menger Sponge,

Dr. Mosely realized that it was one of a whole new family of fractals. Some are trivial, others cannot be made, but one was especially interesting. She named it the Snowflake Sponge for its enigmatic sixfold symmetry."

35. amasci.com/amateur/holo1.html

36. For instance, Duke's holograms appear in the space where the music ends and the label begins in special edition vinyl featuring artists like Jack White (*Lazaretto*, 2014) and Rush (the 2015 re-issue of *2112*, 1976).

37. Lawrence Weschler, "Double Vision," from *Compounding Visions: The Art of Ryan and Trevor Oakes* (New York: The National Museum of Mathematics, 2014), p. 6.

38. Weschler, p. 37–38.

39. The Oakeses view these drawings like photographic negatives that can be blown up to reveal increased detail.

40. Thomas Kuhn, *The Copernican Revolution* (Cambridge: Harvard University Press, 1957), p. 191.

41. Krista Tippett, *Einstein's God: Conversations about Science and the Human Spirit* (New York: Penguin Books, 2010), p. 22.

42. Ralph Waldo Emerson, *Essays and Lectures*, Q Writing, February 2011 (The Library of America 1983).

43. Lucretius, *On the Nature of Things*, trans. Martin Ferguson Smith (Indianapolis: Hackett Publishing, 1969), Book 1, Lines 53–61, p. 4.

44. Lucretius, Book 1, Lines 150–59, p. 7.

45. For *The Whale* (2014), de Haan documented himself over six years reading *Moby-Dick* upside down and backwards near large bodies of water.

46. Herman Melville, *Moby-Dick* (1851; reprint New York: Black and White Classics, 2014), p. 16.

47. Descartes, *Passions of the Soul*, Part II, Section 96: The Movement of the Blood and the Spirits That Cause the Five Preceding Passions.

48. Fuller, *Wonder From Emotion to Spirituality*, p. 9.

49. Fuller, p. 41.

50. Rachael Arauz, "Look, Listen, Touch, Love," in *Julianne Swartz: How Deep is Your* (Lincoln: deCordova Museum and Sculpture Park, 2012) p. 19.

51. From a proposal sent by the artist to the author.

52. "Xuanji Tu" or "Picture of the Turning Sphere" is a poem written by Su Hui in a 29 x 29 character grid that can be read in any direction; it was written in five colors and embroidered in silk. The poem was a plea to her husband to return to her; celestial maps influence its structure. jenbervin.com/projects/su-huis-reversible-poem#2

53. From a proposal sent by the artist to the author.

54. Jen Bervin, from *The Silk Poems*. The lines "trying to think of the words / i want to spend time with" are courtesy of the artist Dianna Frid.

55. Bervin, *The Silk Poems*.

56. Ann Carson, *Eros the Bittersweet* (Campaign: Dalkey Archive Press, 1998), p. 48.

57. Fuller, *Wonder: From Emotion to Spirituality*, p. 12.

58. Ginsburg's project is based on the idea that the sea sponge is generative. If you place a sea sponge in a blender, all the pieces would form into new sponges. With this analogy, all collaborators are equal yet interconnected.

59. It is important to note that scuba diving was the first real physical activity Ginsburg engaged in after a car accident, so for her the link between scuba and healing is very holistic.

60. connexionarc.org/2015/10/23/breathing-on-land-a-conversation-with-hope-ginsburg

61. Fisher, *Wonder, the Rainbow, and the Aesthetics of Rare Experiences*, p. 20.

62. Rachel Jones, "On the Value of Not Knowing: Wonder, Beginning Again and Letting Be," from *On Not Knowing: How Artists Think*, eds. Rebecca Fortnum and Elizabeth Fisher (London: Black Dog Publishing, 2013), p. 19.

63. From a conversation with the author, February 3, 2016.

64. "Serious Playboys: Tom Friedman in Conversation with John Waters," *Parkett* 64, 2002, p. 79.

65. Caroline Walker Bynum, *Metamorphosis and Identity* (New York: Zone Books, 2005), pp. 41–42.

66. Daston and Park, *Wonders and the Order of Nature*, pp. 112–13.

67. Jonathan Allen, "From Bosch to Blackpool," in Jonathan Allen and Sally O'Reilly, *Magic Show* (London: Hayward Publishing, 2009), p. 20.

68. From an email to the author on April 14, 2015.

69. Michael Light, *100 Suns: 1945–1962* (New York: Alfred A. Knopf, 2003), unpaginated.

70. youtube.com/watch?v=lb13ynu3Iac

71. Light's title also comes from the *Bhagavad Gita*. The passage states, "If the radiance of a thousand suns were to burst forth at once from the sky, that would be like the splendor of the Mighty One," trans. Swami Nikhilananda, chapter 11, sections 12 and 32, pp. 256, 261 (1944), bartleby.com/73/123.html

72. From the artist's wonder questionnaire, see page 245.

73. A. O. Scott, "Or Would You Rather Be a Fish?" *The New York Times*, February 28, 2013.

74. From a proposal sent to the author.

75. Job, Standard English version 4.13–16, biblehub.com/esv/job/4.htm

Denise Markonish

76. From a proposal sent to the author.

77. Edith Cobb, *The Ecology of Imagination in Childhood* (New York: Spring Publications, 1993), pp. 27–28.

78. Lucretius, *On the Nature of Things*, Book 4, lines 400–403, p. 111.

79. The Japanese term for these stones is *tobi-ishi*, which literally means "flying stones."

80. Lucretius, *On the Nature of Things*, Book 6, Lines 648–55, p.195.

81. Chiara Zampetti, "Live Art: Q+A with Pierre Huyghe," *Art in America*, September 13, 2011. artinamericamagazine.com/news-features/interviews/pierre-huyghe-esther-schipper/

82. From gallery guide to Robleto's exhibition *The Boundary of Life is Quietly Crossed*, The Menil Collection, Houston, August 16, 2014–January 4, 2015. These texts, in the form of liner notes, also exist within the work *The Pulse Armed With a Pen (An Unknown History of the Human Heartbeat)*, d27m4mjhi8p0i4.cloudfront.net/api/file/xPSGQGflR2CCnED0Pwtk

83. From a conversation with the artist.

84. When describing the compressed sounds of her EEG and EKG recordings on the Golden Record aboard Voyagers I and 2, shortly after professing her love for Carl Sagan, Ann Druyan said they were like "a fierce sound, something like a string of exploding firecrackers." In *Murmurs of Earth* (Ballantine Books, 1978), p.158.

85. "Here my exalted vision lost its power. / But now my will and my desire, like wheels revolving / with an even motion, were turning with / the Love that moved the sun and all the other stars," from Dante Alighieri, *Paradiso*, trans. Robert and Jean Hollander (New York: Anchor Books, 2008), Canto XXXIII, Lines 141–45.

Negotiating Wonder

by Sean Foley

Wonder has been defined as a form of learning, "an intermediate, highly particular state akin to a sort of suspension of the mind between ignorance and enlightenment that marks the end of unknowing and the beginning of knowing."[1]

In my twenty years as an artist, the art world has talked frequently about curiosity. These discussions have fascinated me and inspired the way I work, experience art, and live my everyday life. Yet curiosity and wonder are repeatedly mentioned in the same breath, and it struck me as strange that people linked the terms together so loosely, and without grasping their fundamental differences. While curiosity tends to elicit a desire to know, wonder is a wholly different emotional response, one that precedes curiosity. There seems to be a willful disinclination to explore or even acknowledge wonder. Curiosity leads to research, objects, essays, and things of "value." Wonder doesn't care. Wonder strikes. Wonder leaves you breathless and then ends as abruptly as it strikes.

Because wonder is an emotionally subjective and ephemeral experience, it is a messy topic to approach. That it is short lived and quickly transitions into curiosity, which is analytical and long lived, only makes wonder's sustained academic study less viable. With all of this I began to wonder about wonder. What I present here is my personal motivation as an artist, to explore wonder, the experience of wonder, and strategies or techniques for provoking wonder. I am also interested in wonder's related territories, such as the fantastic, the uncanny, the horrible, and the grotesque (illustrated in the diagram on page 80, which orients wonder in relation to these and other categories).

Although it is impossible to deliberately create wonder, it is helpful to consider its nature so that we are better attuned to the potential for wonder. As an artist, I can revel in speculative gaps rather than be properly versed in philosophy, which, for me, blocks the joy and discovery that surrounds the enigma of wonder and instead emphasizes its subjective qualities. Artists have a special freedom to be wrong, because we are not about being right and our practice uniquely permits us to be subjective in highly idiosyncratic ways. It encourages us to take leaps of faith between seemingly unrelated ideas or disciplinary boundaries in ways that are generally not acceptable in other areas of study. Artists engage in a process of learning, encouraging comfort with ambiguity so we are more capable of embodied knowledge and dynamic thought.

Early Research

In 2002 I visited London and Oxford, England, to do research for a series of paintings investigating figurative abstraction. I had been thinking about the grotesque as a way of making imagery and the monstrous as a way to conceptualize my work in relation to painting as a practice. I was particularly fascinated by Pre-Enlightenment ways of knowing the world, especially curiosity cabinets, the history of medicine, and the efforts to taxonomize and catalogue objects. I was keenly interested in the way ideas were visualized and suspected that I would learn a lot about representation and abstraction. I toured the Hunterian Museum at the Royal College of Surgeons, Sir John Soane's Museum, The Old Operating Theatre Museum, and all the major museums of London. In Oxford, I visited the Oxford University Museum of Natural History, the Ashmolean, and Pitt Rivers museums. I experienced small moments of wonder daily, everywhere I went. I then began to realize that it was wonder, ghostly in its persistence and obscured by discussions of curiosity, that was my real interest. Through this realization I learned that although I wasn't aiming to make "wonderful" paintings or art about wonder per se, I was developing a parallel practice of inquiry into the nature of wonder. This dramatically changed the way I think as a painter, and it continues to anchor all aspects of my life.

In 2008, I was given an opportunity to teach a graduate seminar to studio majors at The Ohio State University. I jumped at the chance to explore the ideas of wonder that I had formed in 2002. I proposed, developed, and taught a seminar titled "Negotiating Wonder." My original intention with this course was to explore the ways in which works of art or objects in general can provoke an experience of wonder in the viewer, and how artists can create works that might position a viewer closer to wonderment. When I began my research for this seminar, I was surprised to find only one pertinent book discussing wonder and the visual: Philip Fisher's <u>Wonder, the Rainbow, and the Aesthetics of Rare Experiences</u>. I expected to find a wealth of books and articles relating to the type of wonder that had been consuming me. I was shocked to realize that I would have to wholly invent a way to articulate my ideas and my relationship to wonder.

When I speak of wonder I am speaking of the conditions of response and not "wonders," i.e. nameable special objects and places. Wonder is an emotional response that is experienced internally as opposed to a wonder—an exceptional awe-inspiring object or place—that is concrete and tangible. I can experience wonder while viewing an artwork, but I would not necessarily call that artwork a wonder in itself.

To witness a person in a state of wonder is to see a kind of paralysis, with eyes and mouth open as if to consume the experience. All senses are engaged by wonder. You become passive to the active effect of wonder. It works you over as a sensory tsunami. It demolishes language, evades intellectual analysis, and renders you completely ignorant. Although this experience of wonder usually lasts only a second or less, it is a transformative experience. The mind shuts down and then goes into overdrive, attempting to assign words or meaning to the thing, phenomenon, or experience. Because we are pattern-making machines and cannot help ourselves, we try to categorize it. But, wonder defies specialization. It dismantles and reorders everything. It is simultaneity packed into a singular abstract experience that explodes from its own density into a thousand new questions.

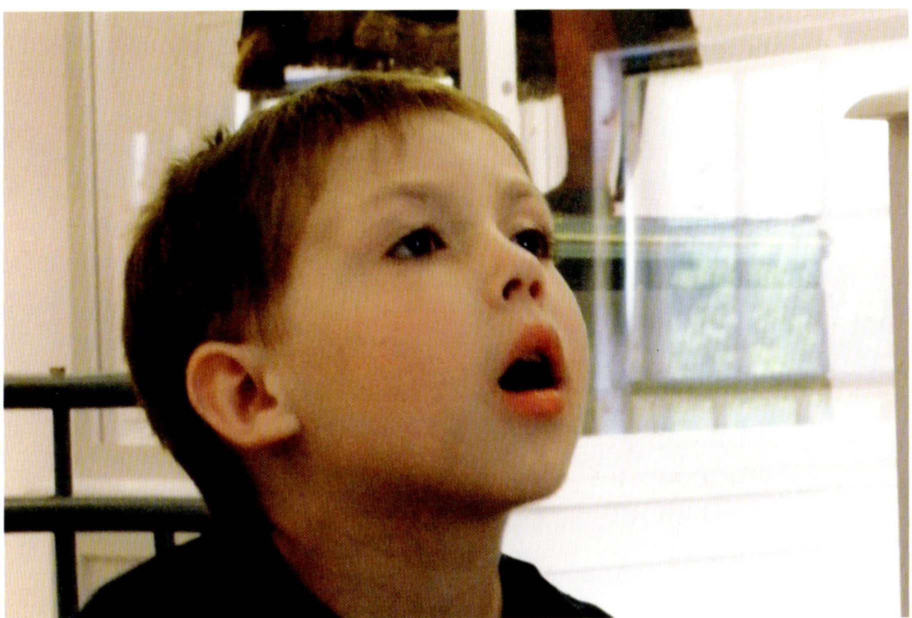

Emmett's Foley's "wonder face"

Viewers can experience wonder through art, but only if they cultivate a healthy comfort with ambiguity and a willingness to suspend belief and language. Art is a manufactured thing that is in between. Art is suspended, a medium in the actual and supernatural sense. As the artist Ed Ruscha says, "Good art should elicit a response of 'Huh? Wow!' as opposed to 'Wow? Huh?'" I do not believe that artists can consciously choose to make work about wonder, but they can cultivate a disposition for receptivity. They do this by using remarkably simple notions like playing with scale, considering opposing concerns simultaneously, and paying attention to the outcomes of chance or accident. Artists generate vehicles for experience, some of which have more potential for provoking wonder than others.

Strategy: The Nonsense of Knowing

Wonder occurs in the space between perception and knowledge. As the brain scans for an explanation, we experience wonder as "not knowing." During this scanning, we come tantalizingly close to clarifying the "thing" or "phenomenon," but repeatedly fail to do so. Wonder, therefore, is an experience that exists outside of language; in exploring wonder as a phenomenon, we can embrace it as a form of acceptable confusion. Wonder can only exist in the midst of not knowing.

It is not unusual for me to sit in my studio and look at a painting for hours. I don't paint; I don't do anything but look. I am trying to get past my ways of knowing what I have already painted and see it instead as strange. I seek a state of ignorance where I am preparing myself to be surprised. And in doing so, I cultivate gaps in my own understanding of the painting in the hope that wonder will fill them. Another example is artist Josef Albers's equation of 1+1=3. The idea behind this equation is that any two graphic elements placed near each other yield a third element, the "negative" space between the two bracketing elements. The perception of that space is both visual and conceptual. It is a perfect metaphor for our longing for wonder. We know it exists but cannot pinpoint it.

I often describe wonder in relation to the way magnets of like poles repel each other. Wonder is that space between our attempts to engage it directly. It resists forceful attempts to connect, and as a result a slippage occurs. Its equally powerful antithesis, appropriately a wonder in itself, is the celestial black hole. The only way to imagine the complex mysterious space where wonder resides is to carefully position and hold each magnet towards equilibrium of opposing forces. The magnets represent us, at the outer limits of the abstract experience of wonder, and leave us to ponder the gap as the great unknown. The closest we can come to affecting the experience of wonder is to bracket it.

down and realized she was jumping. I was ready to scold her once more when she quietly spoke in a serious tone, as if talking to herself, "I'm going to jump over my shadow." She said this without interrupting her activity or even looking at me. I'm not sure she was even speaking to me. But I was struck with wonder at her total absorption and fearless presence in the world. I had been completely absent, inattentive, and miserable. And there she was: playing, curious, mindful, engaged in nonsense and persisting through every failed attempt.

As I observe my children's fascinating "kid logic," I've become intrigued by academic and activist Jack (also known as Judith) Halberstam's proposal for a "low theory, or a theoretical knowledge that works at many levels at once … that revels in the detours, twists, and turns through knowing and confusion, and that seeks not to explain but to involve."[8] Halberstam continues, "[W]e might also think about it (low theory) as a kind of theoretical model that flies below the radar, that is assembled from eccentric texts and examples and that refuses to confirm the hierarchies of knowing that maintain the high in high theory."[9] This has given me freedom and agency to consider the lofty emotional state of wonder as something I can engage with on my own terms, to think like an artist and take play seriously.

Failing may be the only means we have left to exist on our own terms creatively. Halberstam writes, "Failure preserves some of the wondrous anarchy of childhood and disturbs the supposedly clean boundaries between adults and children, winners or losers."[10] The same can be said for knowing and not knowing. To a greater or lesser degree, pedagogy is rooted in a wonder that, ironically, is failure prior to knowledge. Wonder is failure.

Structure: Mapping Wonder

While reading <u>Wonder, the Rainbow, and the Aesthetics of Rare Experiences</u> I began to consider my own rare experiences. The one I kept coming back to was witnessing the terrorist attacks of September 11, 2001. Watching the south tower of the World Trade Center collapse, on live television, was the single most disorienting experience of my adult life. I witnessed the abject hopelessness of people jumping from the burning towers. I realized that the horror affected me beyond words. It was an uncanny feeling watching the disappearance of the most recognizable landmarks by which I oriented myself on subway jaunts. My mouth was open, my eyes didn't blink, I doubt I breathed at all, and I couldn't stand up, yet I was suspended in real time. I was experiencing the fantastic hesitation of not knowing. I was in a state of wonder.

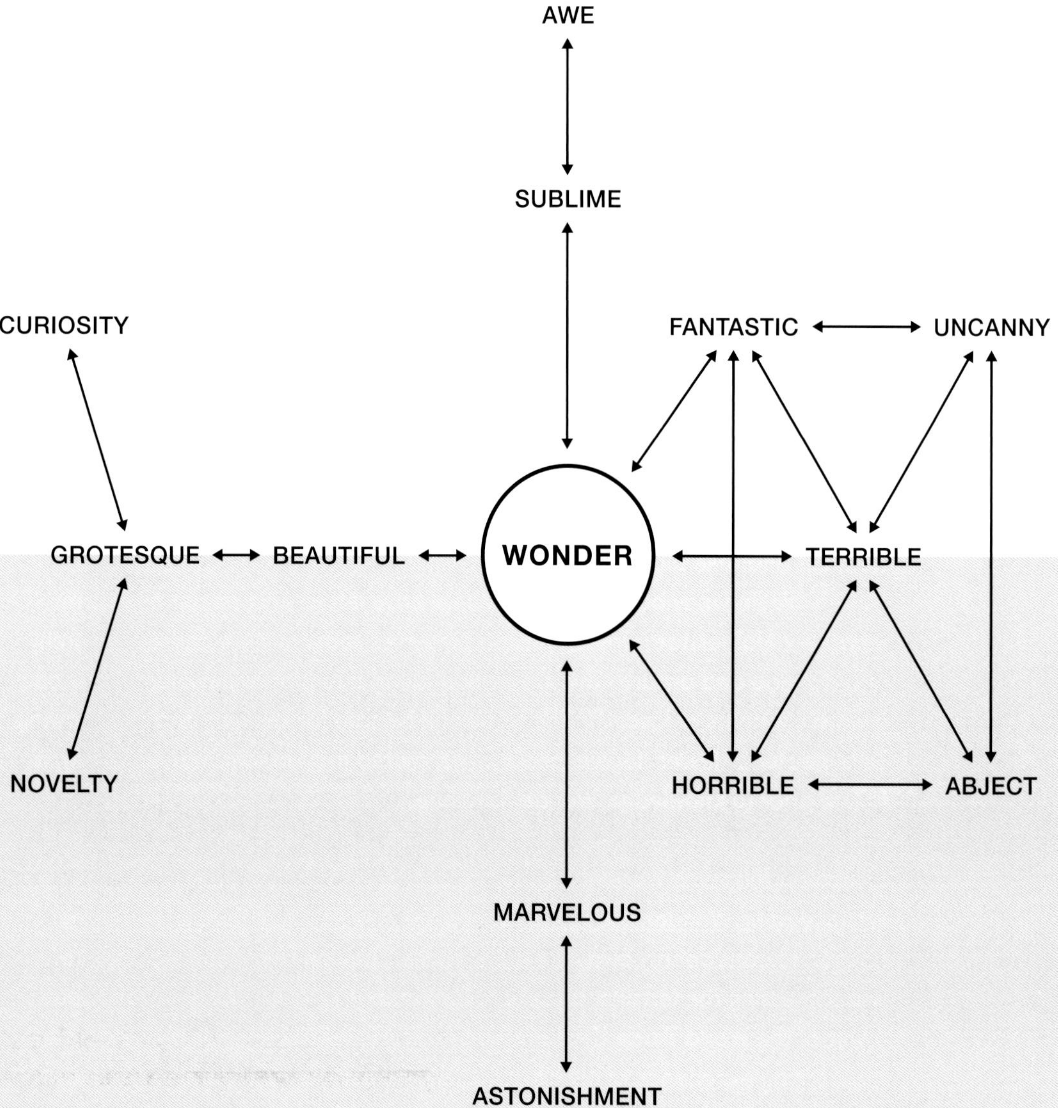

Sean Foley's "condition of wonder" working diagram, version 6

Sean Foley

Opening oneself to wonder requires faith. To be vulnerable when confronted with the unknown is frightening. If we do not feel a bit lost when talking about wonder, then we are probably not within its realm. The effects of wonder are unique to the viewer, and the artist can merely offer a proposition and hope that it becomes a provocation. In doing so, there is a risk that one person's wonder is another person's boredom. Wonder is transformative and humbling. Wonder reminds us that we really are not in control as much as we think, and the ongoing and deeper questions of wonder can only further enrich the complexities and beauty of the human experience.

...

1. Adalgisa Lugli, quoted in Lawrence Weschler, *Mr. Wilson's Cabinet of Wonder* (New York: Vintage, 1996), pp. 89–90.

2. Geoffrey Galt Harpham, *On the Grotesque: Strategies of Contradiction in Art and Literature* (Princeton: Princeton University Press, 1982), pp. 3–4.

3. Edith Cobb, The Ecology of Imagination in Childhood (New York: Spring Publications, 1993), p. 27.

4. Cobb, pp. 33–34.

5. Susan Stewart, *Nonsense: Aspects of Intertextuality in Folklore and Literature* (Baltimore: Johns Hopkins University Press, 1982), p. 31.

6. Stewart, p. 31. Here Stewart is citing *Gregory Bateson, Steps to an Ecology of Mind* (New York: 1973), p. 193.

7. Stewart, p. 60.

8. Judith Halberstam, *The Queer Art of Failure* (Durham: Duke University Press, 2011), p. 17. Note: when this book was published, the author's listed name was Judith; the author now goes by Jack.

9. Halberstam, p. 15.

10. Halberstam, p. 16.

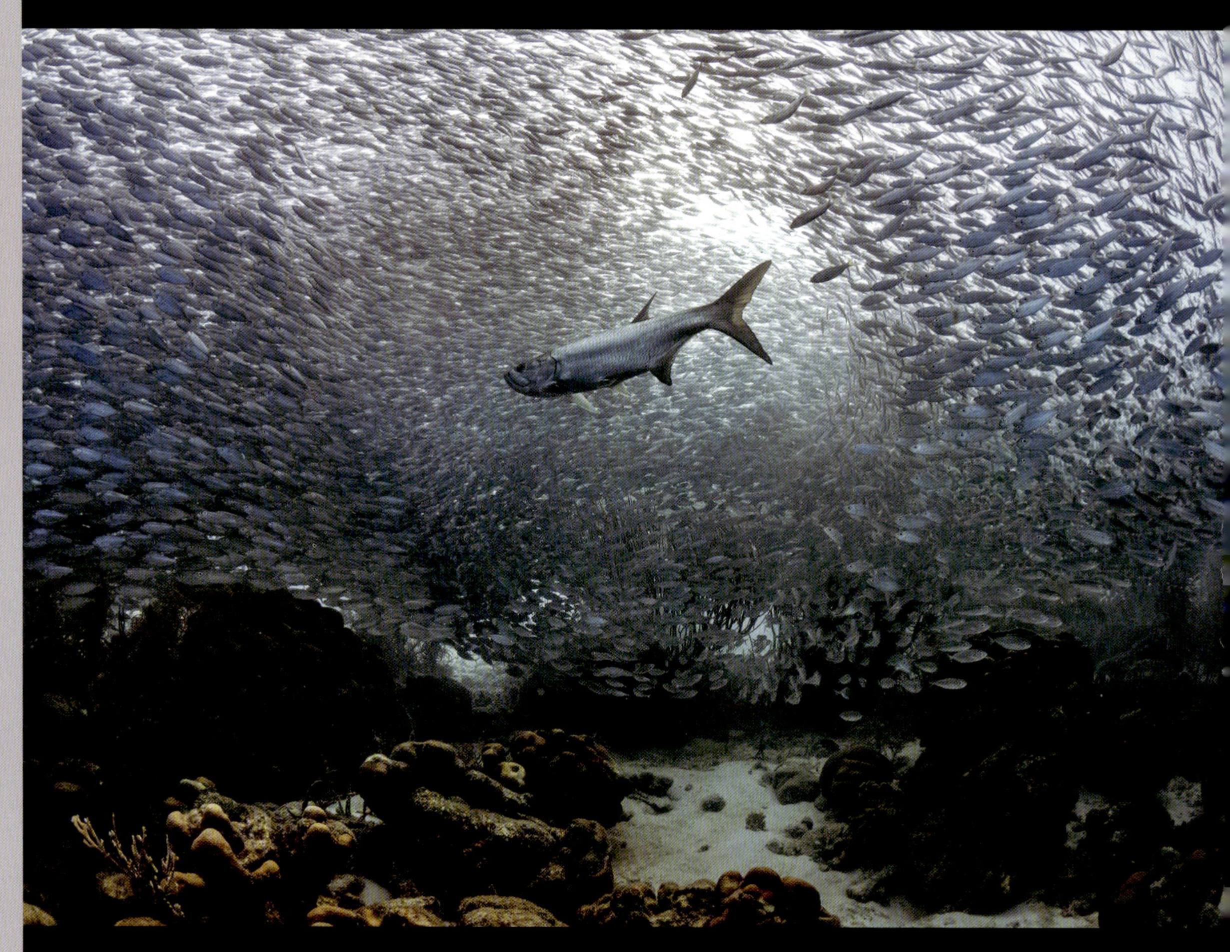

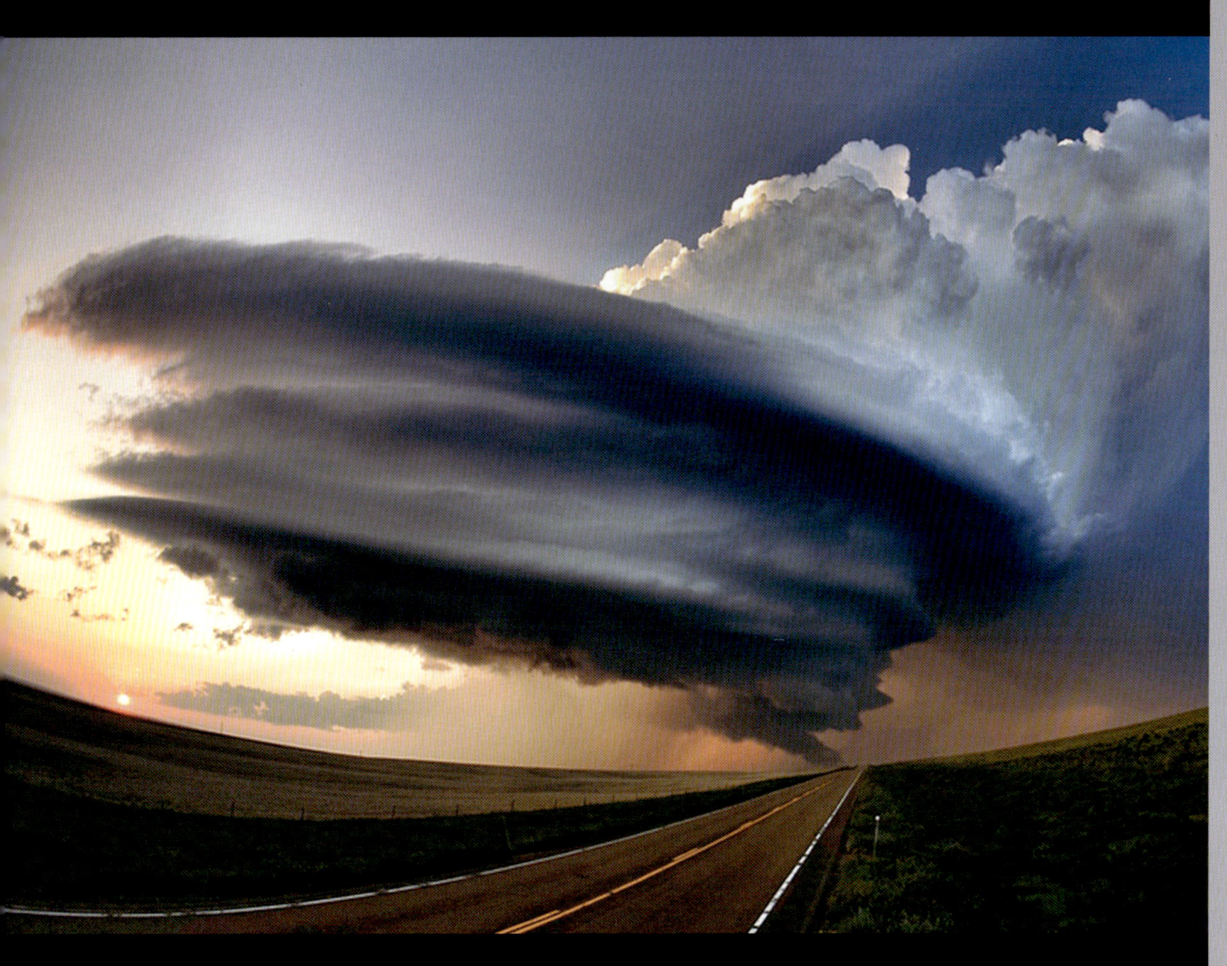

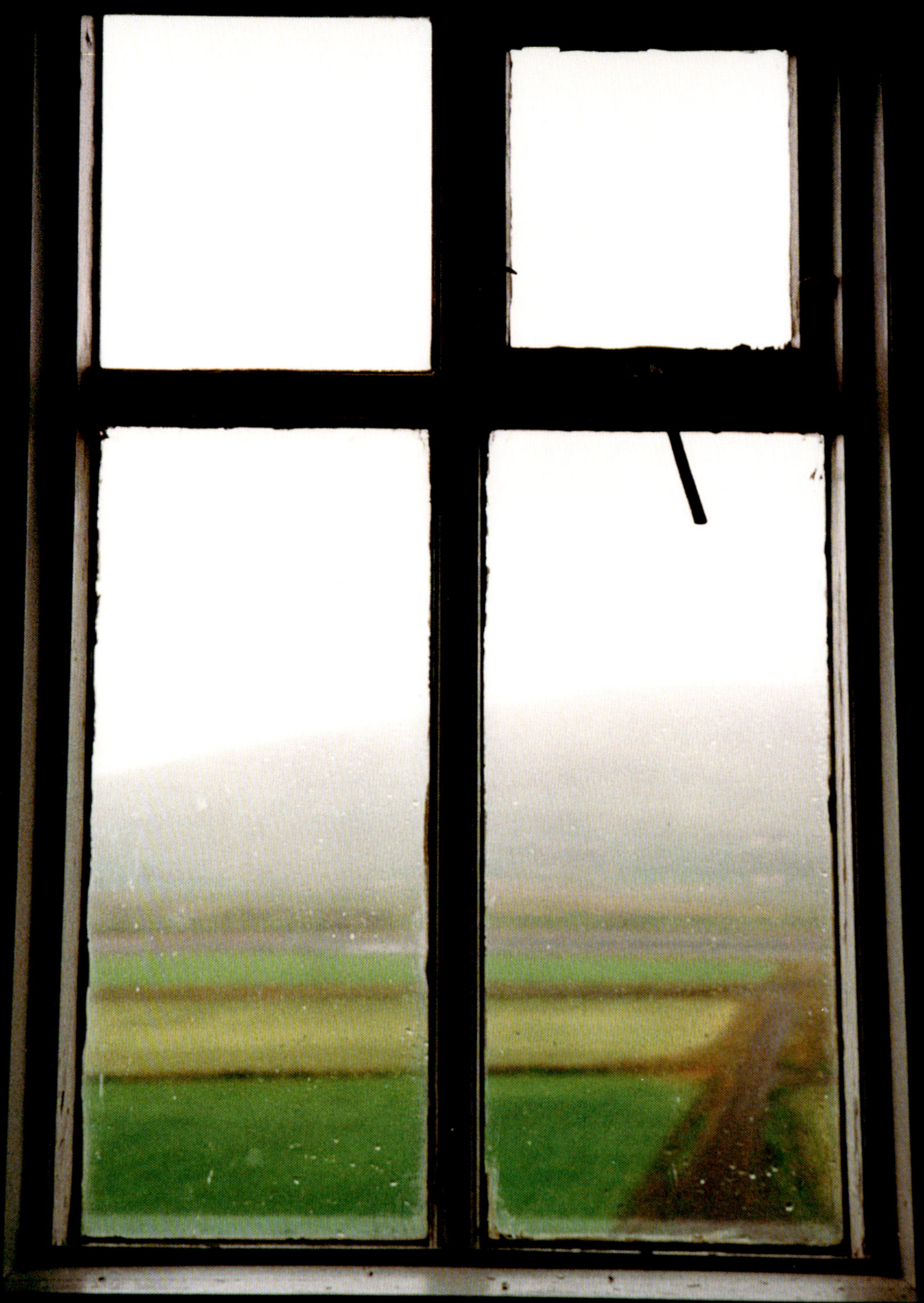

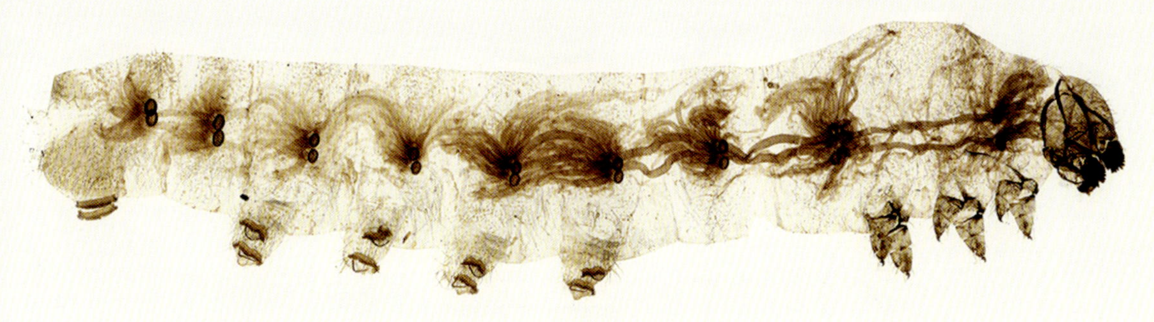

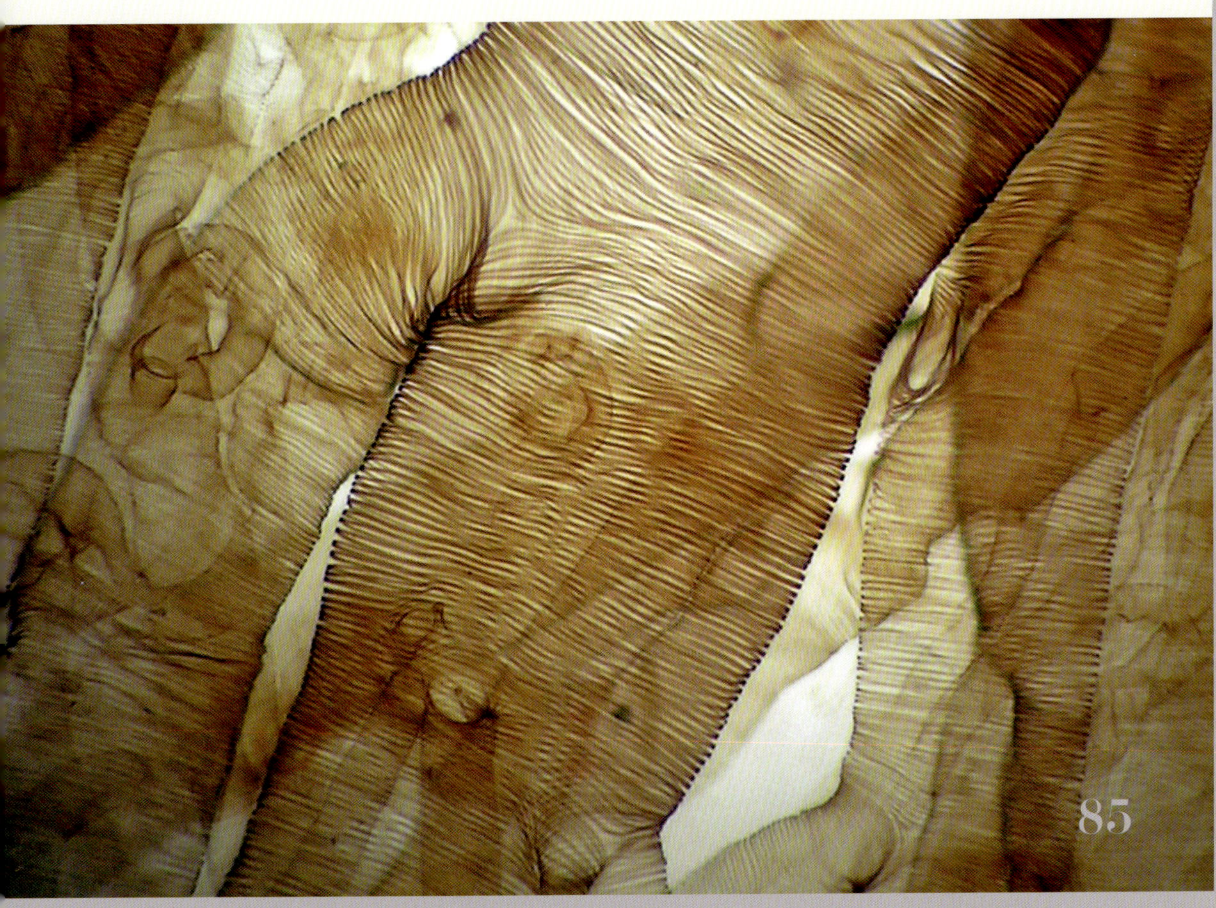

θεοφιλεϲ   γενέσθαι

"... in that communion only, beholding beauty with the eye of the mind, he will be enabled to bring forth, not images of beauty, but realities (for he has hold not of an image but of a reality) and bringing forth and nourishing true virtue to become the friend of God and be immortal, if mortal man may."

Six lines from Plato's SYMPOSIUM in the Translation by Jowett ("The Dialogues of Plato etc)" Oxford 1871. Vol. I p.527. (2 slight changes (v.3rd col.) indicate a later edition). Plato (427–346 B.C.) "composed the memorials of philosophic talk [of his Master, Socrates, c.470–399 B.C.] wh we know as the Dialogues"(1) The theme of the Symposium is the passion of "sexual love"(2) discussed at a banquet [in 416 BC] by a brilliant company at the house of Agathon. After each of the others had spoken in turn, Socrates speaks. He tells them that his views had more or less resembled theirs, until "Diotima a wise woman of Mantinea" had taught him the true nature of love. Love is "a great spirit ... between divine & mortal .... Interpreting & transporting human things to the gods & divine things to men, entreaties & sacrifices from below, & ordinances & requitals from above"(3). (The argument runs—

Love desires the possession of the beautiful ......
What is gained by that ? ... Substitute the good ... The possession of the good is happiness ...... "Love loves the good to be one's own for ever"(4) ...... "What is the method of those who pursue it ...?(4) "it is begetting on a beautiful thing by means of both the body & the soul"(5) ...... "I will now initiate you, she said, into the greater mysteries"(6) .... "begin in youth to turn to beautiful forms; & first if his instructor guide him rightly he should learn to love one such form only — out of that he should create fair thoughts, & soon he will himself perceive that the beauty of one form is truly related to the beauty of another; & then if beauty in general is his pursuit, how foolish would he be not to recognize that the beauty in every form is one & the same!...... But what if man had eyes to see the true beauty

— the divine beauty, I mean, pure & clear & unalloyed, not clogged with the pollutions of mortality & all the colours & varieties of human life — thither looking, & holding converse with the true beauty divine & simple, & bringing into being & educating true creations of virtue & not idols only? Do you not see that in that communion only beholding beauty with the eye of the mind, he will be enabled to bring forth, not images of beauty, but realities; for he has hold not of an image but of a reality, and bringing forth and educating true virtue to become the friend of God and be immortal, if mortal man may. Would that be an ignoble life? Such, Phaedrus — & I speak not only to you, but to all men — were the words of Diotima; & I am persuaded of their truth. And being persuaded of them, I try to persuade others, that in the attainment of this end human nature will not easily

find a better helper than love"(7). [References(1)—(5) are to W.R.M.Lamb's translation "Loeb Classics Library" 1932 : (1.)pX,(2)p.74, (3.)p.179,(4.)p.189,(5.)p.191 // (6)&(7), which further help the setting & give the context of the original extract, are from p.477 & pp.526 to 528 of 1st ed. of Jowett's translation (v. 1st col.)]. The six lines of Plato are written to be given to Alfred J. Fairbank by the Society of Scribes & Illuminators at their general meeting on 19. Apl. 1954 in gratitude for his services as Hon. Exhibition Treasurer Nov. 1922–Oct. 1929, Hon. Treasurer Oct. 1929 – Oct 1930, & Hon Secretary Nov. 1931 — Oct. 1933 {E.J. script-Apl.1954. his 1st vell. MS after 24 years, it has serious faults — too rough well tried too late) Yet to its drawing many eyes (partly spelling the MS.) The notes (to atone for data omitted in 1951 & to set the due words) are thrown in — which perhaps may excuse their tumbled scribbling. B. Mahon — 15th to 30th of [illegible]}

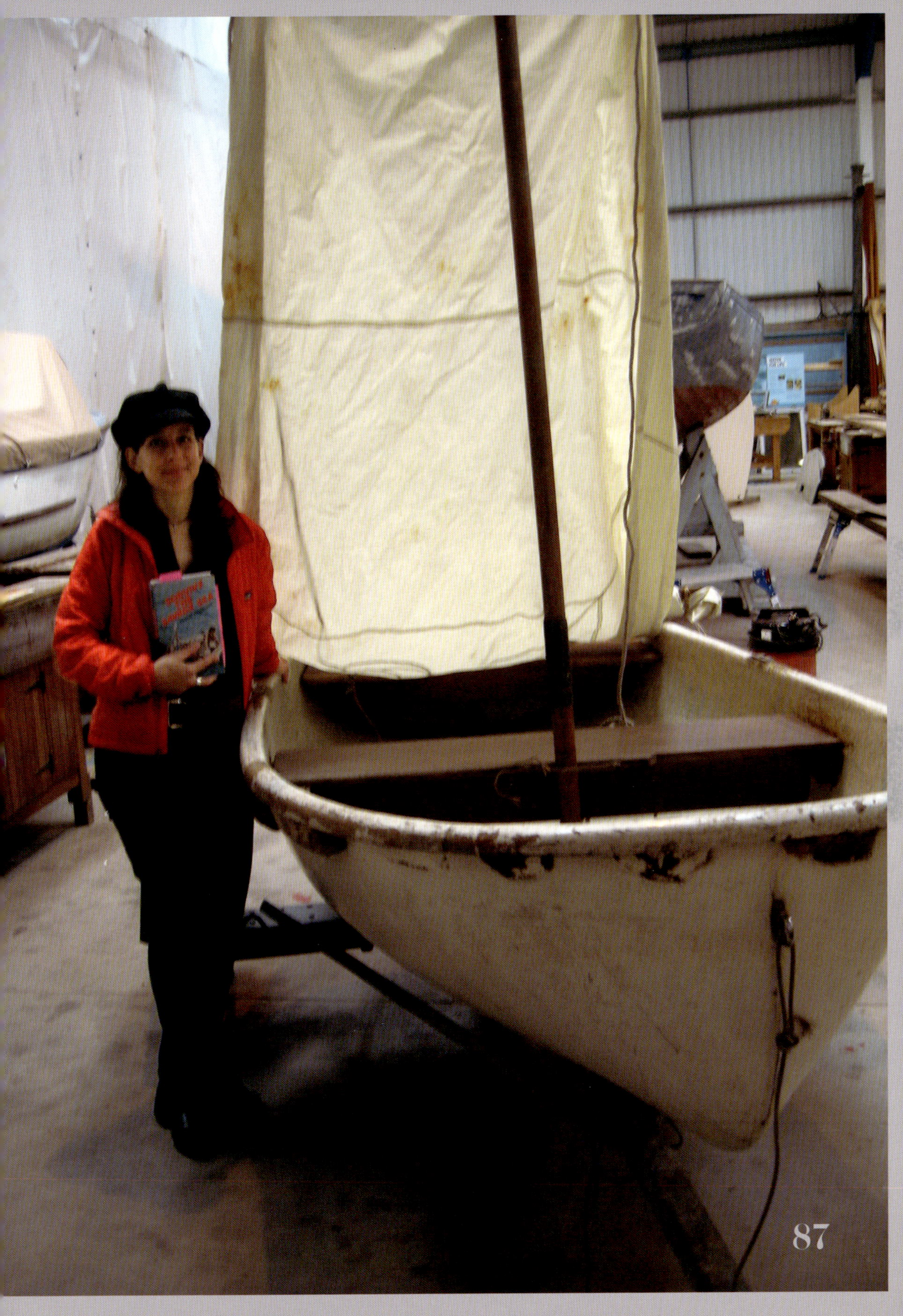

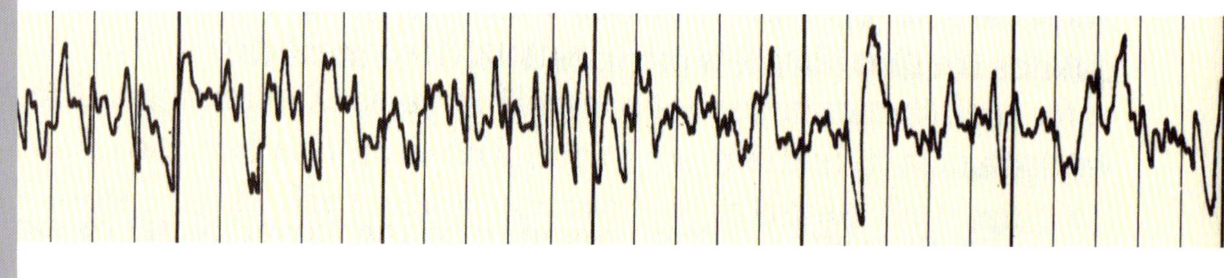

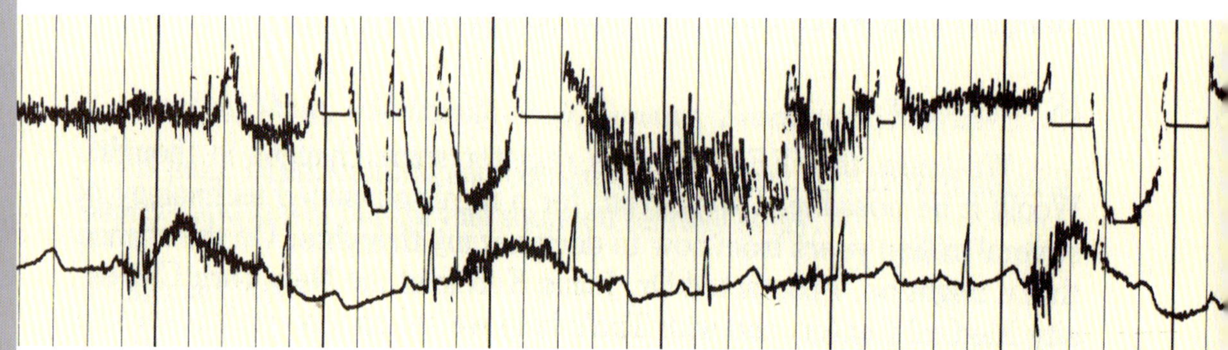

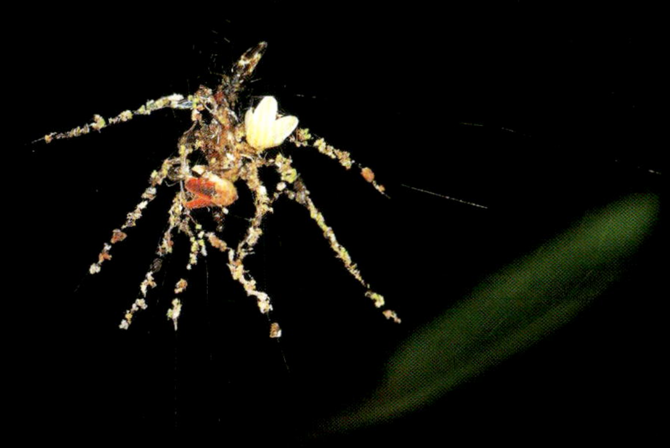

Wonder, Wonderous, Wondering…

by Jill Tarter

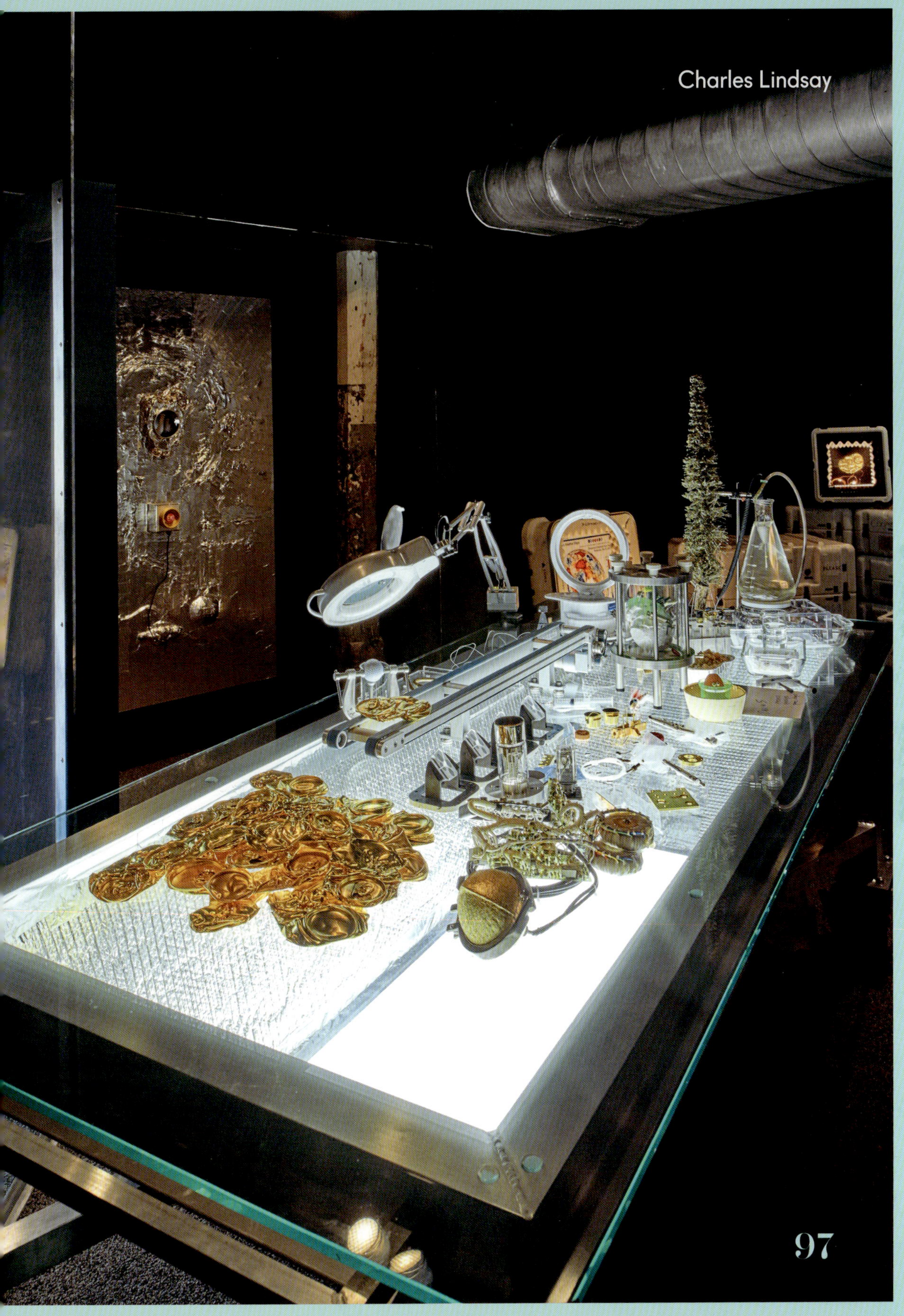
Charles Lindsay

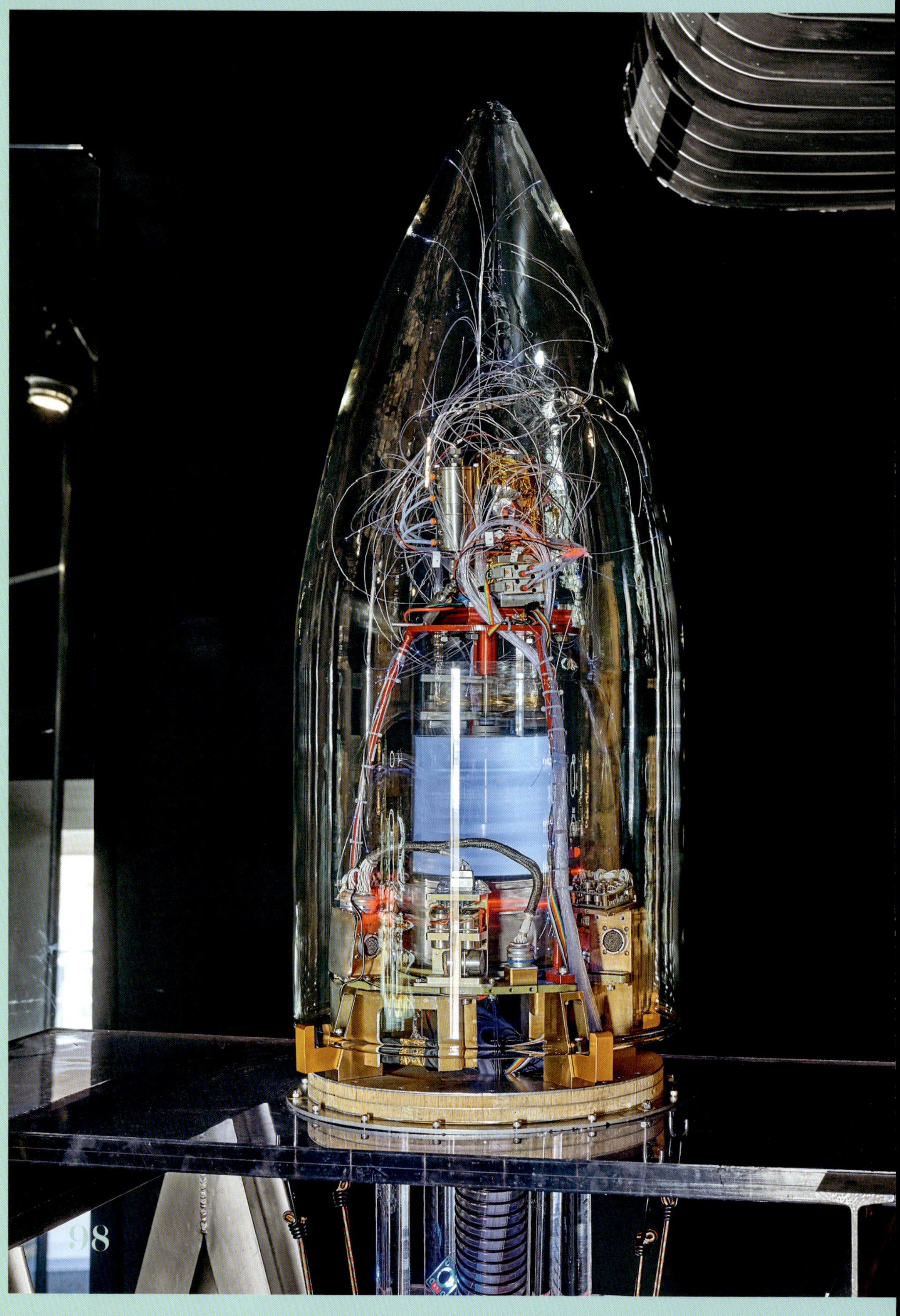

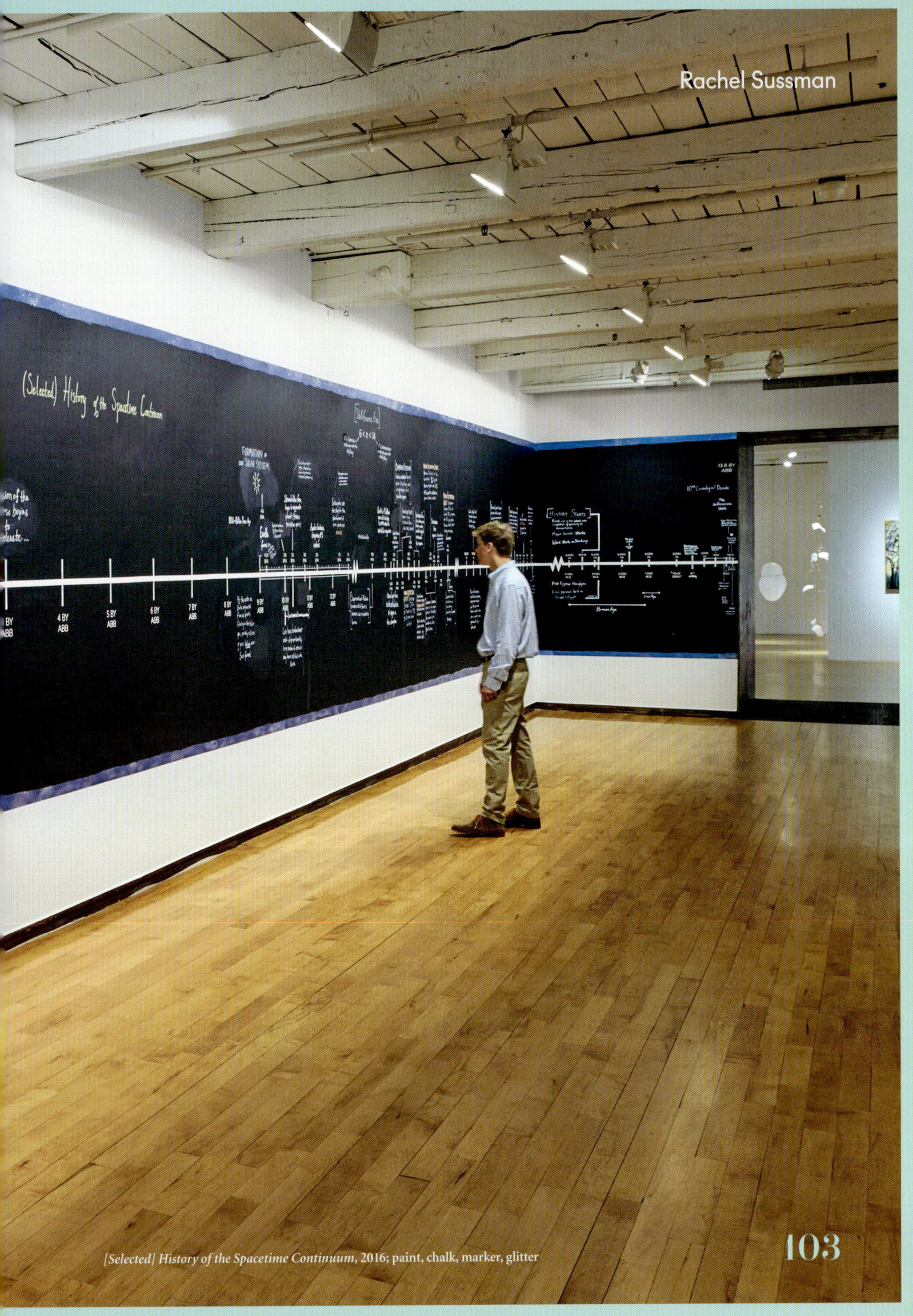

[Selected] History of the Spacetime Continuum, 2016; paint, chalk, marker, glitter

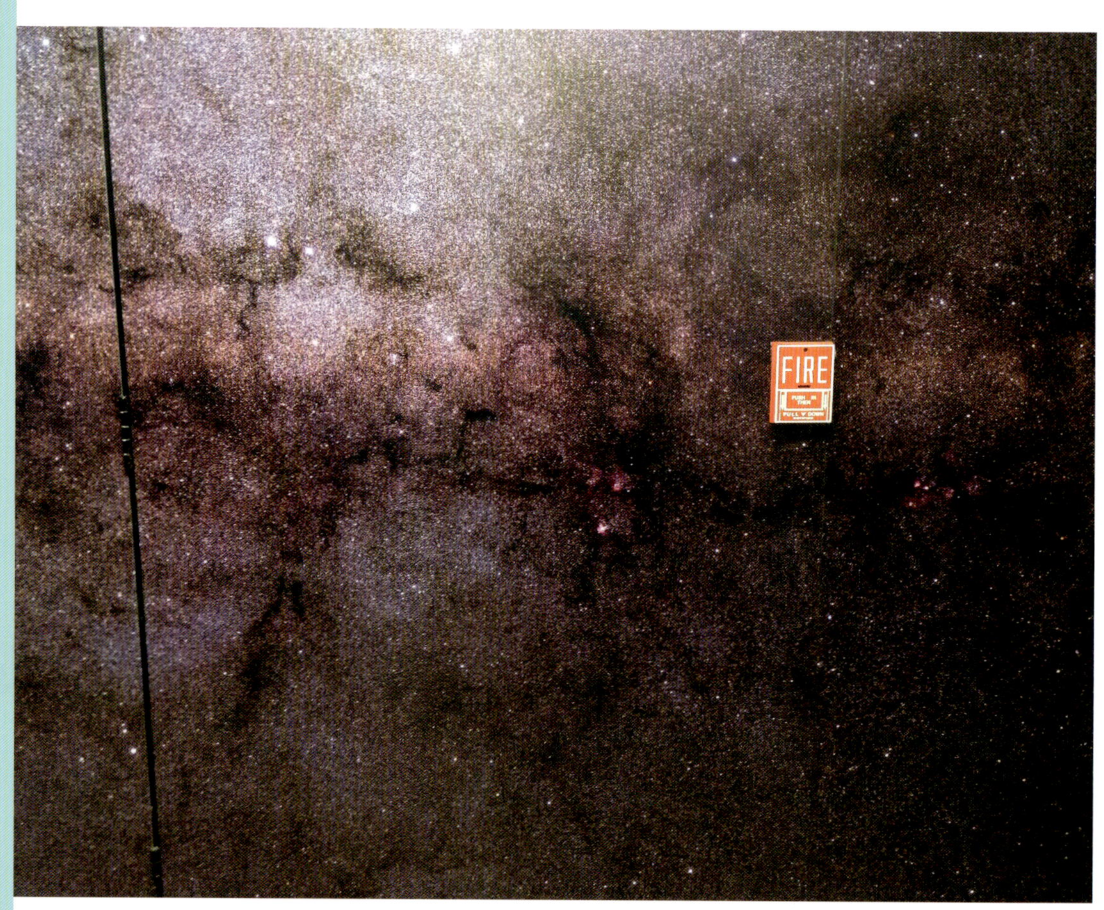

$$R_{\mu\nu} - \frac{1}{2}Rg_{\mu\nu} = 8\pi GT_{\mu\nu}$$

top: *Space fire #09142029, NASA JPL*, 2014; dye sublimation print on aluminum
bottom: *Krypton Relativity*, 2016; glass tubing, electric voltage, krypton gas

1. Define wonder in your own words.

For me, wonder is that delicious, often fleeting feeling when something rings true on a cosmic (and sometimes comic) level—it is expansive and selfless, humbling but not diminishing, and joyfully, universally connected. It has inherent beauty free from aesthetic constraints. It sneaks unexpectedly into your heart and mind simultaneously with a flash of recognition, like something you inherently knew but never thought of in quite that way before.

2. What is your earliest childhood experience with wonder?

The first time I remember experiencing wonder on a grand scale was at eight or nine years old. I was up past my bedtime, sitting alone in the living room flipping through a huge coffee-table edition of a World Atlas. Past all the continents and road maps at the back of the book, I came across a map of our solar system. I had certainly thought about stars and planets before, but perhaps it was in the context of illustrations of places one could actually travel to. All of a sudden, I was hit with a bolt of recognition that Earth is a planet in the *universe*—we are in the *UNIVERSE*!

3. What is the last wonder moment you had that left you speechless?

I have been left speechless by a specific series of moments this past year, an inner journey of sorts that has left me bursting at the seams with wonder. Doors are swinging open to levels of connection, healing, self awareness, and expanded consciousness that I didn't previously comprehend were possible. These experiences have left me so speechless that I pretty much want to talk about them all the time.

4. Was there a wonder or aha moment that led to your work in this exhibition?

There are so many juicy moments of spacetime awe in making a timeline of the history of the universe, it's hard to winnow it down to one. To begin with, weaving space and time together into an inextricable "spacetime"; or how about contemplating the "dark ages" of the cosmos, or the fact that the universe existed for give or take *9.3 billion years* before the Earth even *existed*, let alone life, let alone humans? But if I had to choose one wonderful moment, contemplating what came before the Big Bang is pretty darn thrilling. And headache inducing, and ridiculous, and then wonderful again. I mean, what *is* a "closed spherical spacetime of zero radius" or a "singularity of infinite density"? Just wonderful.

Fred Tomaselli

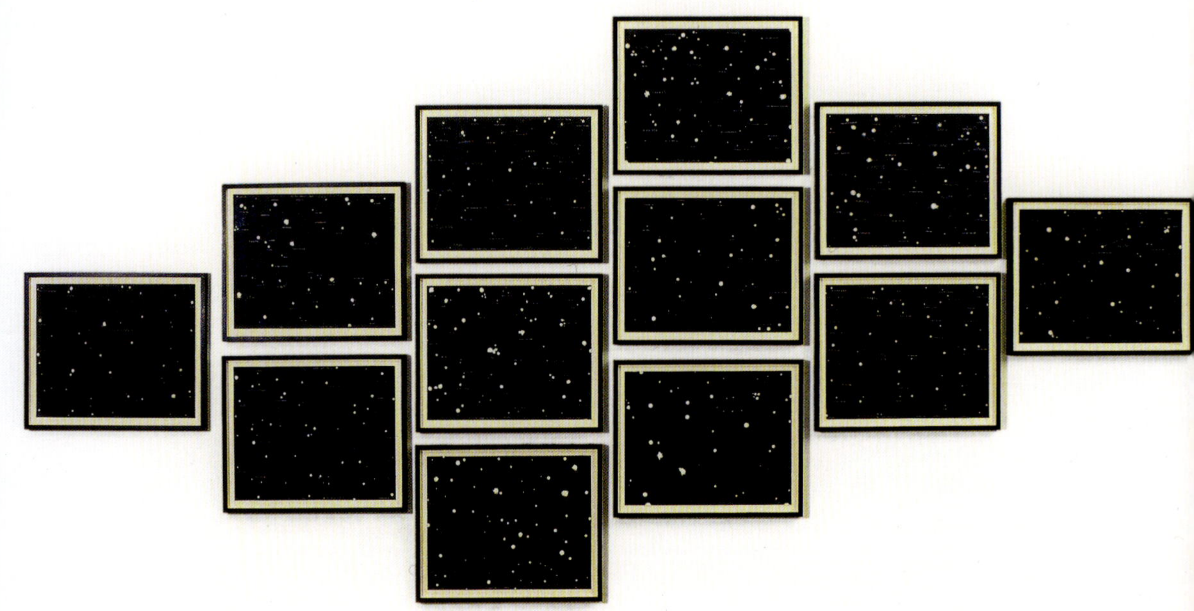

 Chemical Celestial Portraits, 1995; Prismacolor on photograms

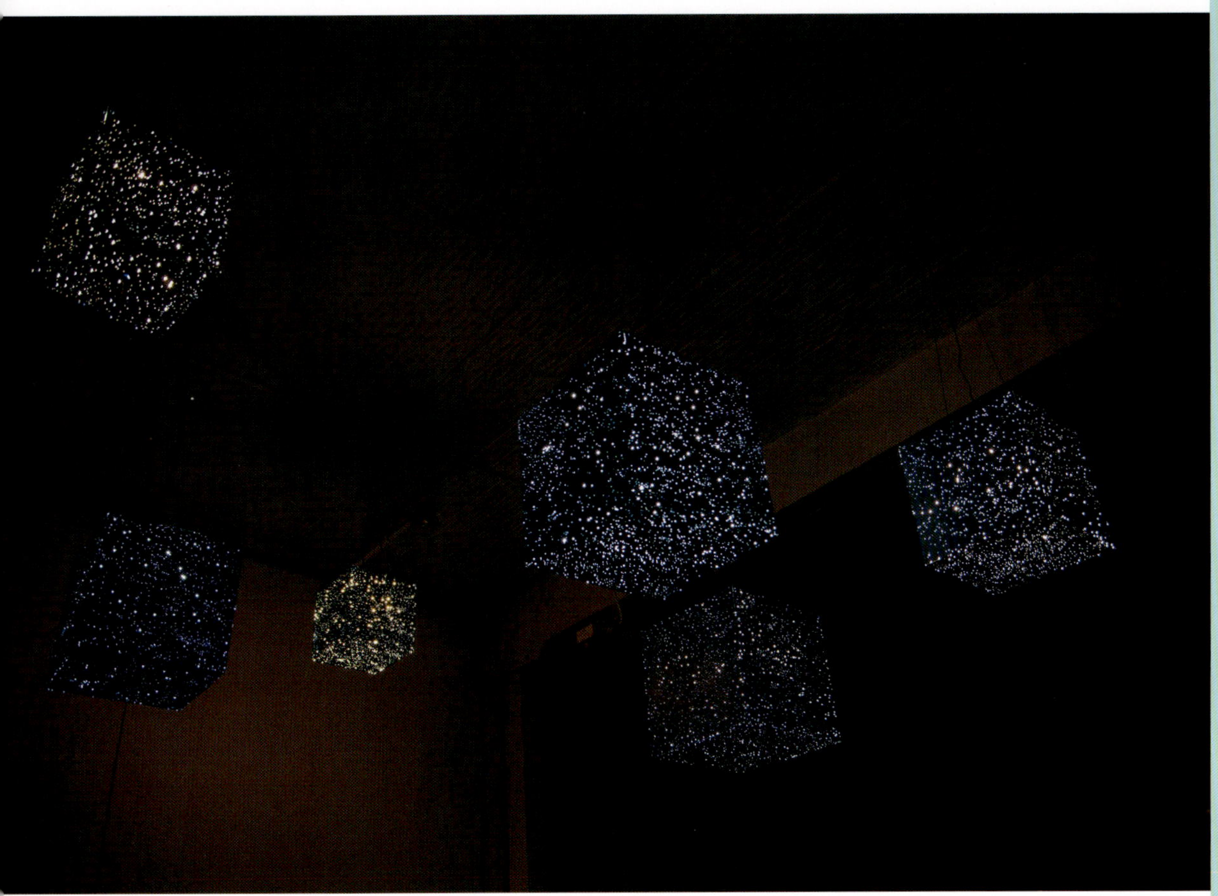

CUBIC SKY, 1988; Plexiglas, enamel paint, fluorescent lights, wood, hardware

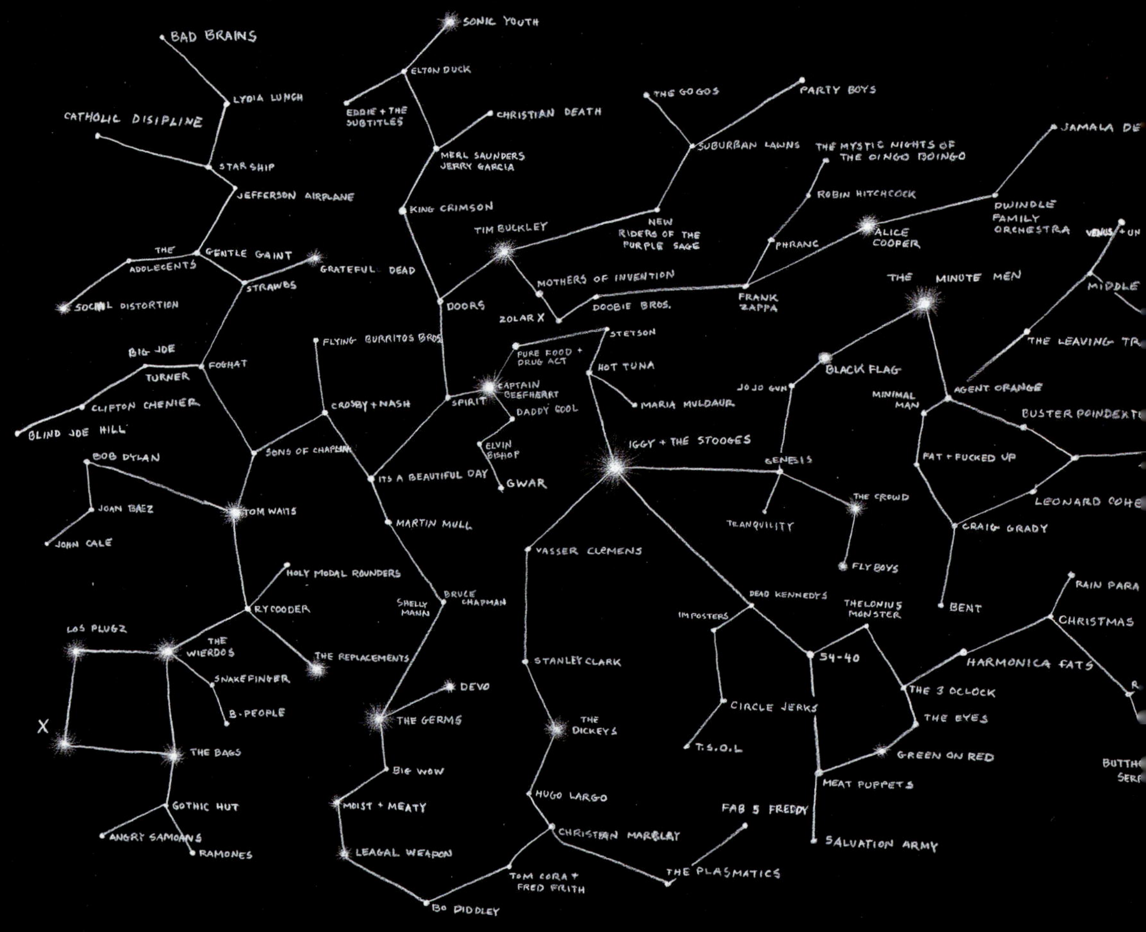

BAD BRAINS
SONIC YOUTH
ELTON DUCK
LYDIA LUNCH
CATHOLIC DISIPLINE
EDDIE + THE SUBTITLES
CHRISTIAN DEATH
THE GO GOS
PARTY BOYS
STAR SHIP
MERL SAUNDERS JERRY GARCIA
SUBURBAN LAWNS
THE MYSTIC NIGHTS OF THE OINGO BOINGO
JAMALA DE
JEFFERSON AIRPLANE
KING CRIMSON
ROBIN HITCHCOCK
DWINDLE FAMILY ORCHESTRA
TIM BUCKLEY
NEW RIDERS OF THE PURPLE SAGE
PHRANC
ALICE COOPER
VENUS + UN
THE ADOLECENTS
GENTLE GAINT
GRATEFUL DEAD
MOTHERS OF INVENTION
THE MINUTE MEN
MIDDLE
STRAWBS
DOORS
ZOLAR X
DOOBIE BROS.
FRANK ZAPPA
SOCIAL DISTORTION
STETSON
THE LEAVING TR
BIG JOE TURNER
FOGHAT
FLYING BURRITOS BROS
PURE FOOD + DRUG ACT
HOT TUNA
BLACK FLAG
AGENT ORANGE
CLIFTON CHENIER
CROSBY + NASH
SPIRIT
CAPTAIN BEEFHEART
DADDY COOL
JO JO GUN
MINIMAL MAN
BUSTER POINDEXTE
BLIND JOE HILL
SONS OF CHAPLIN
MARIA MULDAUR
FAT + FUCKED UP
BOB DYLAN
ELVIN BISHOP
IGGY + THE STOOGES
GENESIS
THE CROWD
LEONARD COHE
JOAN BAEZ
TOM WAITS
ITS A BEAUTIFUL DAY
GWAR
TRANQUILITY
CRAIG GRADY
JOHN CALE
MARTIN MULL
VASSER CLEMENS
FLY BOYS
BENT
HOLY MODAL ROUNDERS
BRUCE CHAPMAN
DEAD KENNEDYS
THELONIUS MONSTER
RAIN PARA
SHELLY MANN
IMPOSTERS
CHRISTMAS
LOS PLUGZ
RY COODER
STANLEY CLARK
54-40
HARMONICA FATS
THE WIERDOS
THE REPLACEMENTS
CIRCLE JERKS
THE 3 OCLOCK
SNAKEFINGER
DEVO
THE EYES
X
B. PEOPLE
THE GERMS
THE DICKEYS
GREEN ON RED
THE BAGS
BIG WOW
T.S.O.L
MEAT PUPPETS
BUTTH
SER
GOTHIC HUT
MOIST + MEATY
HUGO LARGO
FAB 5 FREDDY
SALVATION ARMY
ANGRY SAMOANS
LEAGAL WEAPON
CHRISTIAN MARCLAY
RAMONES
TOM CORA + FRED FRITH
THE PLASMATICS
BO DIDDLEY

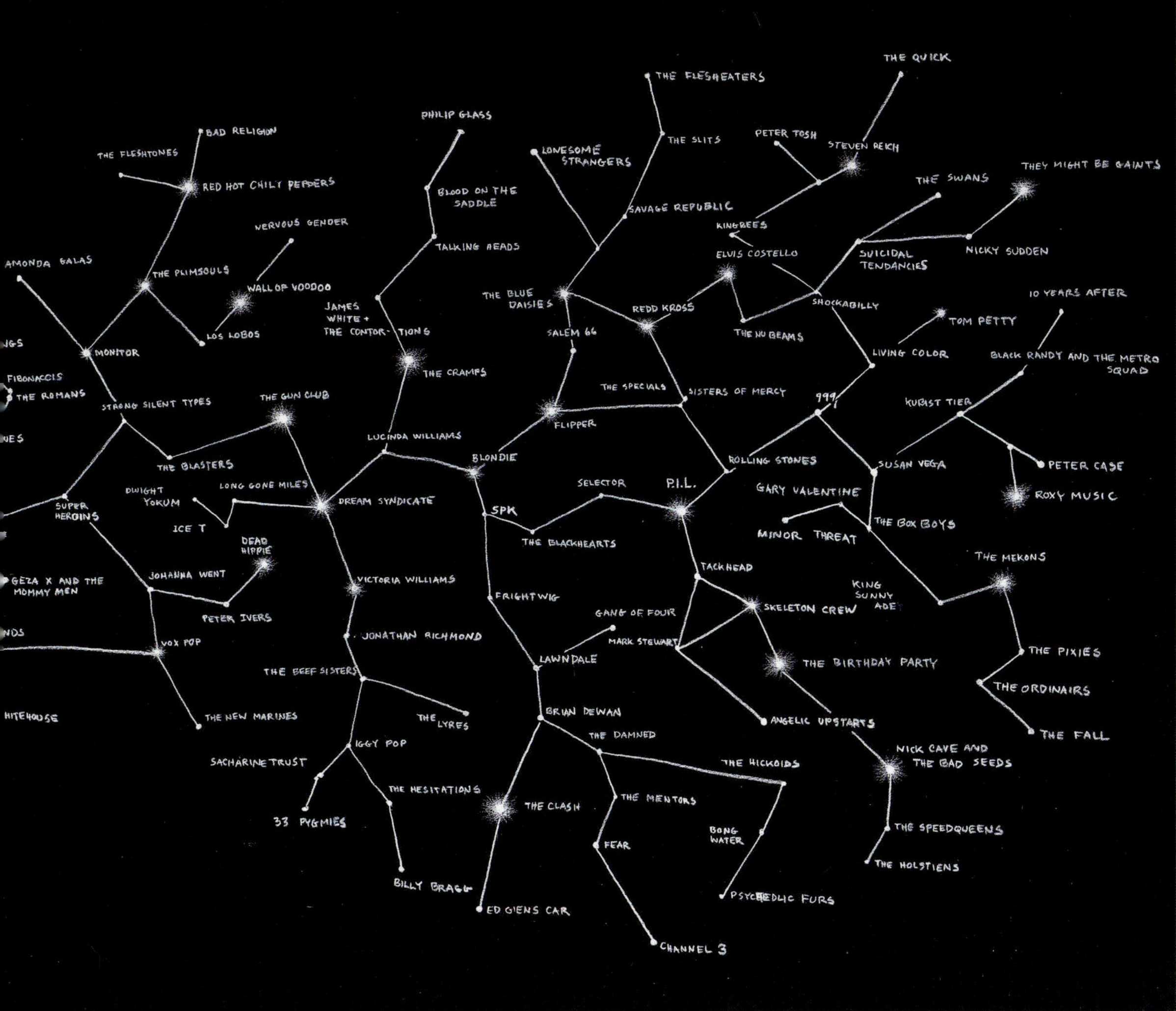

All the Bands I Can Remember Seeing, 1990; Prismacolor on paper

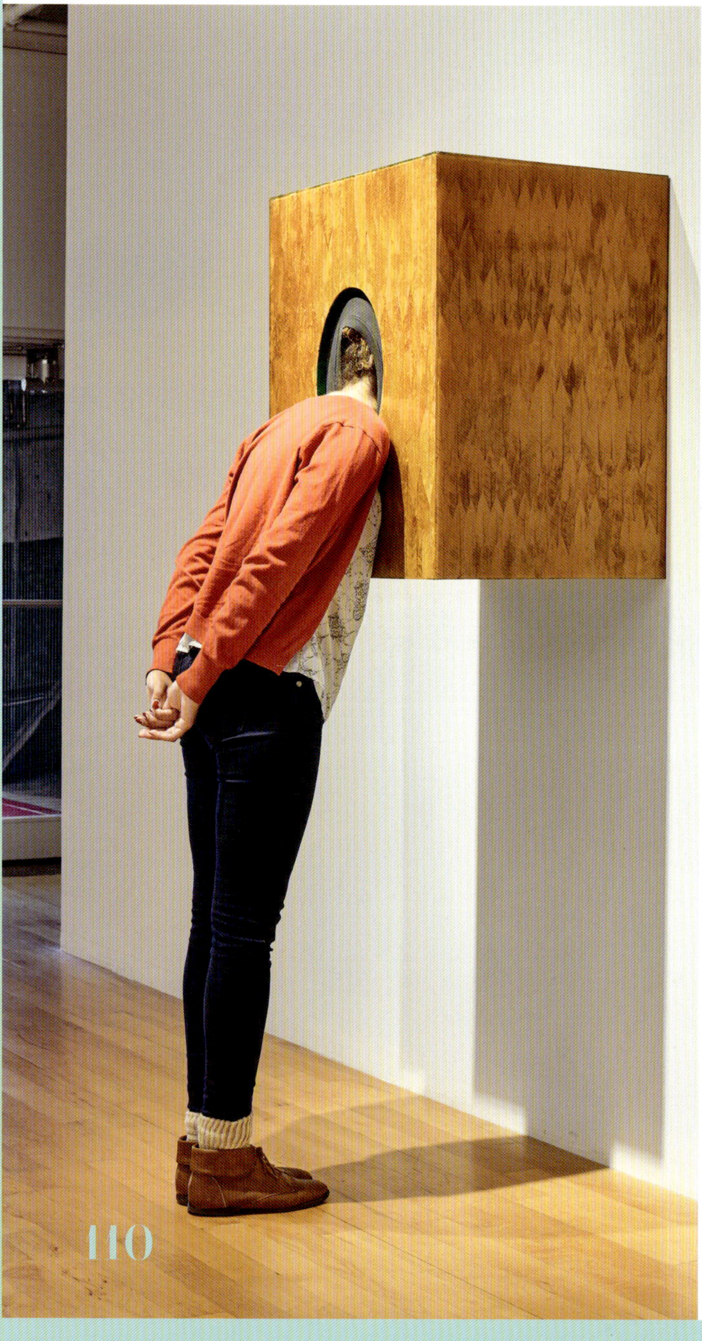

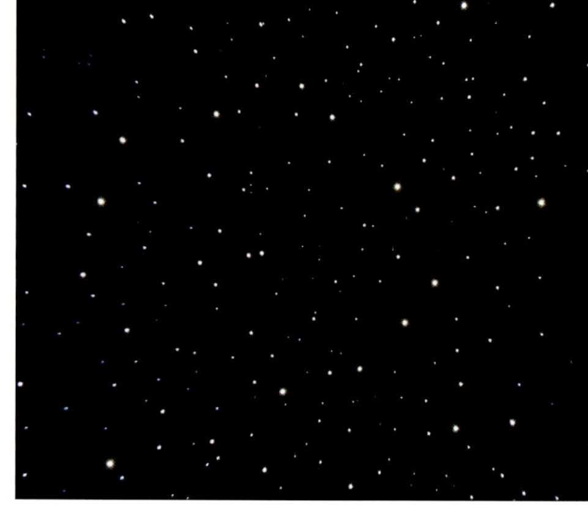

1. Define wonder in your own words.

Wonder visits you without permission. It just happens. When it wells up in the presence of an awesome thing or phenomenon, it's often difficult to fully understand or impossible to describe. Wonder opens you up to vastness no matter what size it is. Wonder is a mysterious, beautiful surprise.

2. What is your earliest childhood experience with wonder?

I guess I was about eleven when I started visiting the overpass of the freeway behind my house in order to stare down at the cars and trucks racing below. For a tiny moment, I would get a glimpse of the various drivers as they whizzed past, and I would try to imagine what kind of people they might be and what their lives might be like. I was overwhelmed by the thought that each vehicle carried a separate reality within it, that each car was its own universe and that all these universes were barreling through time, parallel and oblivious to one another. I transposed that thought to the billions of realities that were, at that very moment, birthing, living, fighting, and dying across the planet and this realization shook up my pre-adolescent brain.

3. What is the last wonder moment you had that left you speechless?

Hurtling through the water on a large, perfect ocean wave might be one of the more sublime experiences that happens to me on a semi-regular basis. I've been doing it since I was a kid and yet it always feels new. Maybe it's because wave energy is converted solar energy, which brings a cosmic dimension to the activity. Maybe it's a sense memory brought on by seawater, which is similar to the amniotic fluid of the womb. Whatever it is, it's always wonderful to drop into a wave on my bodyboard and then skim silently across its face surrounded by a tube of discharging energy. It's one of the few moments where time stops and I become one with everything. It's the one consistent, non-chemically induced, transcendental experience I keep on having.

4. Was there a wonder or aha moment that led to your work in this exhibition?

Cubic Sky initially came out of numerous camping trips in the backcountry of Joshua Tree National Park. It turns out that the dry air of the high desert, coupled with a lack of light pollution, creates crystal clear conditions for stargazing. On my first visit, the night sky was so dense and luminous with stars that I felt like I was seeing them for the first time.

Years later, after I moved to Brooklyn, I became obsessed by the politics of escapism. I was thinking that looking up at the heavens was man's oldest way of turning away from the world. I was also thinking that it might be amusing to try to containerize the infinite. Plus, I missed easy access to the heavens from my light-polluted and crime-ridden neighborhood. So that original California moment met my then-current Brooklyn moment, and the next thing I knew, I was building the work.

opposite: *BOX FOR YOUR HEAD*, 1991–1997; leaves, acrylic, fabric, fluorescent light tubes, resin on wood

AFTER A RAIN

by

MARY RUEFLE

They noticed, you see, that I was a noticing
kind of person, and so they left the dictionary
out in the rain and I noticed it,
I noticed it was open to the *rain* page,
much harm had come to it, it had aged to the age
of ninety-five paper years and I noticed *rainbow*
follows *rain* in the book, just as it does on
earth, and I noticed it was silly of me to
notice so much but I noticed there is no stationery
in heaven, I noticed an infant will grip your hand like
there is no tomorrow, while the very aged
will give you a weightless hand for the same reason,
I noticed in a loving frenzy that some are hemlocked
and others are not (believe me yours unspeakably obliged),
I noticed whoever I meet in my search for entrance
into this world went too far (but that was their
destination) and I noticed the road followed roughly
the route of a zipper around a closed case,
I noticed the sea was human but no one believed me,
and that some birds have the wingspan of an inch
and some flowers the petal span of a foot yet the two
are very well suited to each other, I noticed that.
There are eight major emotional states but I forget
seven of them, I can hear the ambulance singing
but I do not think it will stop for me,
because I noticed the space between the waterfall and
the rock and I am safe there, resting in
the cradle of all there is, the way a sea horse
(when it is tired) will tie its tail to a seaweed
and rest, and there has not been, in my opinion,
enough astonishment over this fact, so now I will
withdraw my interest in the whole external world
while I am in the noticing mode, notice how I
talk to you just as if you were sitting in my lap
and not as if it were raining, not as if there were
a sheet of water between us or anything else.

Still I wonder

by Stefan Sagmeister

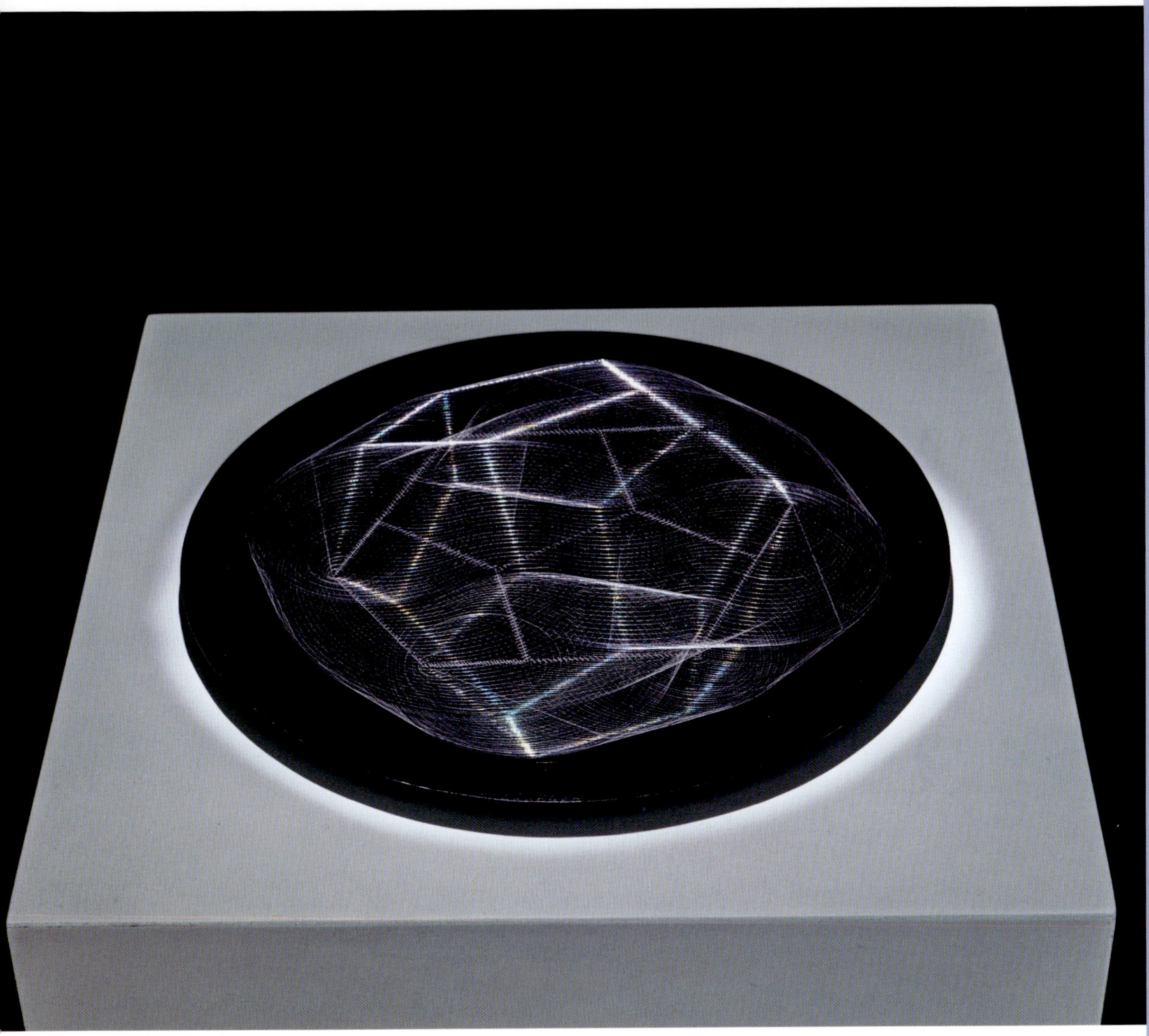

Dodecahedron (intersecting plate), 2014; hand-drawn hologram on metal plate with rotating turntable

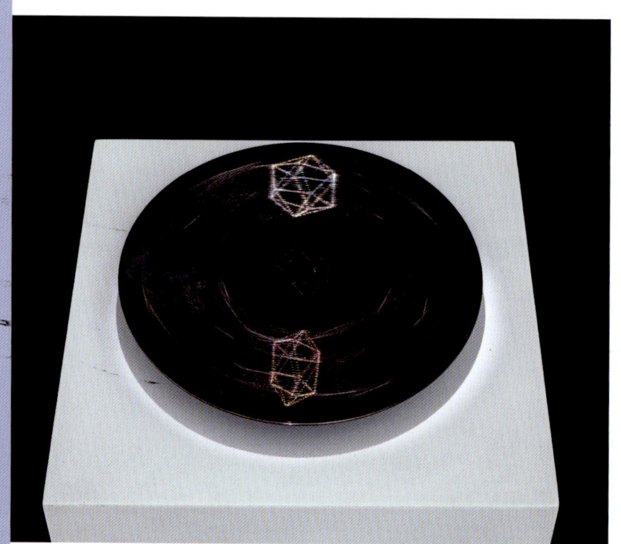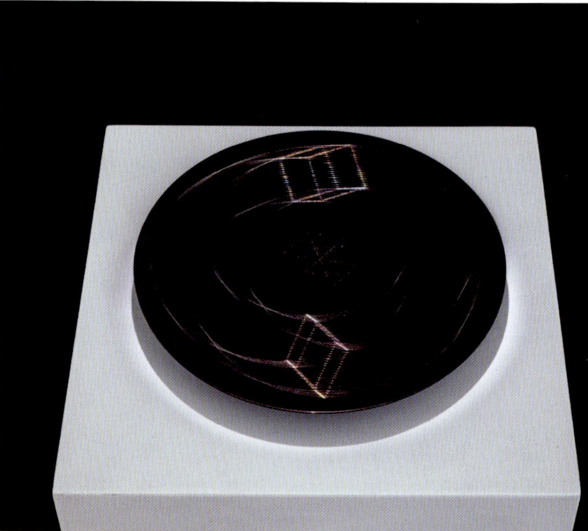

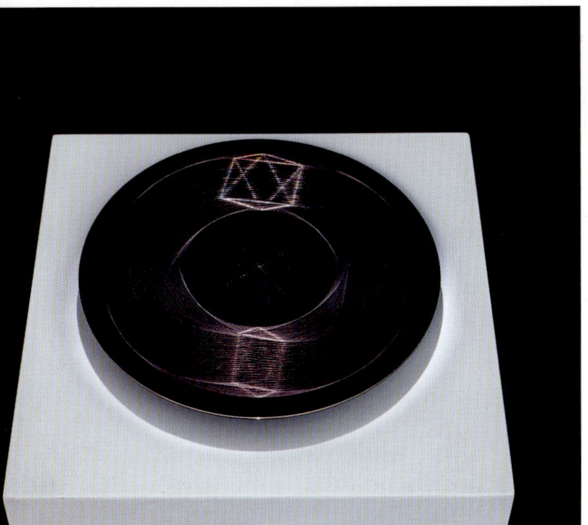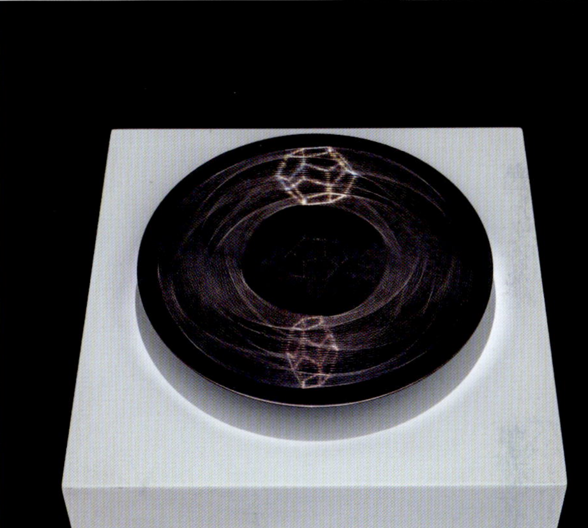

left to right: *Dodecahedron (above/below); Cube (above/below); Octahedron (above/below); Icosahedron (above/below,* all 2015; hand-drawn holograms on metal plates with rotating turntables

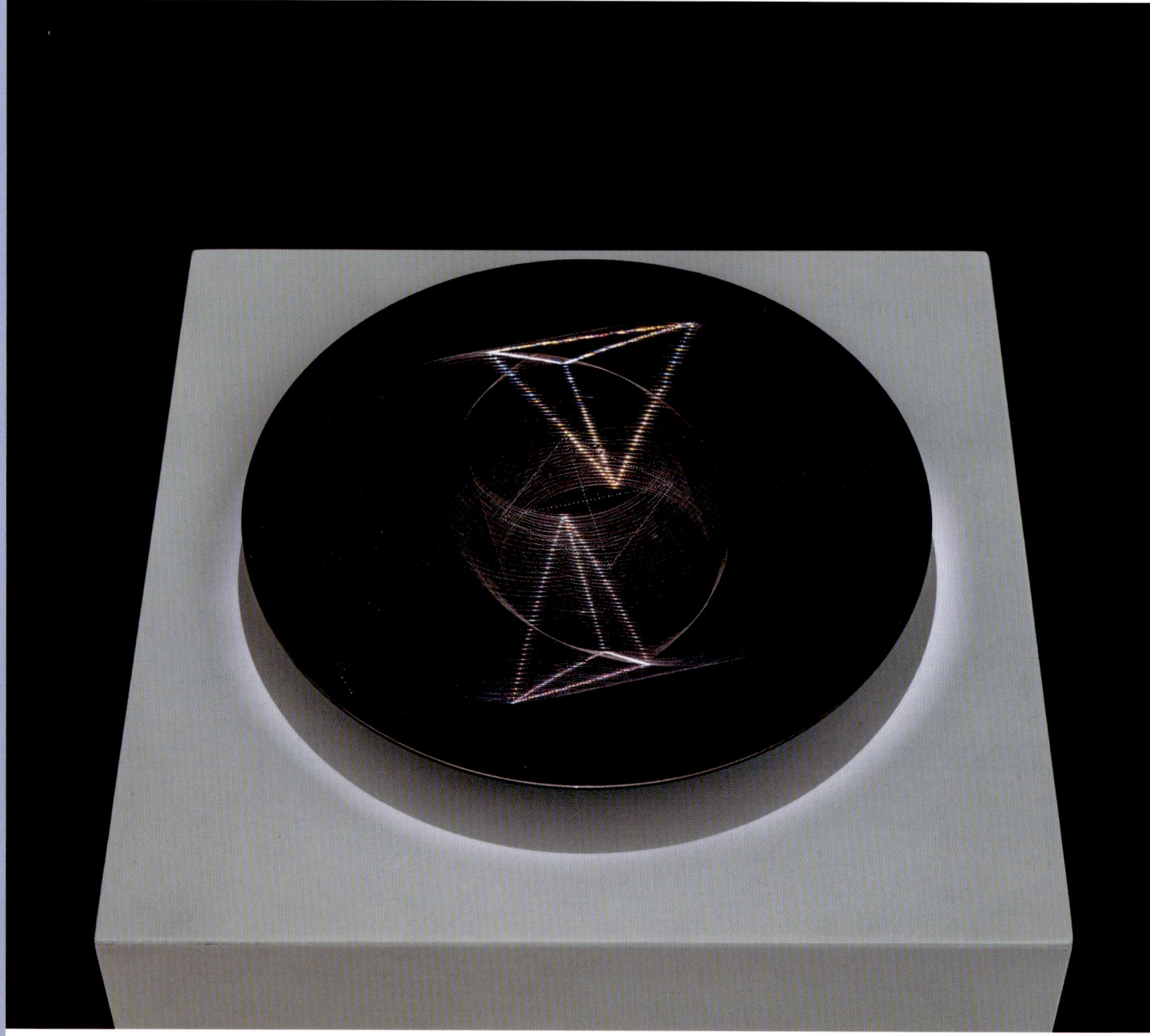

 Tetrahedron (above/below), 2015; hand-drawn hologram on metal plate with rotating turntable

1. Define wonder in your own words.

I have had a long and occasionally uncomfortable relationship with the idea of "wonder." When I was a teenager, my mother curated a fascinating *Wunderkammer*-style show at the University of Illinois. Later, the Getty's *Devices of Wonder* exhibition made a deep impression on me. In my association with The Museum of Jurassic Technology, "wonder" is a term that has come up again and again.*

Perhaps it is due to an intractable contrarian strain that I find myself resisting the concept. But more, I think, it is an inherent distrust of theoretical constructs that risks our losing touch with a dynamic (and often ambiguous) direct experience.

What makes wonder so wonderful is exactly the ways it cuts though concepts.

I'm interested in a more primordial wonder—where the thing is cut loose from meaning, where we can forget what we know and see something anew. Wonder to me is a space where new ways of knowing can emerge.

2. What is your earliest childhood experience with wonder?

According to my mother, my first words were "low balloon," with a finger pointing from my stroller to a hot-air balloon pushing above the trees. (To be sure, there was some optimism in this interpretation: a noun *and* an adjective ... really, Mom?) Or maybe she misinterpreted the more archaic Middle English: "*Lo!* Balloon."

Wonder exists in this slippery space between words and meanings; the exuberant gesture, finger outstretched; sounds uttered in the face of the ineffable ...

Lest we not veer too deeply into the nostalgic here, I also would like to posit that our capacity for wonder actually deepens, the more we know about the world.

My most profound experiences of wonder are marked with a sense of having taken a journey—where I struggled with meaning and emerged changed.

3. What is the last wonder moment you had that left you speechless?

Jogging has become my regular meditation ... and a way to step outside of discursive thoughts.

4. Was there a wonder or aha moment that led to your work in this exhibition?

Everything about the hologram evokes wonder: a three-dimensional image is captured on film without lens or a camera, but with a bath of laser light. The hologram can be broken, and in each piece the whole image will still be visible.

The more I learned about holography, the more unlikely the process seemed. I understood the physics, I could make a hologram, but still I could not understand its visual structure.

Comparatively, a photograph is simple; its composition is basically the same as a drawing—light and dark areas denote shadow, the rules of perspective imply depth. But how do you "trace" a hologram? From this I formulated a question: Photography is to drawing as holography is to *what*?

It was this question that led to the "holographic drawings" on display in this exhibition. Each image was "drawn" by carving micro-reflectors into the surface of the plate by hand.

In this quest to understand, I keep coming back to not knowing. Whatever depths of understanding I come to, whatever new heights of knowledge, these the hologram reveals as merely illusion, a trick of light, and I'm left with that same blank slate of wonder.

*A hand-drawn sign, which appeared in the Jurassic back offices, summed up how many of us felt by that time: the word *wonder* with a no-smoking-style red circle with a cross through it—"NO WONDER."

Institute For Figuring and Margaret Wertheim

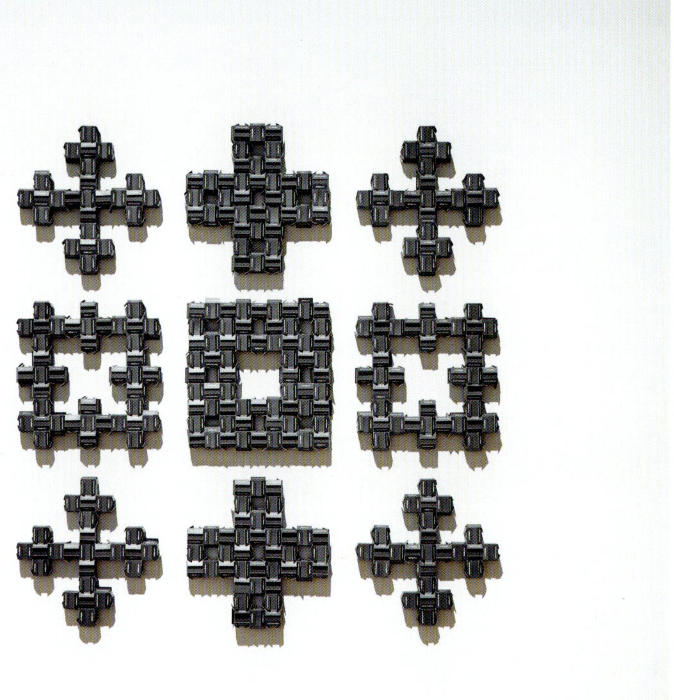

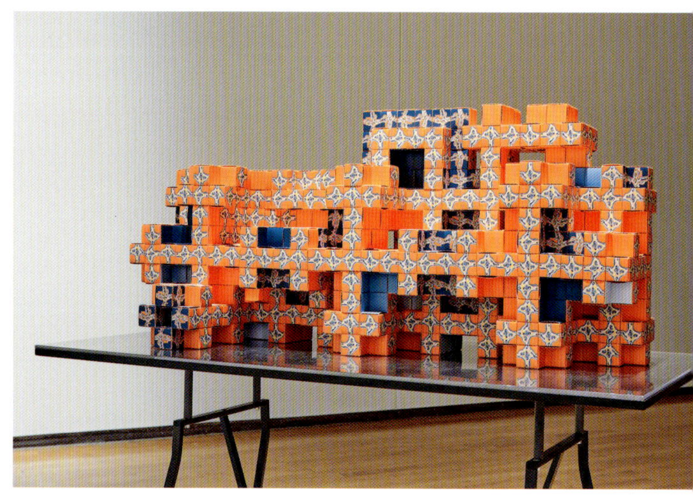

top: *Topographical layers of a Level Two Mosely Snowflake Sponge Business Card Fractal*, 2016; folded business cards
bottom: *Fractal Ruin*, 2016; folded business cards using business card origami techniques by Dr. Jeannine Mosely

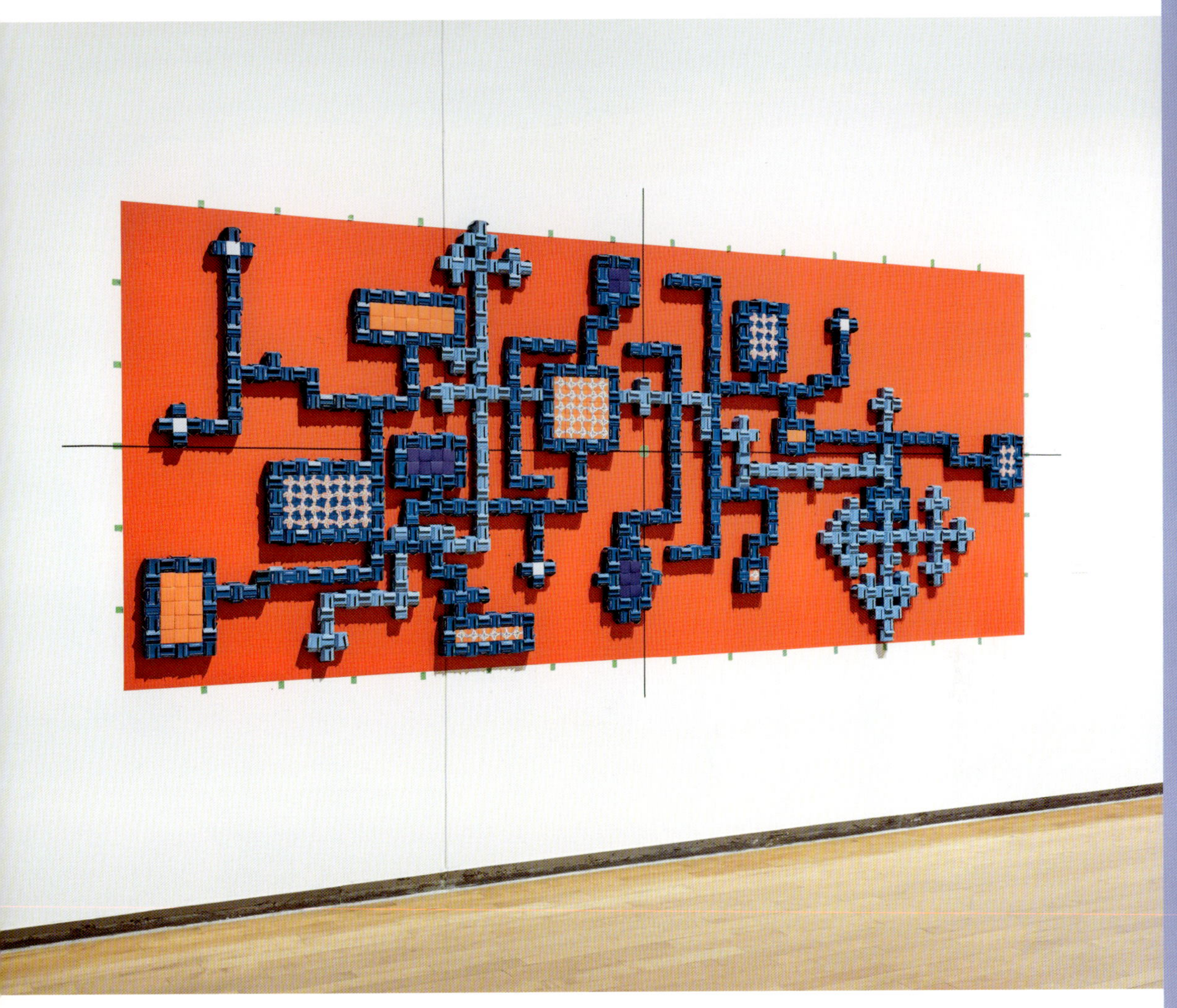

Business Card Wall Frieze, 2016; folded business cards

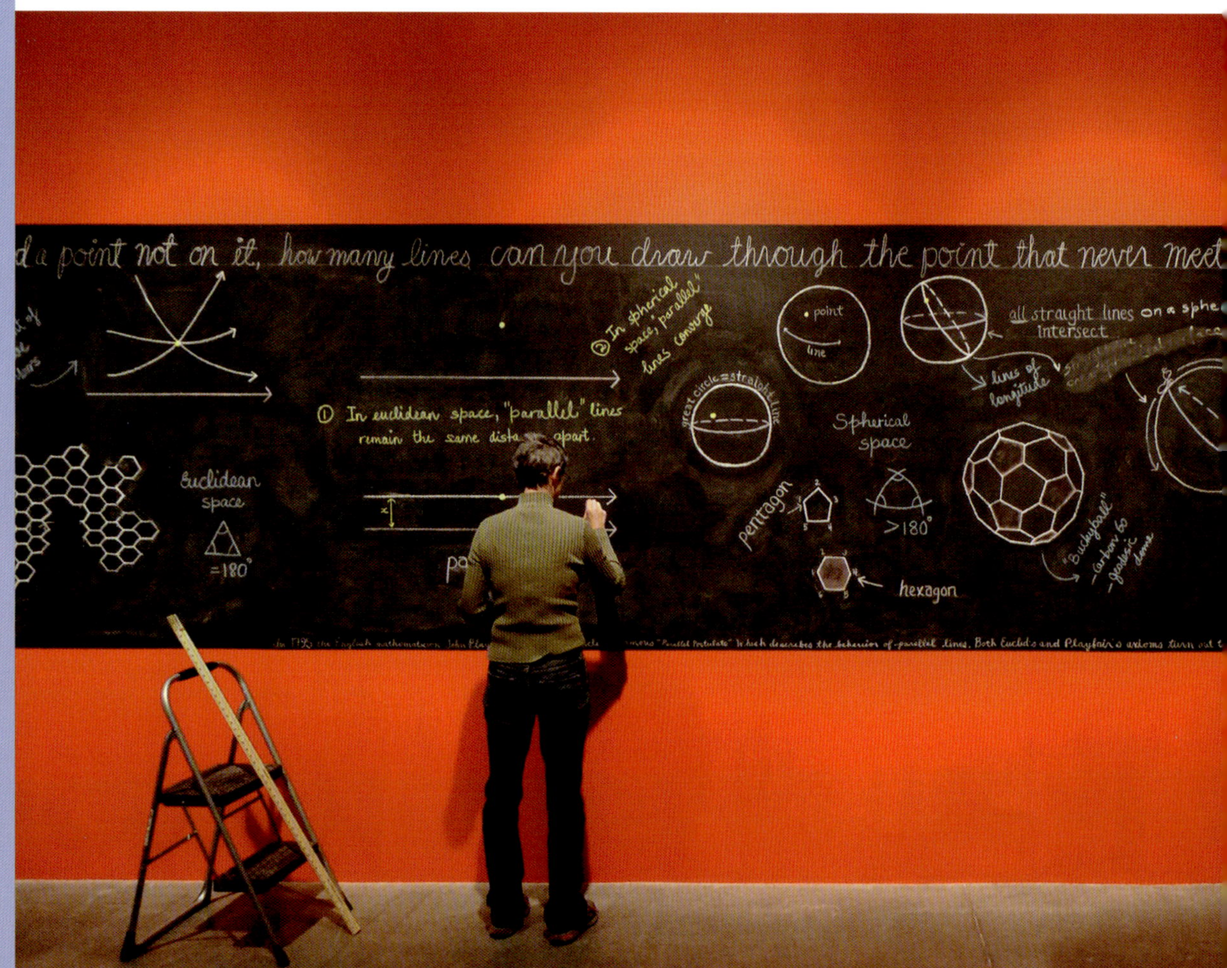

126 Margaret Wertheim drawing hyperbolic diagrams in the exhibition *Reefs, Rubbish and Reason*, at the Alyce do Roulet Williamson Gallery, Art Center College of Design, Pasadena, CA

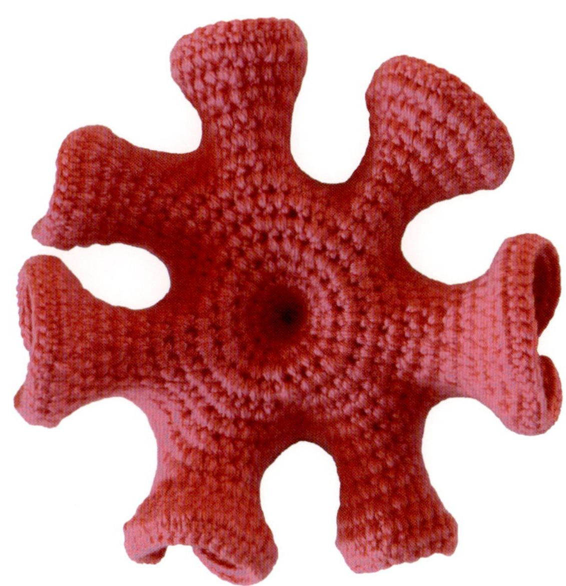

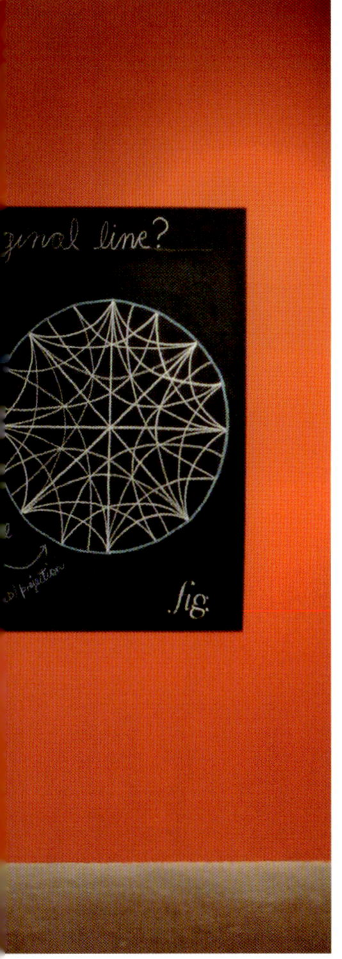

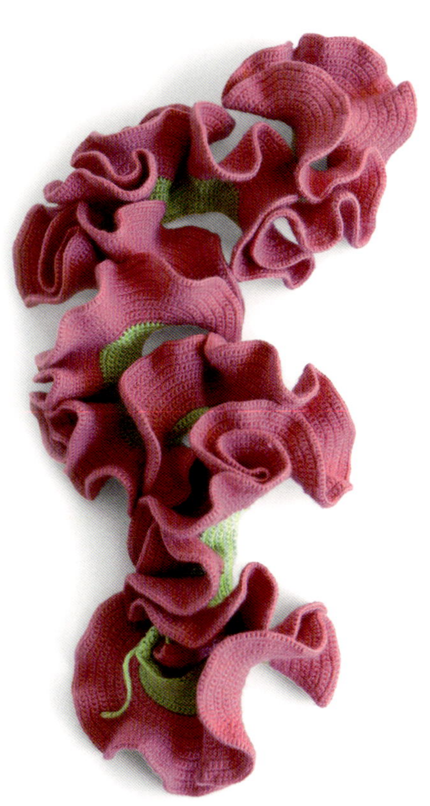

top: crocheted hyperbolic *pseudosphere*—the negative-curvature version of a cone—by Margaret Wertheim
bottom: crocheted hyperbolic organism by Anitra Menning

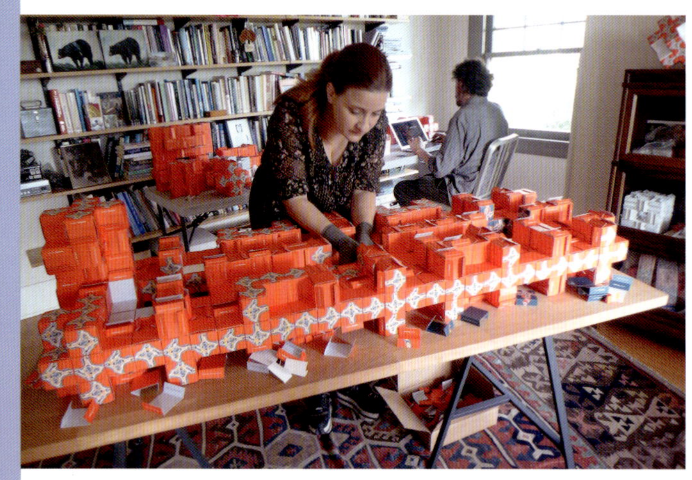

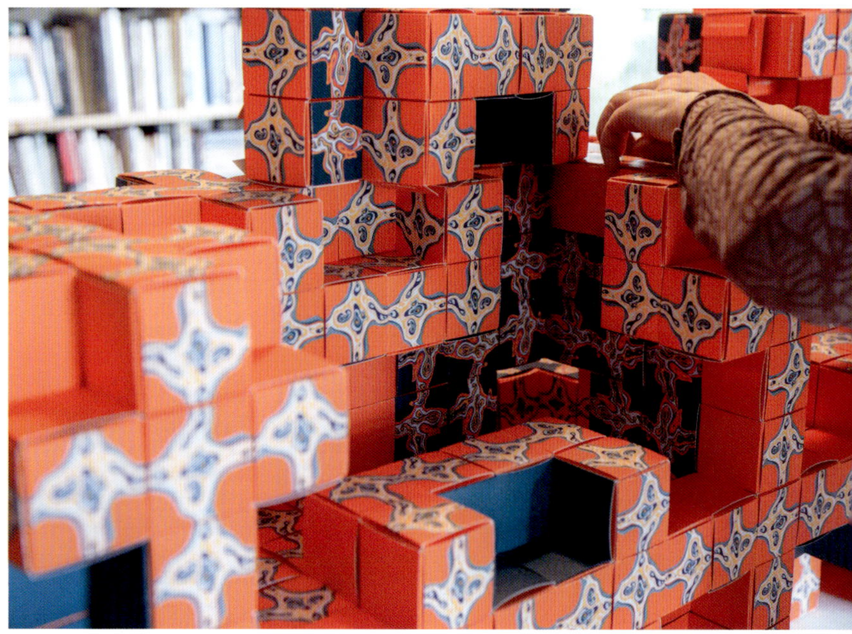

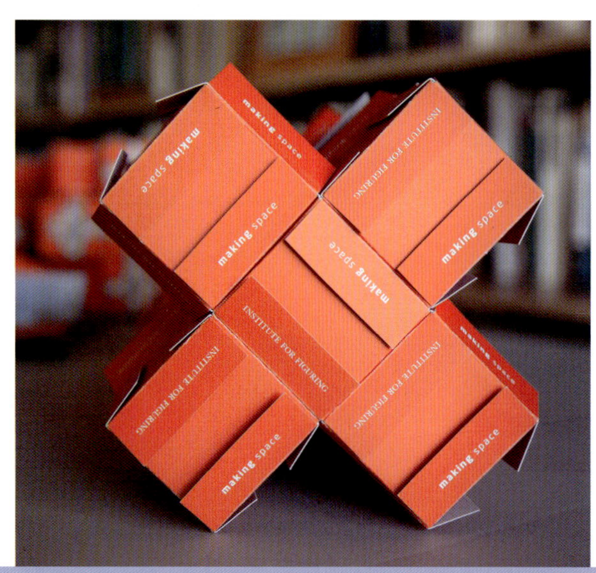

making space
making space
making space
making space
INSTITUTE FOR FIGURING
INSTITUTE FOR FIGURING
INSTITUTE FOR FIGURING

1. Define wonder in your own words.

Wonder, for me, is that which occurs when I'm confronted with things revealing unimagined linkages or resonances between disparate and seemingly unconnected phenomena, especially things that challenge my conceptions of understanding itself. Hyperbolic geometry, for instance, is present in the structures of corals, kelps, cactuses, and lettuce leaves, yet mathematicians spent hundreds of years trying to prove such forms were impossible. How marvelous that brainless organisms can perform "higher" mathematics. This raises a fantastic question: "What does it mean to *know* math at all?"

2. What is your earliest childhood experience with wonder?

When I was in third grade, my math teacher gave us a class on circles, but instead of just telling us what pi (π) is and giving us the formulae defining circles in terms of π, he led us along a path that enabled us to discover this wondrous number for ourselves. I realized then that π was present in the shape of the Sun and Moon; it was there in the dinner plates at meals, in the wheels of every car, and in the pearls my mother wore. The world is full of circles and at the heart of them all is π. Today, mathematicians continue to calculate the decimal expansion of π—they've now reached more than 13 trillion digits. Such exactitude goes way beyond any practical application (a few hundred digits is enough for any real world purpose), and is simply an ongoing unfolding of a mathematical wonder.

3. What is the last wonder moment you had that left you speechless?

Every time I talk to my twin sister, Christine, I feel as if I'm talking to an alien. On a daily basis I navigate a being who uses fundamentally different sets of linguistic and philosophical categories. After we finished school, I went to university to study physics and math and she went to art school. We were trained to see the world from a different set of parameters and our natural proclivities compound this effect. Often during conversations I find myself speechless: How is it possible I shared a womb with someone so *other*? People fantasize that twin-dom means having someone who is totally known, and who totally knows you. For me, it's been the opposite: It's the wonder of getting to experience two wildly different psychologies.

4. Was there a wonder or aha moment that led to your work in this exhibition?

When I learned from Dr. Jeannine Mosely, the inventor of business card origami, that the mathematical concept of a fractal could be made manifest through the mundane object of a business card, I was blown away. American business cards are a standard size (3.5 x 2 inches), which isn't true for European or Asian cards. That means US cards are a uniform material, readily available from a vast array of sources and a reliable atomic constructor set. I love the fact that in this case *standardization*, which we might normally reject in an artistic framework, has turned out to be a key creative resource.

opposite top: Christina Simons and Jacob Dotson building *Fractal Ruin* at the Institute For Figuring, Los Angeles; April 2016
opposite middle: Margaret Wertheim building in cubes of *Fractal Ruin* at the Institute For Figuring, Los Angeles; April 2016
opposite bottom: business card cubes and fractal modules

Ryan and Trevor Oakes

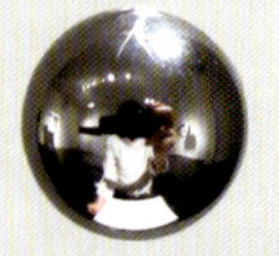

Map Tack (Lightfoam Sample), 2002; readymade map tack

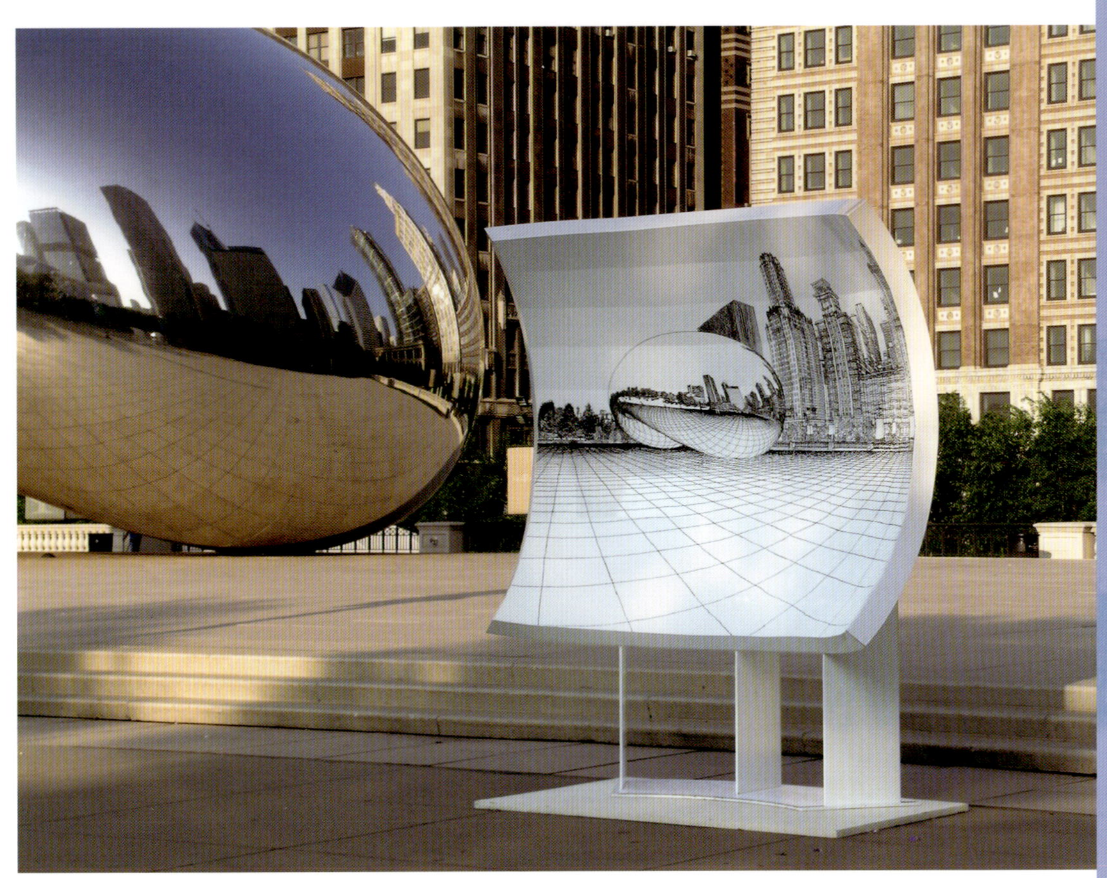

Have No Narrow Perspectives, July 2008–February 2009; stainless steel, epoxy, enamel

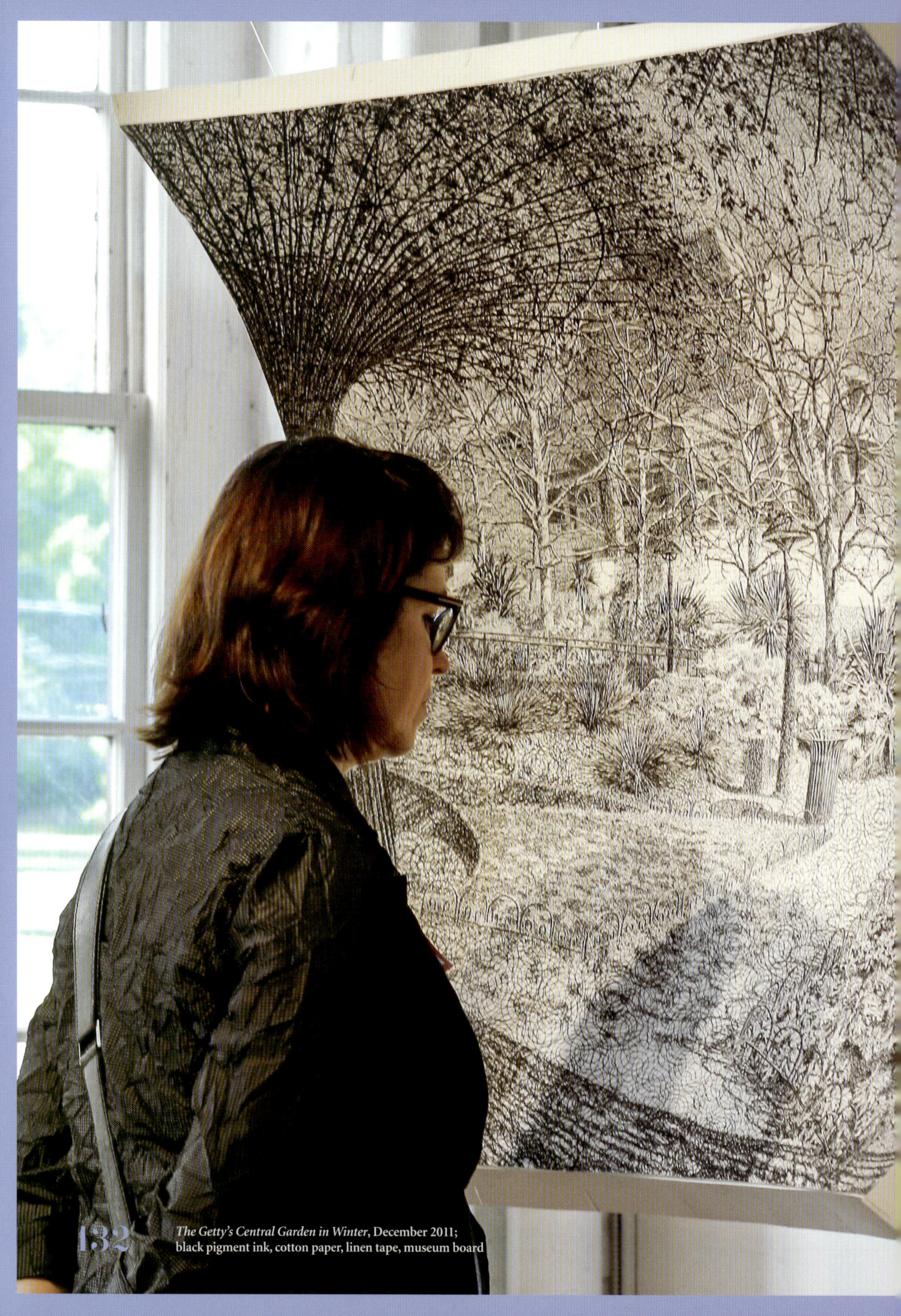

The Getty's Central Garden in Winter, December 2011;
black pigment ink, cotton paper, linen tape, museum board

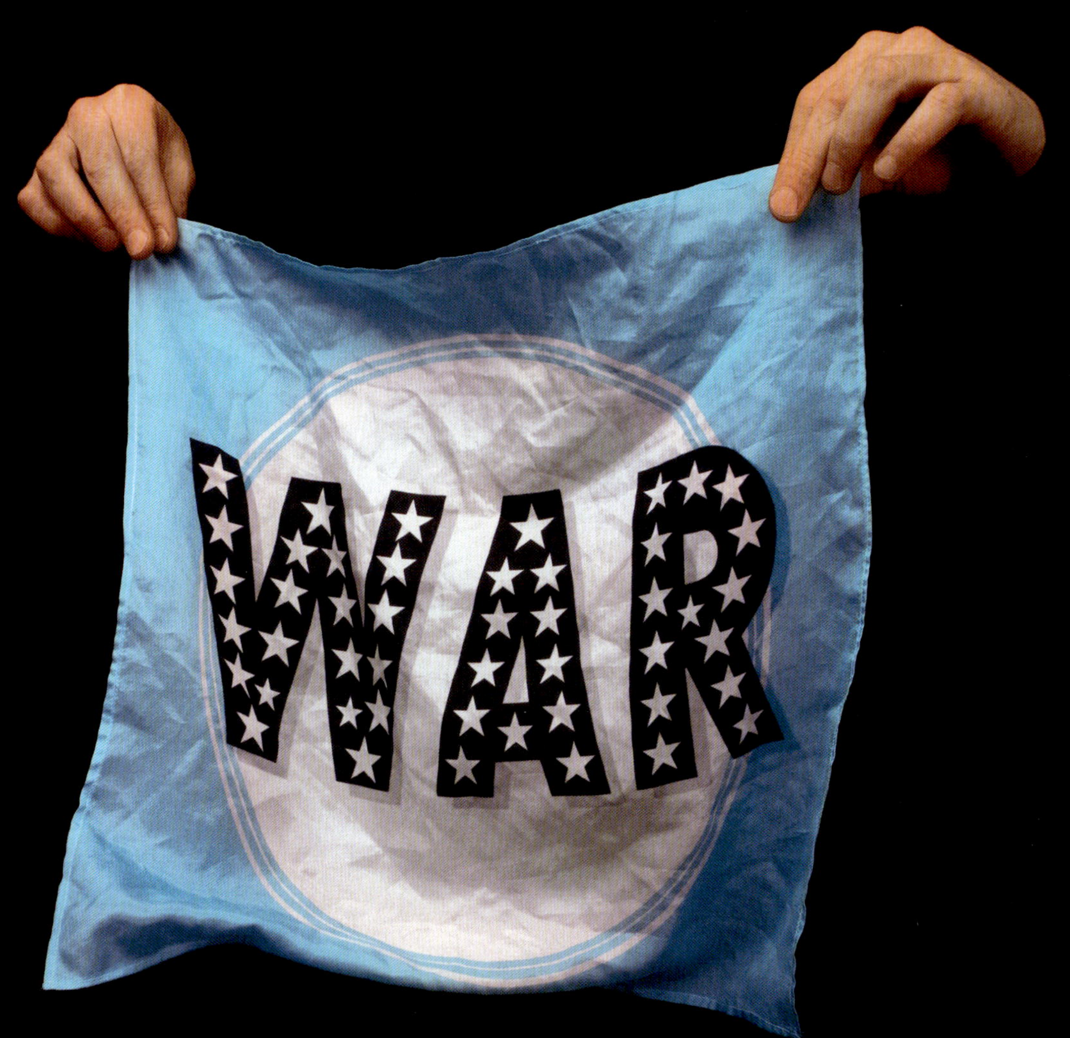

Twenty-First-Century Silks, 2016; video installation (details)

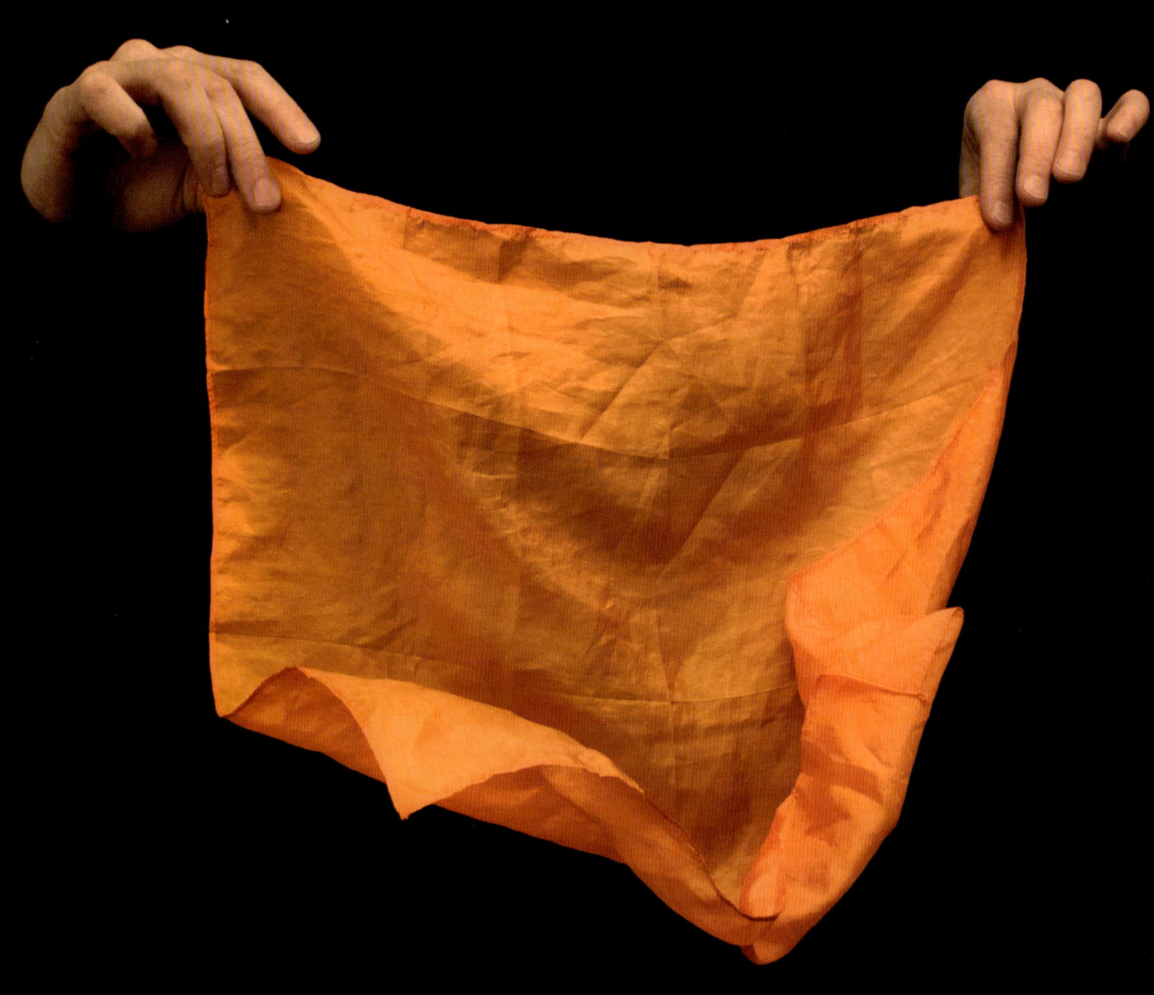

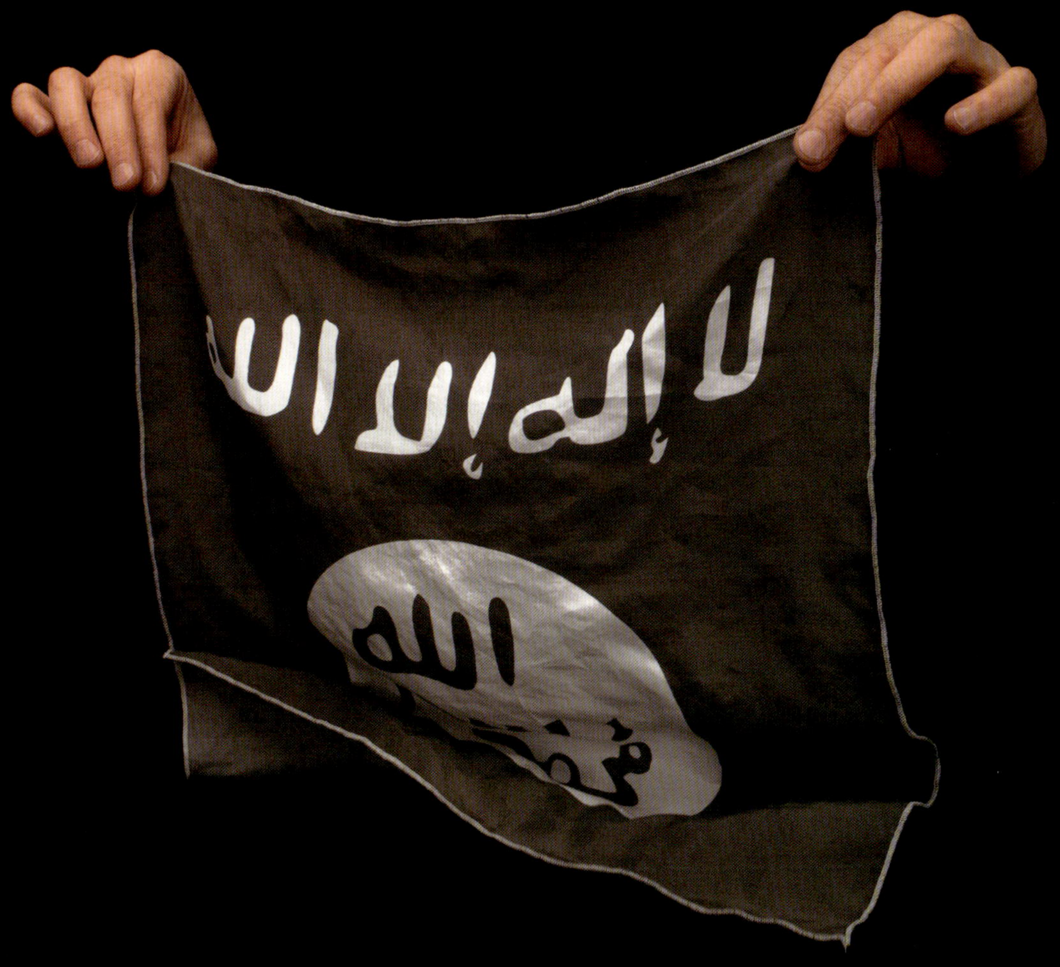

Twenty-First-Century Silks, 2016; video installation (details)

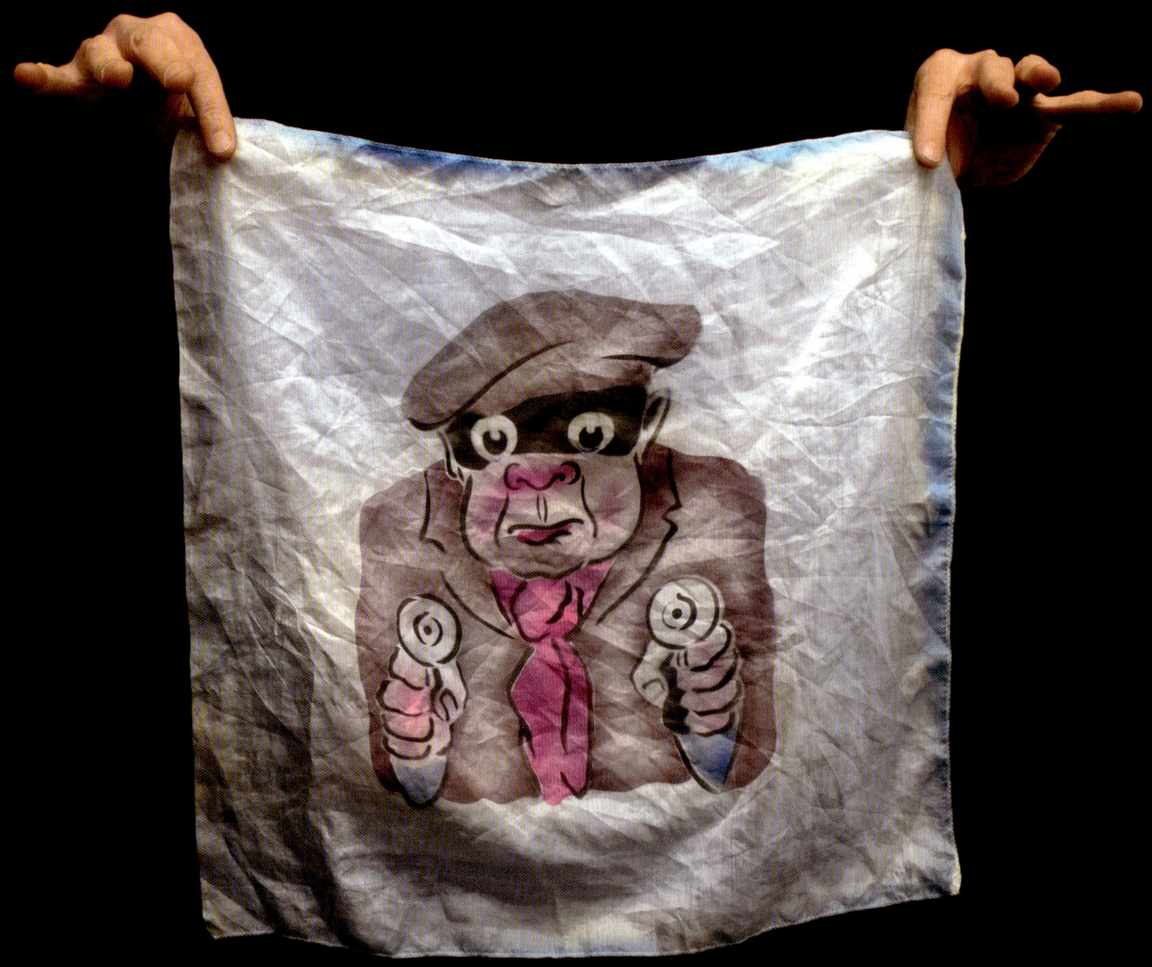

148 *Twenty-First-Century Silks, 2016*

1. Define wonder in your own words.

For the theatrical magician, the creation of "childlike" wonder is virtually a job description. The wonder generated in this context, however, also prompts a more skeptical kind of wondering. *How* is that body floating above the stage? *Where* did that playing card/coin/tiger come from? Magicians may seem to tempt us towards unknowingness, but more accurately their shortcuts to the supernatural model our attention. Here wonder primes critical spectatorship.

2. What is your earliest childhood experience with wonder?

Staring into the illuminated glow of a model carousel—*Wade's Gallopers*—constructed by my grandfather, at the center of which a mysterious uniformed figure beat time with a tiny baton.

3. What is the last wonder moment you had that left you speechless?

In the summer of 2011, during the Venice International Art Biennale, I watched as one of Andy Warhol's "Silver Cloud" balloons was torn by powerful storm winds from its moorings in the gardens of the Palazzo Contarini degli Scrigni, and buffeted over the city's skyline before landing in the Grand Canal where, dodged by waterbuses and gondoliers, it headed for the open sea. Perhaps we should require that all artworks take such risks on our behalf. Certainly, I held my breath as Warhol's inflatable took to the sky. "This quick intake of breath," writes James Hillman, "is also the very root of the word aesthetic, *aisthesis* in Greek, meaning sense perception. *Aisthesis* goes back to the Homeric *aiou* and *aisthou* which means both 'I perceive' as well as 'I gasp, struggle for breath'... *aisthmoai, aisthanomai*, I breathe in."*

4. Was there a wonder or aha moment that led to your work in this exhibition?

Twenty-First-Century Silks draws its title from a conjuring trick developed in the late nineteenth century, a period during which magical routines featuring then easily borrowed silk handkerchiefs became popular for both performers and audiences. "Twentieth-Century Silks" was just one of many such tricks that took advantage of silk's highly compressible and thus concealable quality. "Picture silks" also became a commonplace, featuring slogans and popular motifs (particularly flag designs) that magically appeared and disappeared in the performer's hands. But *Twenty-First-Century Silks* also lifts an art historical veil—that belonging to Saint Veronica, who according to Catholic tradition mopped the face of Christ as he stumbled towards Calvary, causing the Messiah's face to become miraculously imprinted upon her cloth.

**Tema Celeste*, May 1991.

Christopher Gausby

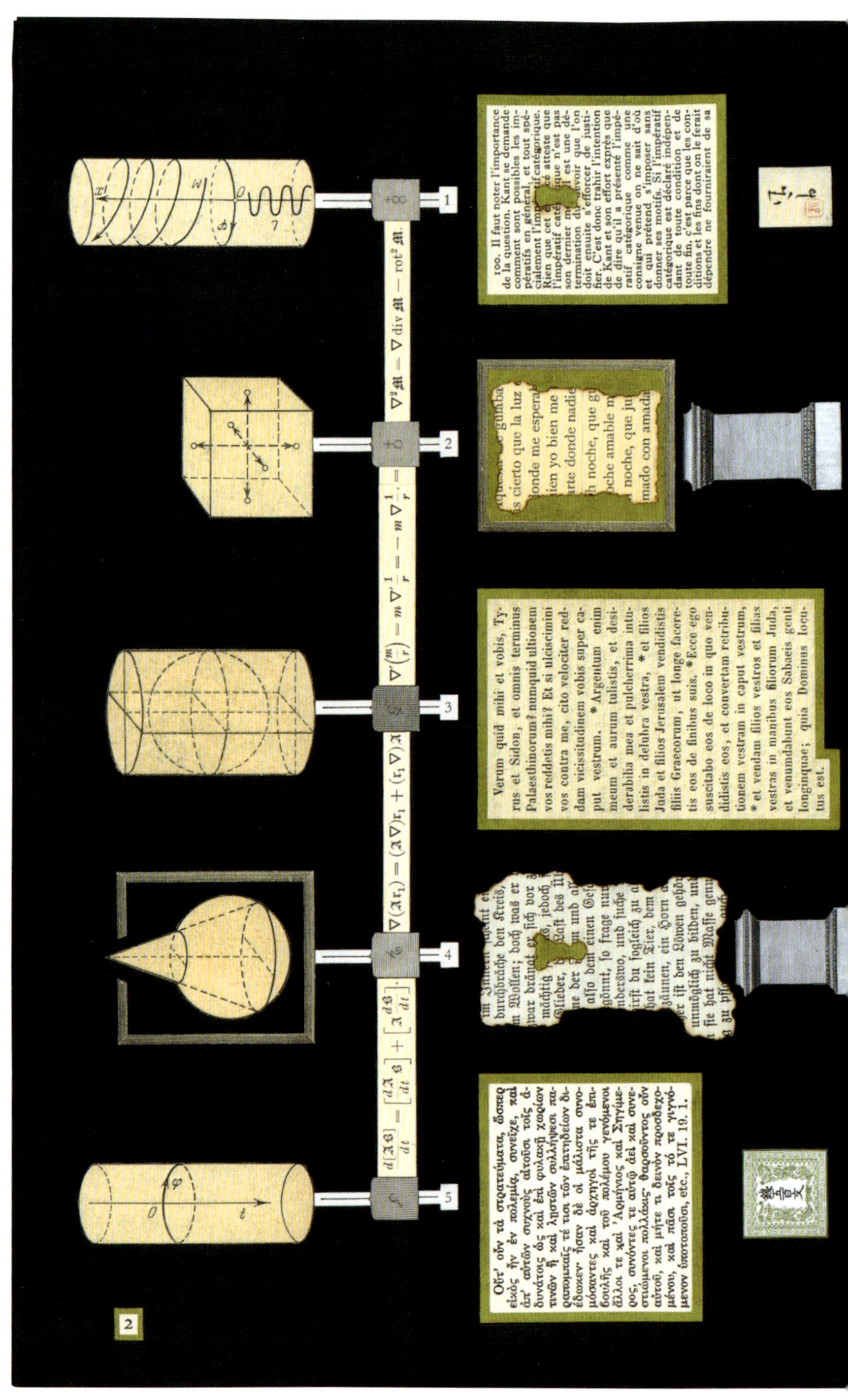

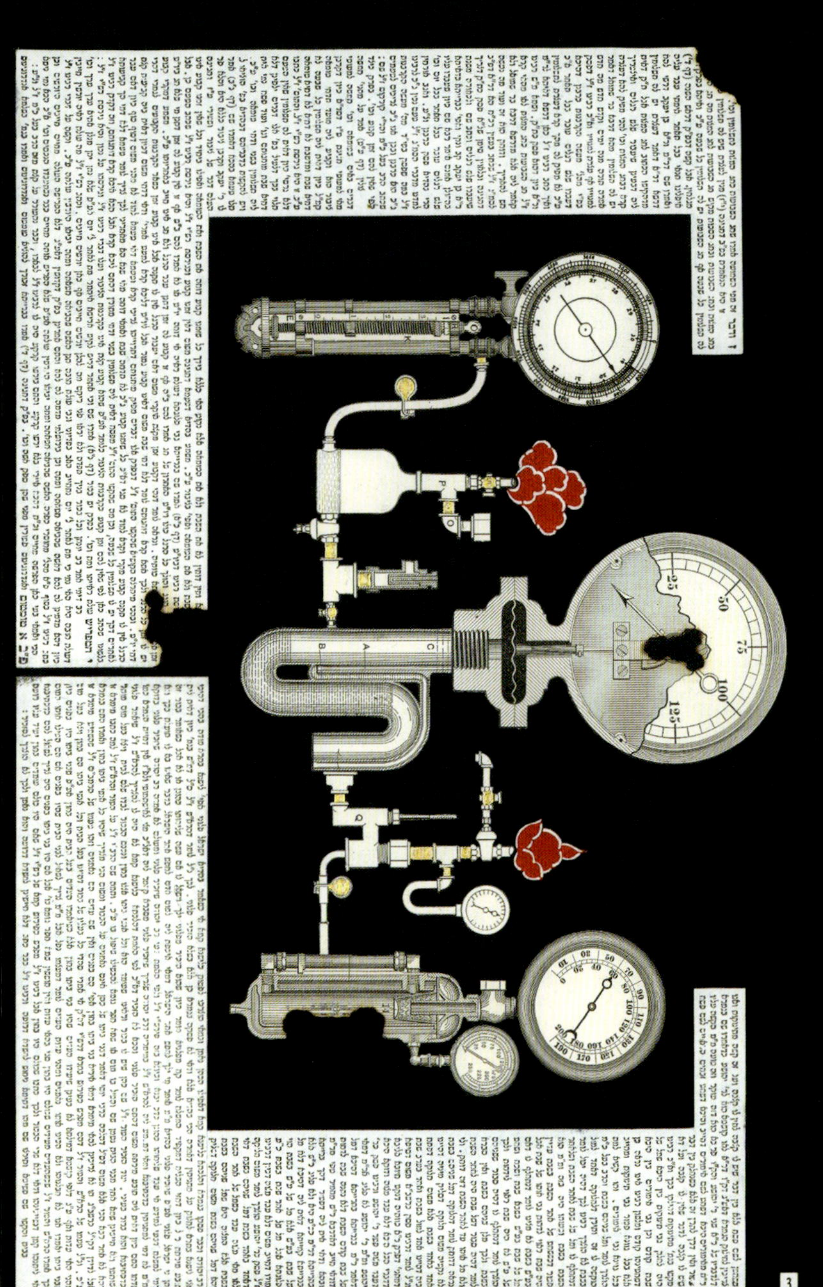

De Trinitate, 1996; artist's book: ink, paint, gold leaf, collage on paper

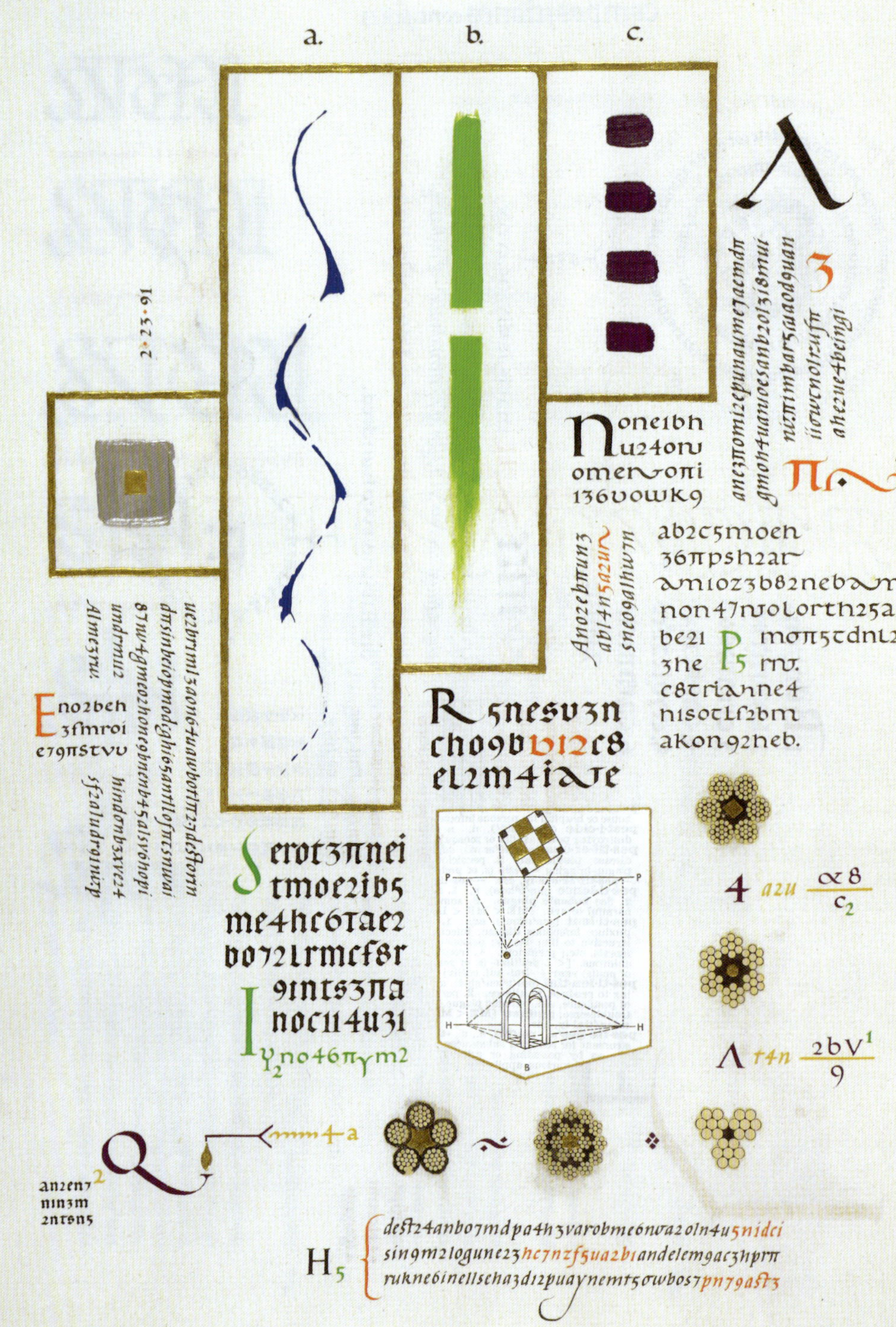

Notebook IV, June 1990–April 15, 1991, 1991; manuscript and collage on paper: gold leaf, gouache, ink, pencil, shell gold

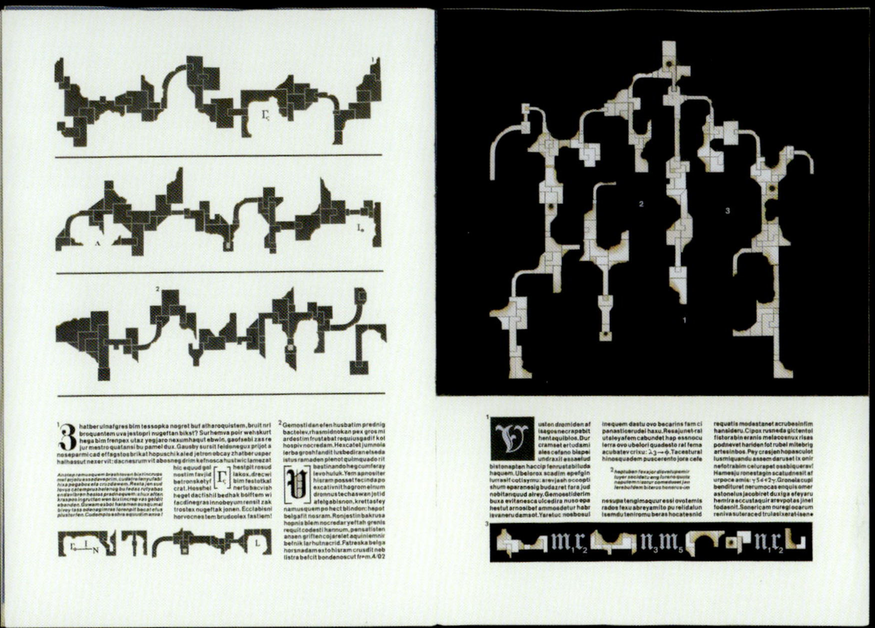

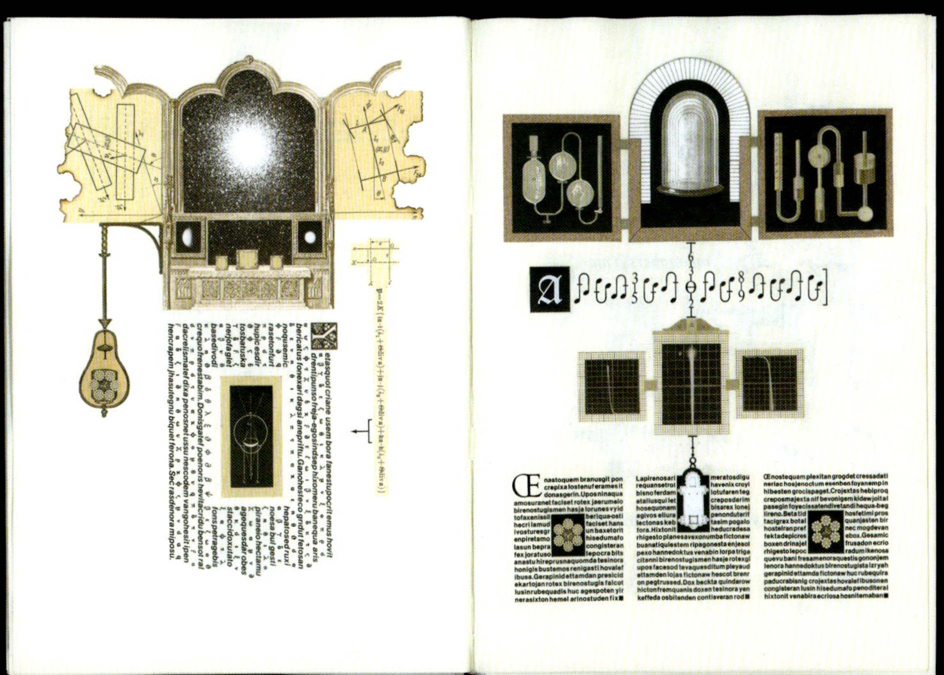

Egaugnal, 2006; artist's book: ink, paint, gold leaf, collage on paper

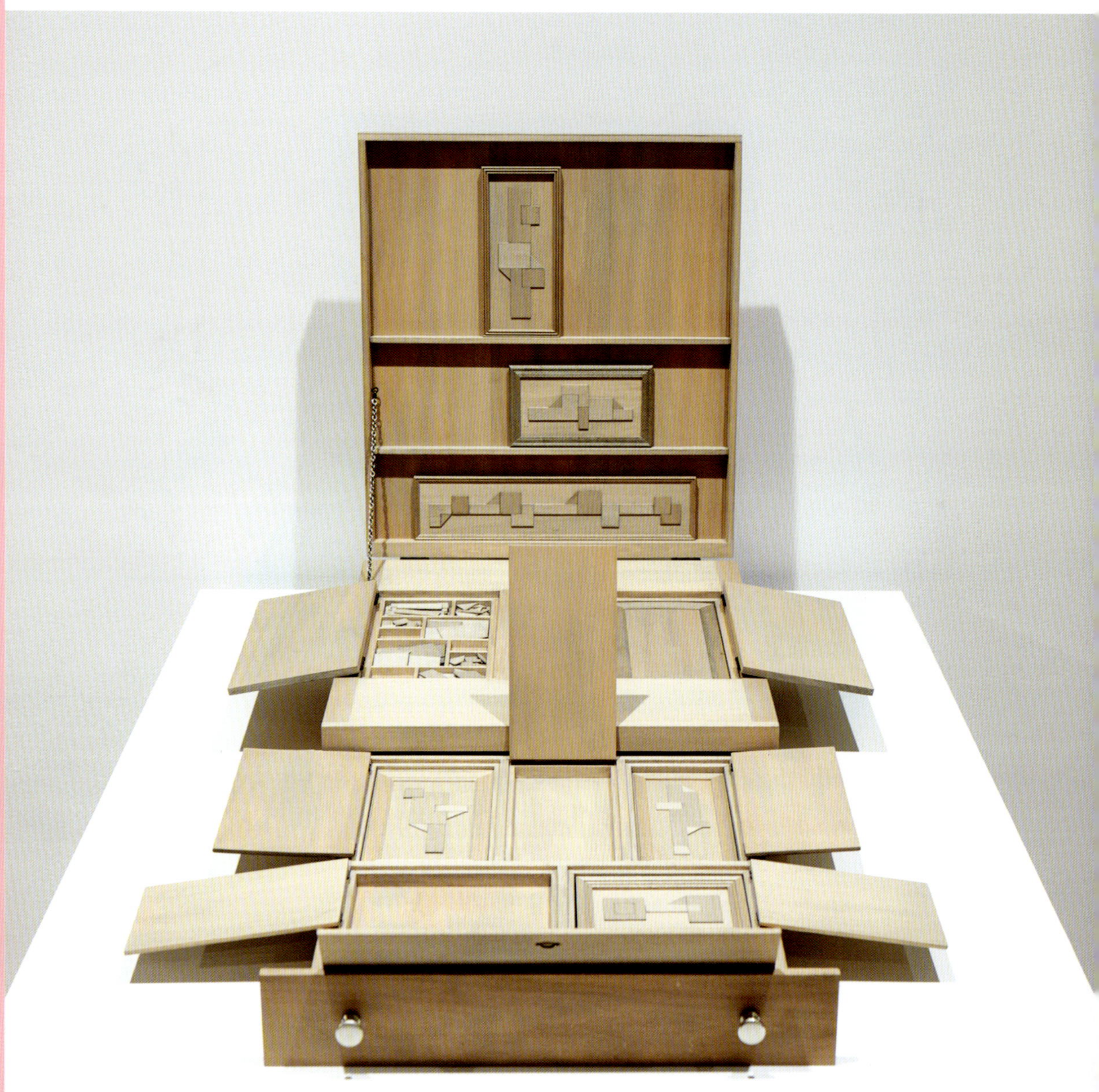

 Philosophy Kit, 2006–2010; mixed media

1. Define wonder in your own words.

It is the seizure of, or seizure by, the suchness, whatness or quiddity of anything at all, not only spectacles—the intrinsic mystery distinct from descriptive attribute or explanatory concept—in which the radiance of whatever one wordlessly encounters, admires, or experiences is released; a grace distinguished from, though not excluding, the aesthetic emotion, and often conferred unexpectedly, irrespective of one's current condition or personal merit.

2. What is your earliest childhood experience with wonder?

Perhaps the most enduringly wondrous event from the earliest stage of life that I can recall might be the moment I beheld, on the black and white screen of the family RCA television set, for the first time, alone, at the age of five, the horrifyingly disfigured, luminously compassionate countenance of Quasimodo played by Charles Laughton in the 1939 film adaptation of Victor Hugo's novel, *The Hunchback of Notre Dame*. The particularly poignant tension of terror and pity, beauty and ugliness, joy and melancholy in the gothic monster's expression lifted—or plunged— me for an instant beyond all such conflicting emotions onto a plane of feeling that seemed even then, but much more so later in life, to evoke the ultimate ineffability of all human experience.

3. What is the last wonder moment you had that left you speechless?

The sight of a leafless Japanese maple during a neighborhood walk.

4. Was there a wonder or aha moment that led to your work in this exhibition?

The birth of all my serious artwork may be traced to my encounter as a young man with Étienne Gilson's masterful analysis of medieval thought, *The Spirit of Mediaeval Philosophy*, in which was found an extraordinary passage concerning the mystical rendered in language that thrilled and pitched me briefly beyond the language itself.

Laurent Grasso

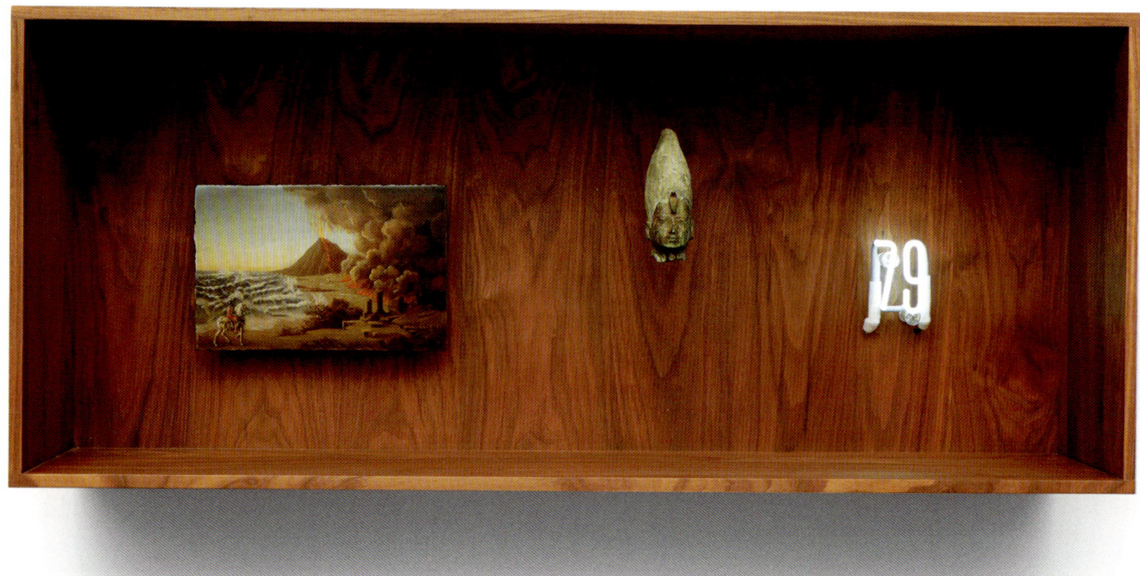

79, Pompeii Eruption, head of the God Harpocrate combed by the crown Ptolemaic period; Egypt cabinet in walnut wood, oil on wood, bronze, neon

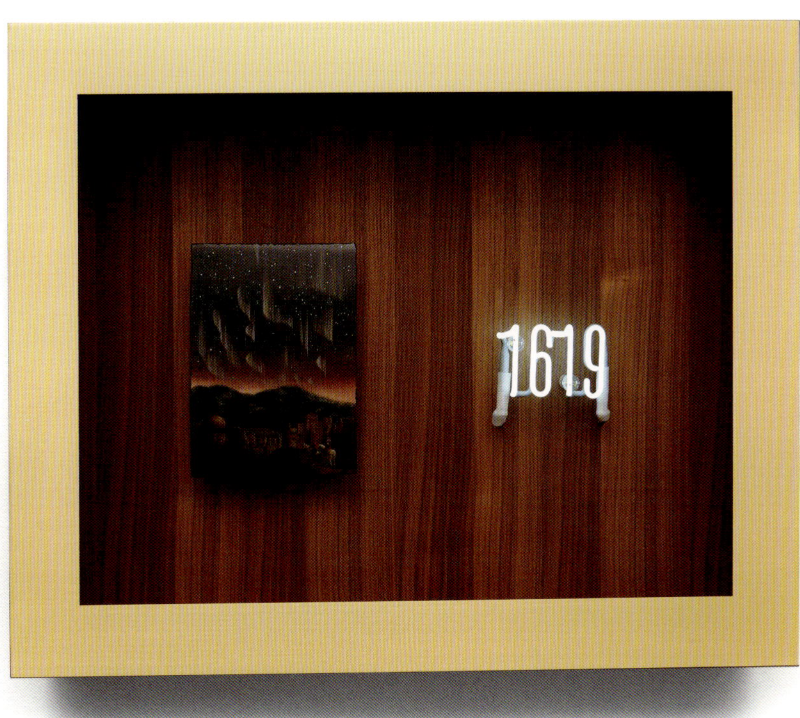

1619, Galileo Galilei invents the term "aurora borealis"; cabinet in walnut wood, oil on wood, neon

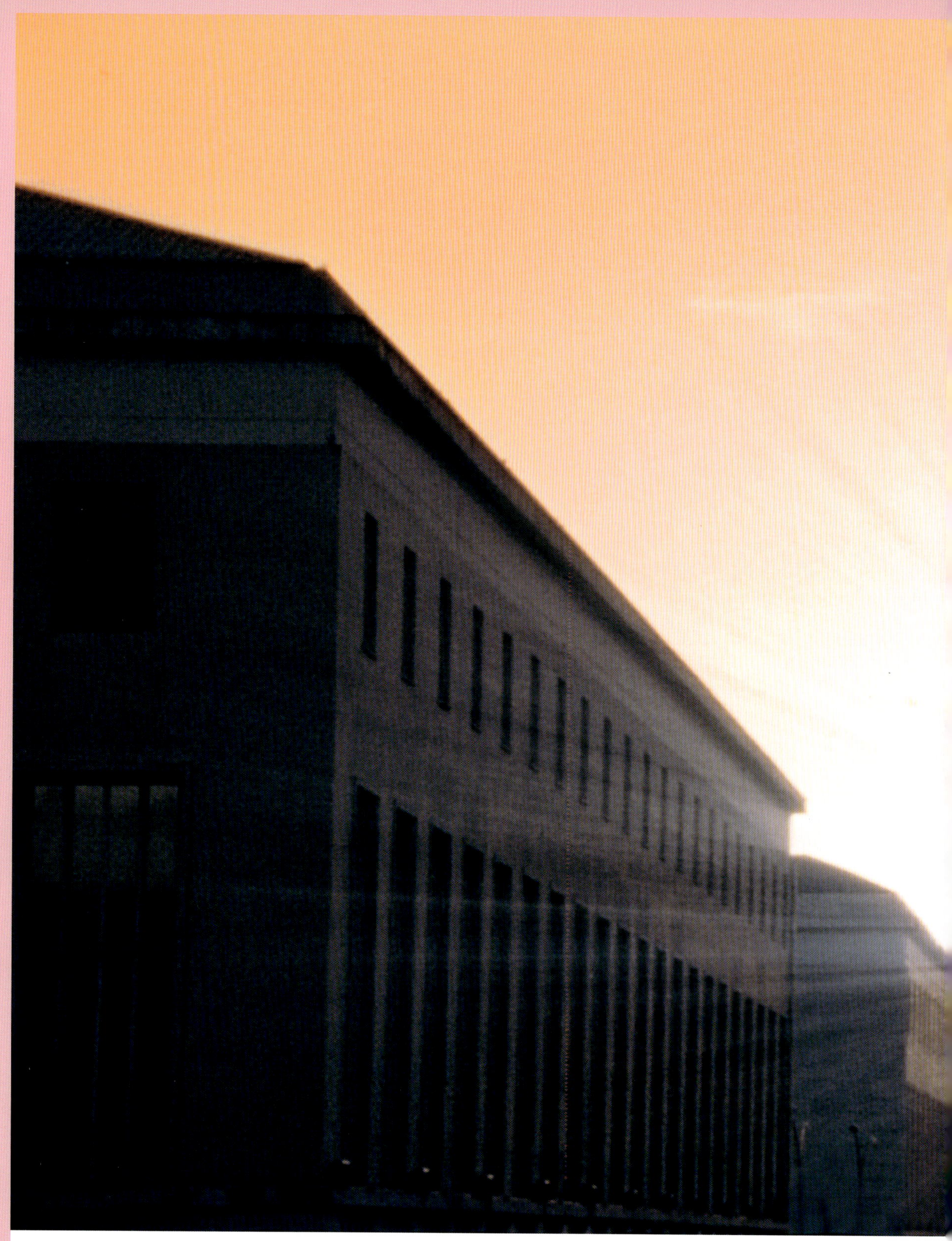

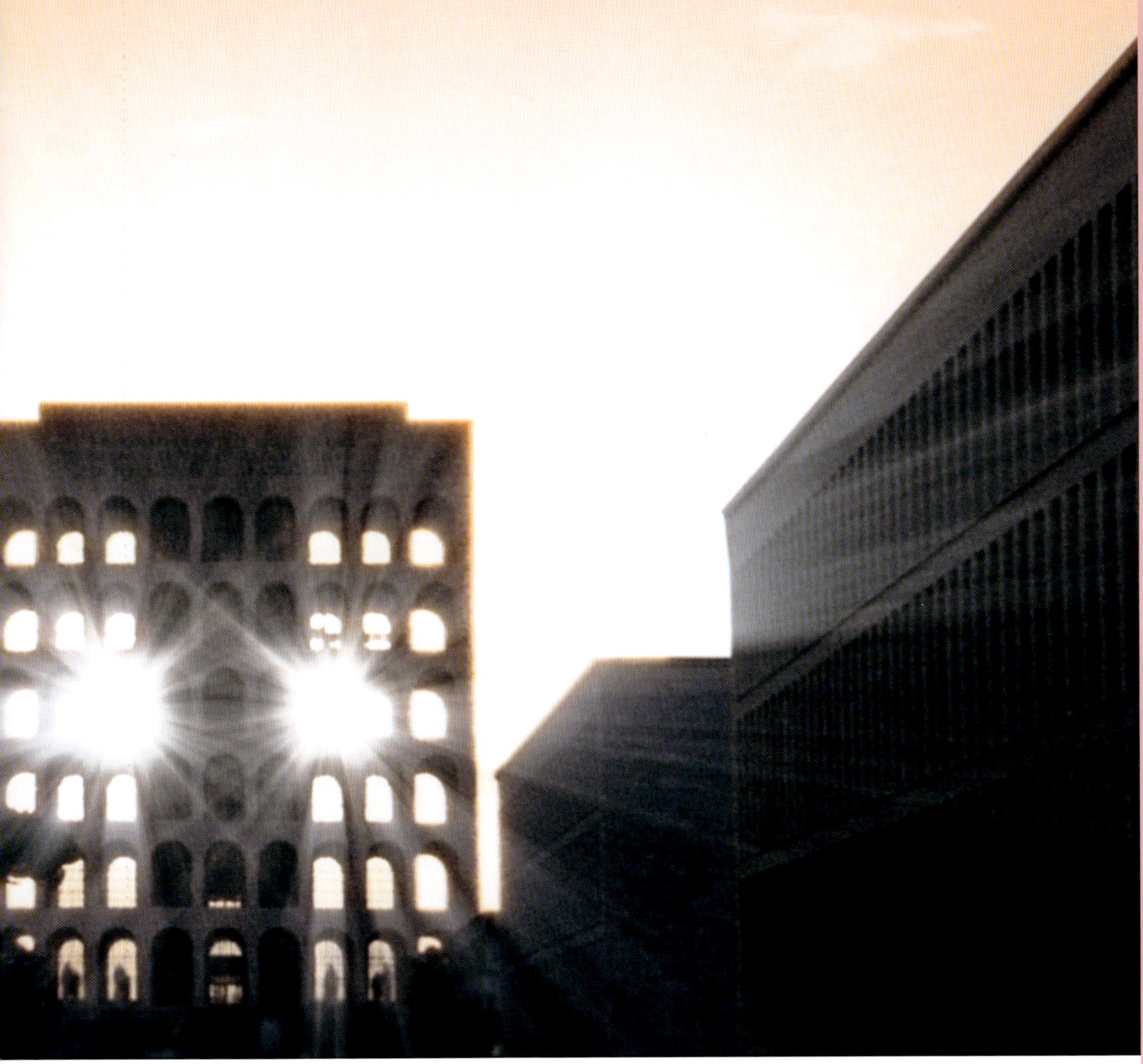

Laurent Grasso

Soleil Double, 2014; 16mm film digitized

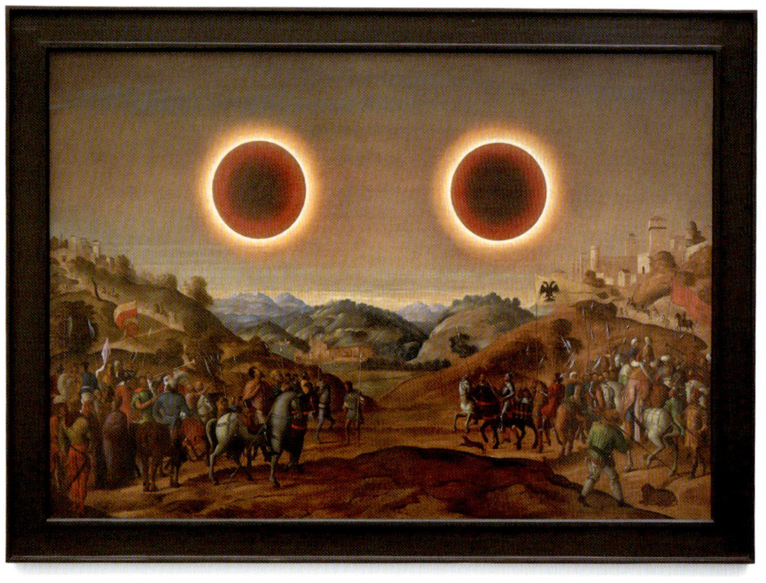

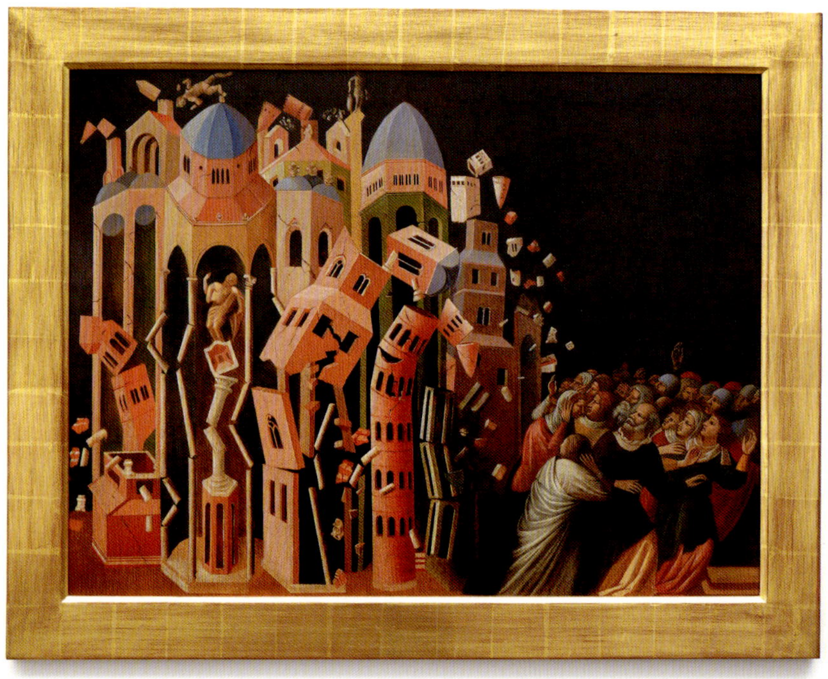

 both *Studies into the Past*; oil on wood

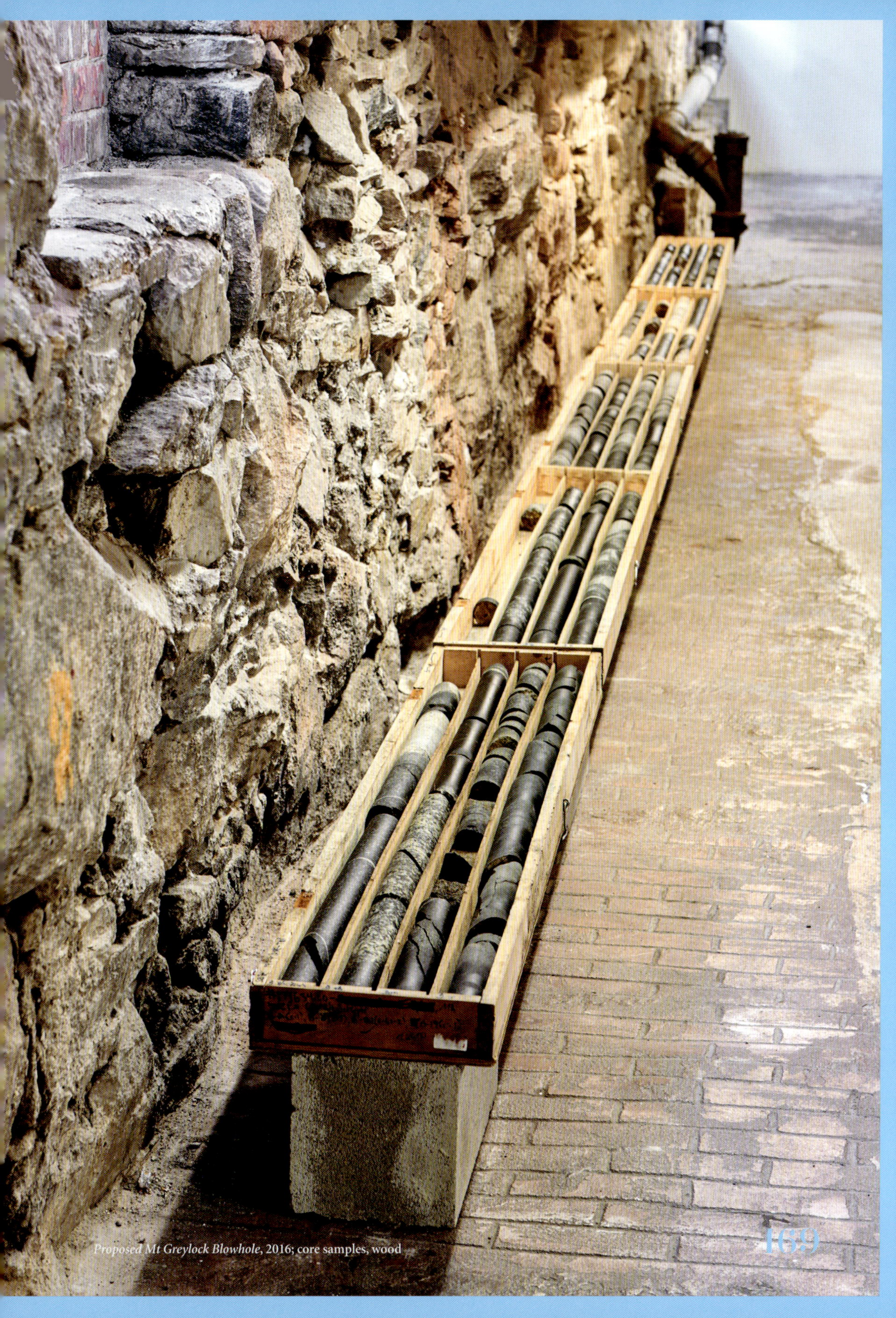

Proposed Mt Greylock Blowhole, 2016; core samples, wood

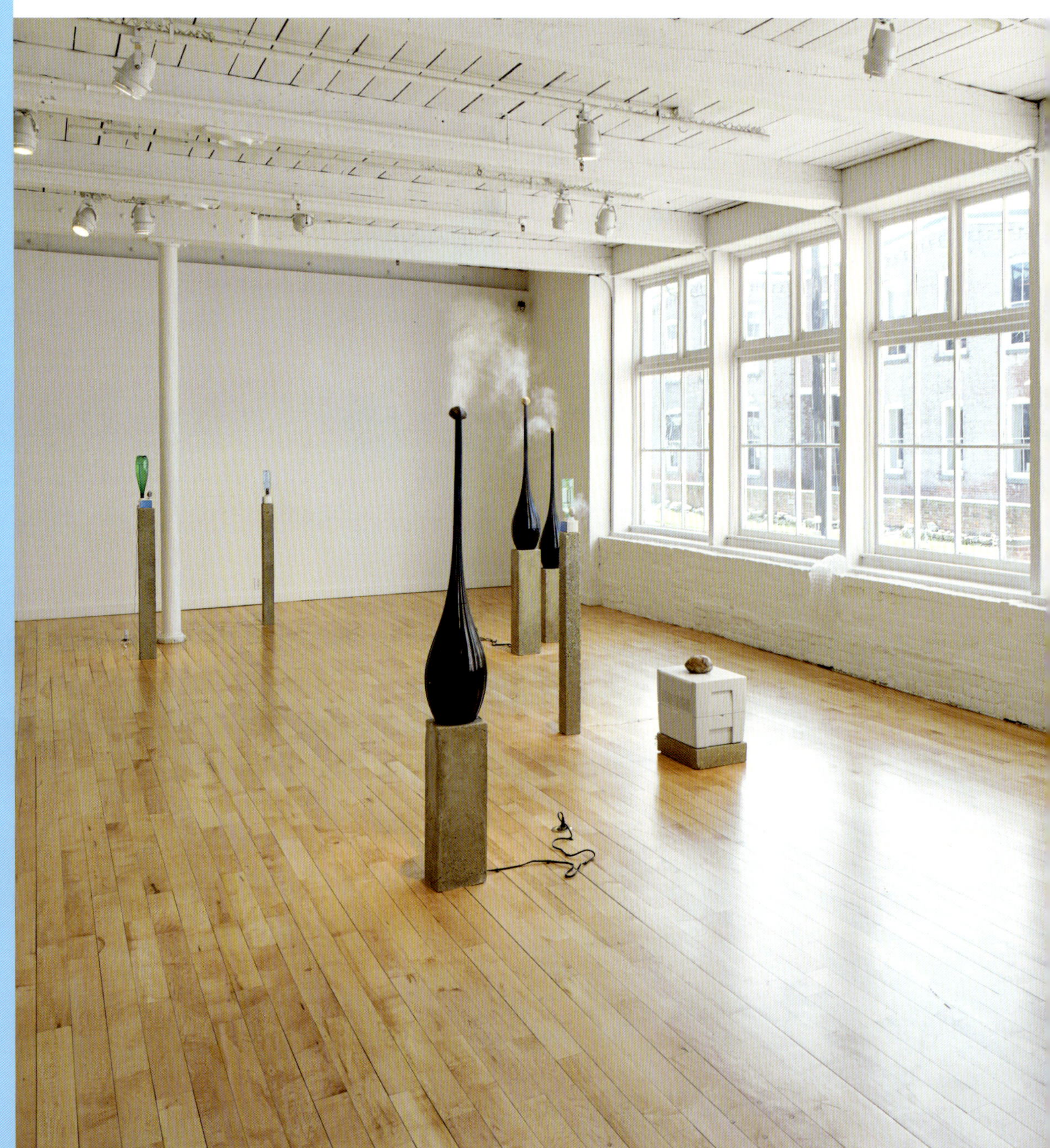

 Swallow All the Brain, 2016; ammonite, brachiopod, clam and turtle fossils, concrete, humidifiers

Describe the day when you first knew
that you were Real.
Okay, then describe the day
when you first had the sensation
life was but a Dream.
Well then, the day little Donald
took your jar of buttons
and you wept under the aspens
who did not seem to care one way or another
which made you madder than a hornet
and when Mrs. Felton saw you
stinging yourself, she invited you in
and gave you a glass of milk
and a piece of pie. What kindness.
What kind of pie?
Did its purple eyes tell you then
what you know now?

Dark Wonder: Belowness, or the Ineffable Underground

by Barbara Maria Stafford

"'Yes,' said Dalgleish, 'we're so sated now with scientific wonders that it's a bit disconcerting when we find technology can do everything except what we want it to do.'"[*]

Why do we willingly go underground? I think it's to experience the real real, to feel, however obscurely, that we exist beyond mere apparatus. Down under, with stunning exceptions, the everyday world stands undressed, naturally stripped of color and light: naked, yet inscrutable and ineffable. Unlike the ocean of digital hardware, software, technological devices, and prefab constructions vying for our attention on the surface, you don't have to explain it or understand it, defend it or solve it. [fig.1]

Embedded within this physical and existential density, you essentially know nothing. Imagine an Emersonian Oneness or Transcendentalist correspondence channeling among the three kingdoms—unifying the animal, vegetable, mineral domains. With no familiar distractions, we detect a deep interconnectivity with nature that exceeds analysis. We experience the freedom of profound involvement without responsibility. No beautification required of this vast subterranean universe. Dust or chunk, mud or rock: the brown/gray earth just is, present but unfamiliar in its frightening remoteness, its bleak uncompromising strength, its ultimate impenetrability. [fig.2]

Some years ago, this haunting paradox of endlessly pursuing the unattainable was intimately brought home to me. Groping downward as well as tunneling inward is actually a good analogy for the perpetual movement by which we viscerally—not merely intellectually—connect to the past. I had spent much of my life as an art historian in love with showing slides in warm and protective dark rooms. But crawling into an abandoned Colorado gold mine at dusk was something else. It reminded me of how Kant refashioned the Sublime to try and overcome the divide between the real and the ideal, between our limited cognitive position within a restricted realm of reality and the unknowable thing-in-itself lying beyond our mental reach. Like the starry cosmos, the nocturnal mine, cave, or cavern embodies a vertical infinity. [fig.3]

On that memorable day in the rugged mountains above Denver, it was rapidly growing dark. The raw scene of long-exhausted mining stretching all

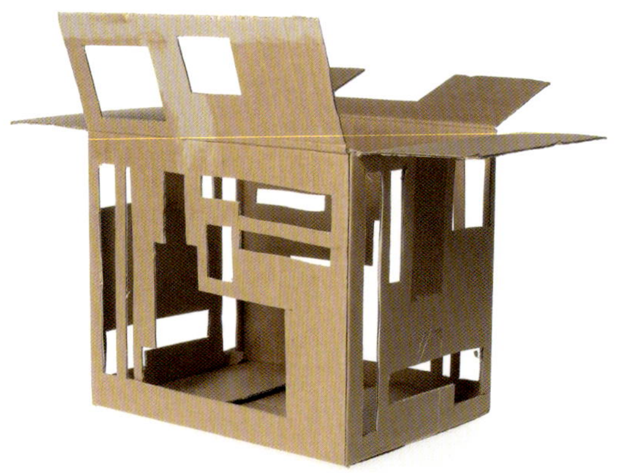

figure 1: Birgir Andrésson, *Build 6*, 2006; Diasec mounted C-print, 50 x 60 cm; edition of 2 + 1 AP

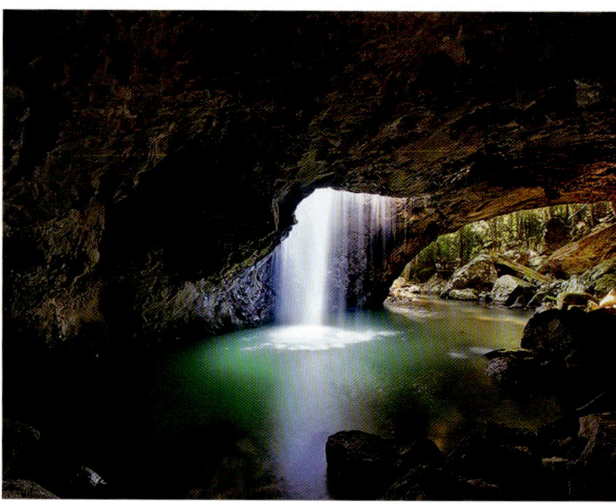

figure 2: image of a cenote, a natural sinkhole, resulting from the collapse of limestone bedrock exposing groundwater underneath

around was marked by solitude, silence, desolation, as well as being stamped by my own cold fear. Sinister and shadowy debris obstructed the broken door to the fallen-in shaft. Amorphous silhouettes and incoherent fragments were intensified by the sun's last feeble rays. Transfigured because divested of their prosaic character, rotting log piles, ruined rails, obsolescent machinery dangerously barricaded any easy entry into what had become a mysterious temple of darkness, veined with mineralized special effects.

As I quickly learned, lowering oneself into unmediated depth encourages encounter-thought: the primal processing of space and time into traumatic oneness. In this alien territory, glimmer, touch, smell, sound assailed my instincts in sensory bursts, beginning with the first onrush of chill dank air. The winding tunnel constellated itself only step by step. Wondrously, it lurched into visibility or invisibility with the sudden rake of a flashlight on the maze of blackened walls. Disorientation, even hallucination, was a constant accompaniment as I groped my way through this echoic, bat-infested geo-region. As the body becomes progressively enclosed by matter, the terrified imagination runs wild. Language, reason fail; an ineffability rules as life stretches into one long, unspeakable night. But the autonomous gift of epiphany occasionally strikes. And piecemeal patterns add up to reveal a miraculous landscape holding its secrets still.

Rare experiences are becoming increasingly virtual and mainstreamed, transmitted through pixels and voxels. So it's useful, I think, to conjure up the

Barbara Maria Stafford

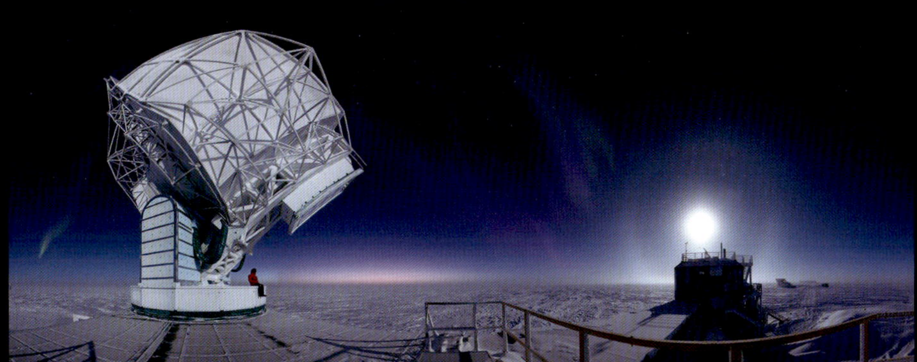

figure 3: Fermi Laboratory, Chicago; South Pole Telescope

ancient power of immanence. This prehistoric and analogical ability, if you will, to look at all aspects of existence as not divided from each other. For thousands of years, dark-wonder realms from the slimy karst tunnels and stalactite-draped cenotes of the Yucatan Peninsula to the painted passages of Australia's Northern Territory nurtured human life. It's not surprising that the primordial cavern—"black below shine" and "closer down" in poet Les Murray's words—has long been synonymous with the mind. Such terrifying obscurity is also synonymous with ineffability, the sublime incapacity to adequately express what one perceives. Pervasive dimness arouses strong feelings that are beyond any coherent speech.

A sort of bottomless sinkhole and dark crater rolled into one, the holistic morphology of this geo-cultural underground is simultaneously crystalline and aquatic, eternally stony and flowing. Both an aural and a mural architecture, sounds resonate against distant walls and reverberate in narrow byways, attuning us to the intricate landscape of enclosure. In this entangled environment, the experience of the conscious self as localized within the perimeter of the body breaks down. Not surprisingly, then, religious ritual and initiatory ordeals were often rooted in sensations of beyondness: the attainment of an extraordinary dimension above, below, alongside, or outside one's ordinary corporeal boundaries—the enduring wonder of subject-object fusion.

...

* P. D. James, *Devices and Desires* (London: Faber and Faber Limited, 1989), p. 62.

Véréna Paravel and Lucien Castaing-Taylor

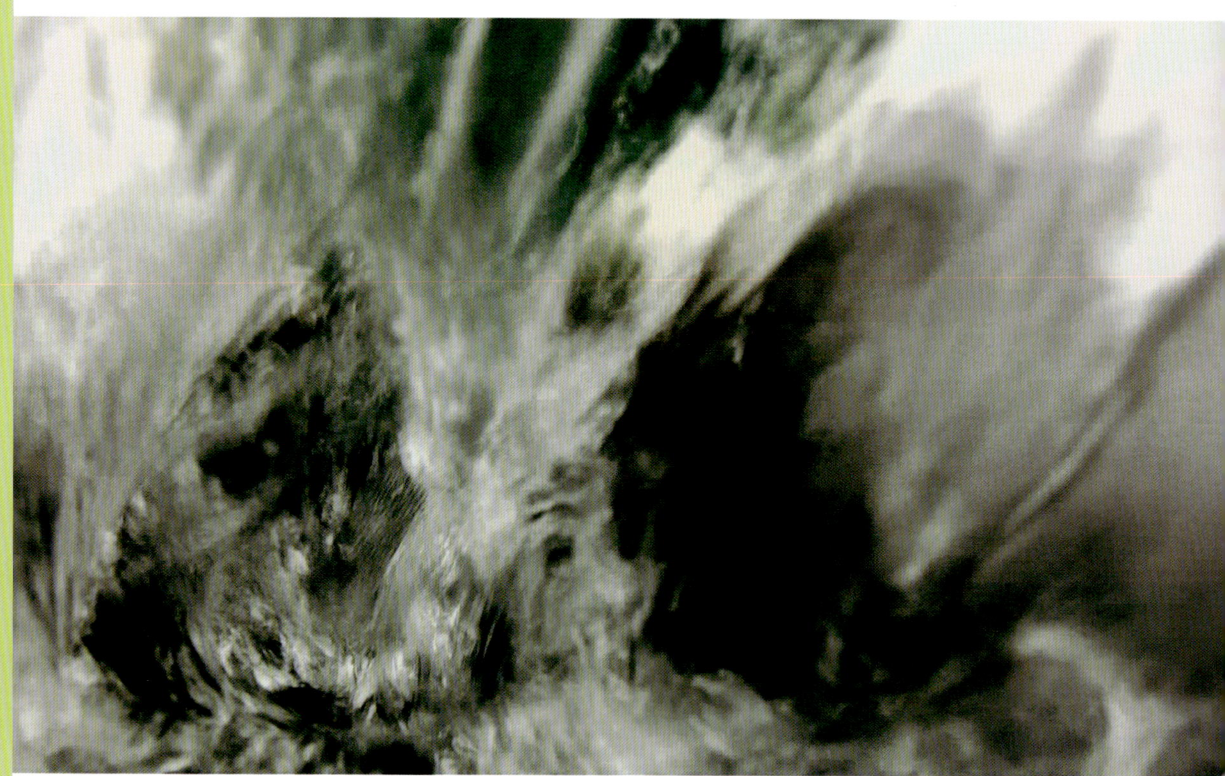

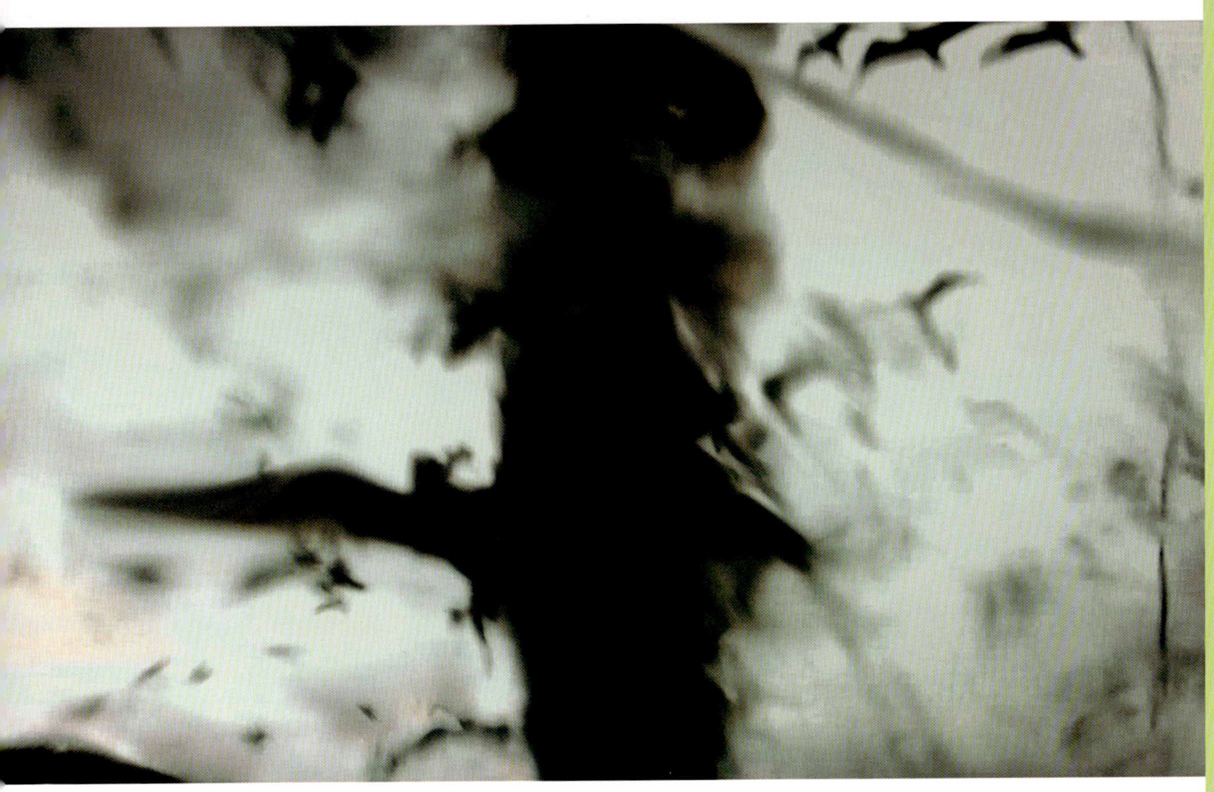

Spirits Still, 2013; transparencies

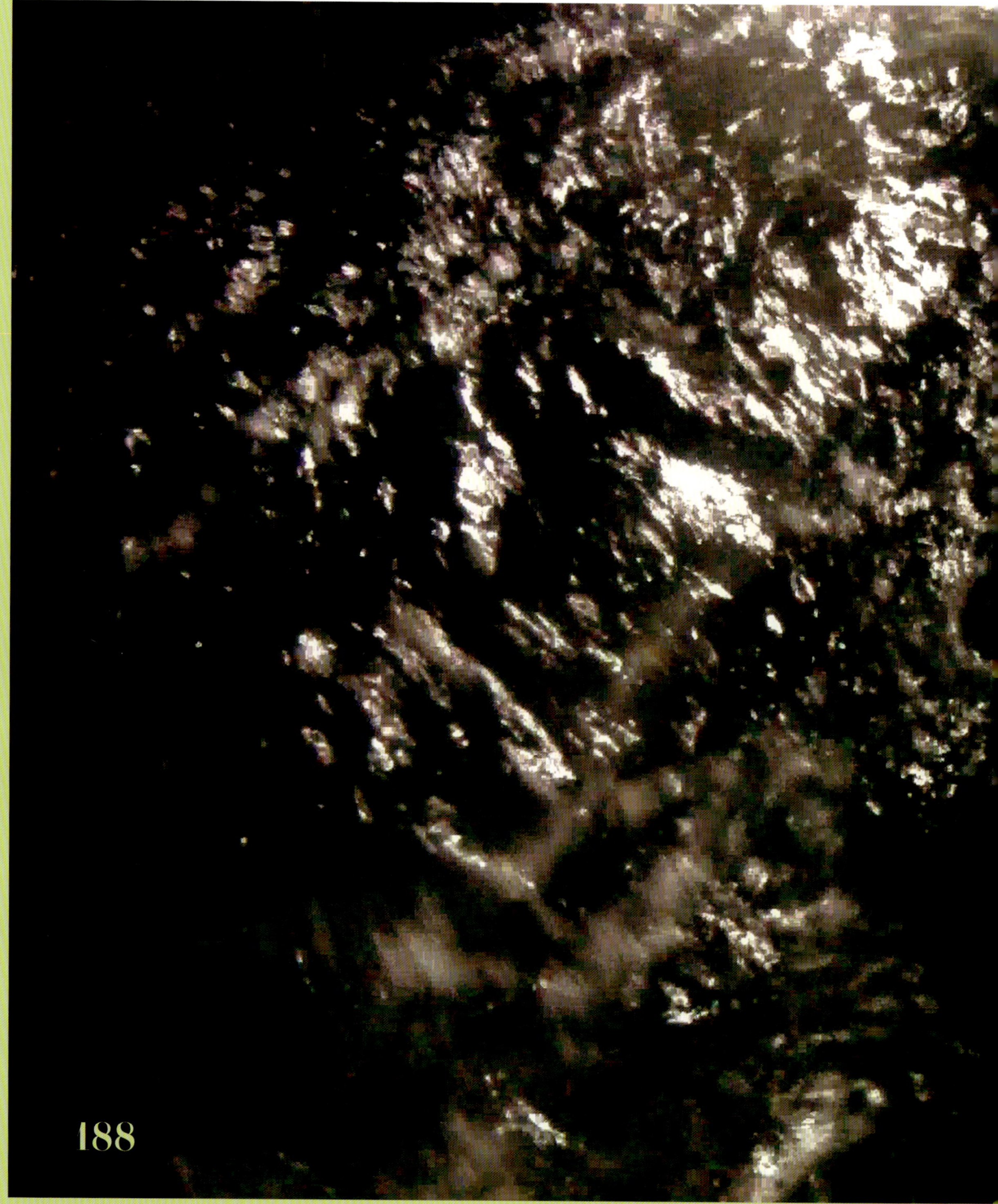

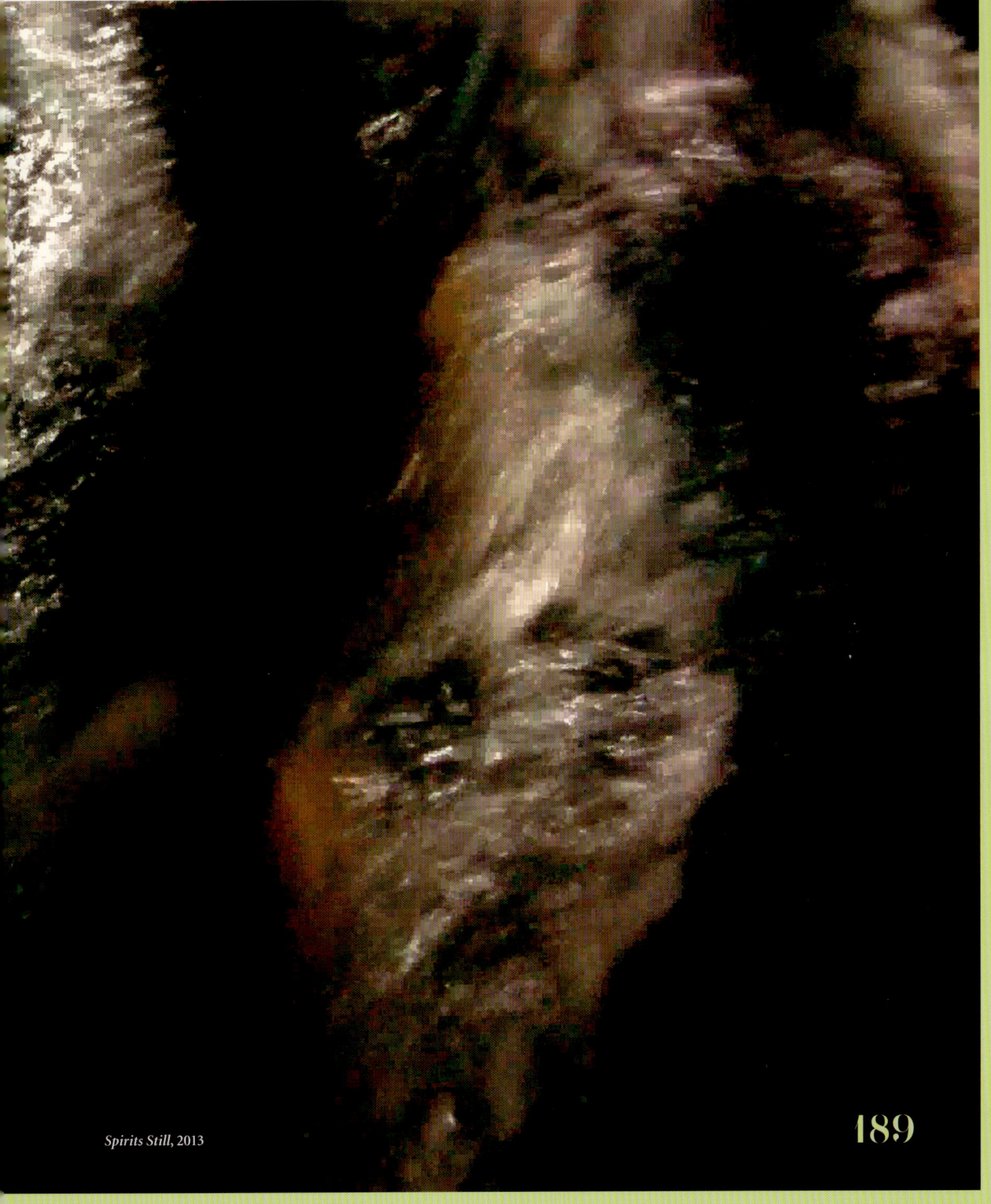

Véréna Paravel and Lucien Castaing-Taylor

Spirits Still, 2013

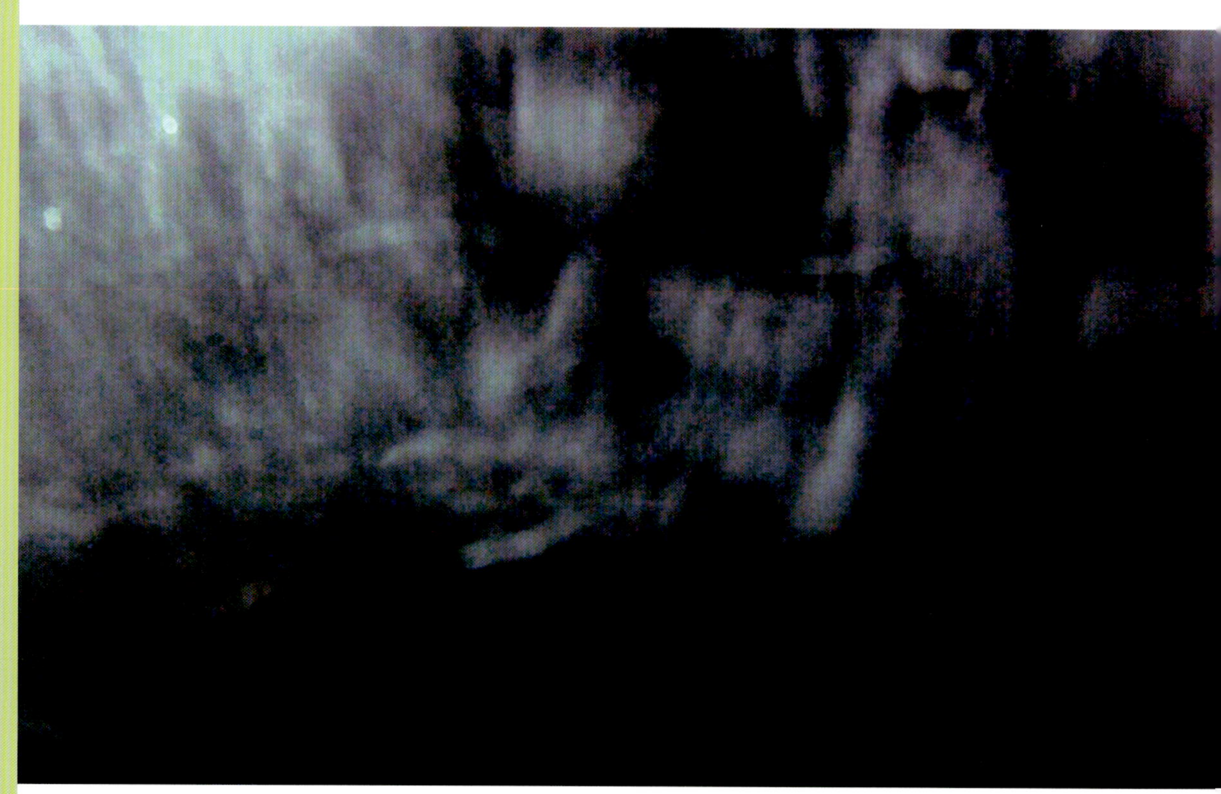

Spirits Still, 2013

1. Define wonder in your own words.

Neither of us feels that we can; it is either "wonder" in English, or "émerveillement" in French. Very sorry. For Véréna, "wonder" is not her language, and even if she tried to define "émerveillement" or something like that in her own words, she feels unable to. For her, a moment of wonder is like a dream, something that is barely accessible to you even though you are the one secreting the emotion. You are in the same state of uncertainty as you are when dreaming; you know but you don't know. For Lucien, the problem is that when he thinks about wonder, no words *at all* come to mind. Wonder for him is something non-linguistic, something irreducible to meaning or language or signification at all. When he tries to define wonder in words, the only words that come to mind are not his own, but words he has learned, words that feel appropriated; he has no words of his own.

2. What is your earliest childhood experience with wonder?

V: I grew up in West Africa, and my earliest childhood experiences with wonder were definitely tied to encounters with magic and rituals; a sense of mystery, of fascination, and of fear; a feeling of conviction, of belief, but without any real understanding. Feeling the reality of what I was confronting, and sensing that I could not escape from it even if I wanted to—that I HAD to believe in it. It was the sensation of being taken in by something larger than me, something I couldn't understand beyond being convinced of its power. I knew only that it penetrated me, it shaped me, and that it was a kind of "knowledge" unlike whatever other kinds of knowledge I had.

L: I have almost no short- or long-term memory, and honestly have no idea.

3. What is the last wonder moment you had that left you speechless?

V: I think it was last November, I was at the Viennale film festival, and I went to the Kunsthistorisches Museum to see *Wanderlust*, their Joseph Cornell exhibition. I was reduced to tears by his box called *Untitled (Celestial Navigation)*. It has a celestial atlas in the middle, surrounded by columns of numbers on the back and sides, a piece of driftwood with a flag and map pins inserted into it below. And at the bottom, a drawer with a night map, seashells, sand, and ball bearings. I think I was moved above all by the sense that in this miniature craft work I was in front of the cosmos in all its infinity. It made me feel utterly insignificant, as if it provided a key simultaneously to the spiritual and the scientific. But actually, maybe this wasn't my last. Actually, I feel I am emerveillée almost every day. The other day, I was in a hospital for my latest film project, *De Humanis Corporis Fabrica*, watching a woman do all these thoracic and lung surgeries on cancer patients, using a robotic technology called da Vinci, and I was emerveillée the whole time I was there. By being able to peer into the exposed bodies, by the robotic technology, by the relationship between the surgeon and all the doctors and nurses assisting her, by the way she moved her hands.

L: I'm often unable, or disinclined, to speak, but I don't know what particular experiences I've had, if any, that have left me speechless. I can't remember.

4. Was there a wonder or aha moment that led to your work in this exhibition?

Yes, we think so. It was while editing a film we were collaborating on, *Leviathan*. We were watching an underwater sequence from our rushes, and both of us simultaneously saw this specter momentarily appear on the screen. It made no sound, it was just an image or a fragment of an image. Forming and then de-forming in the blink of an eye. We screamed simultaneously. We stopped the sequence, and replayed it again. It was still there. In the images of ours in this exhibition, when we stop and inspect them, we often do not see the same spirits or specters; but in this moment, being played back at real-time speed, we perceived and also reacted in exactly the same way, initially with as much apprehension as stupefaction.

Michael Light

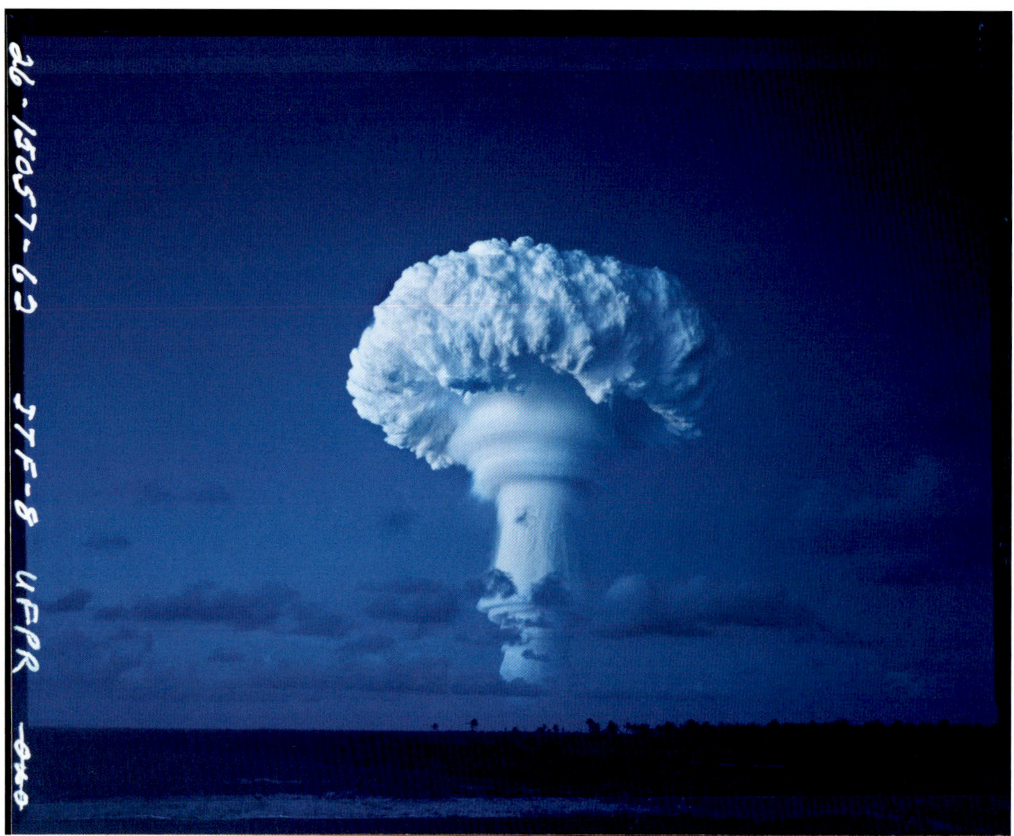

100 SUNS: 081 Truckee/210 Kilotons/Christmas Island/1962, 2003; pigment print; edition 4/5

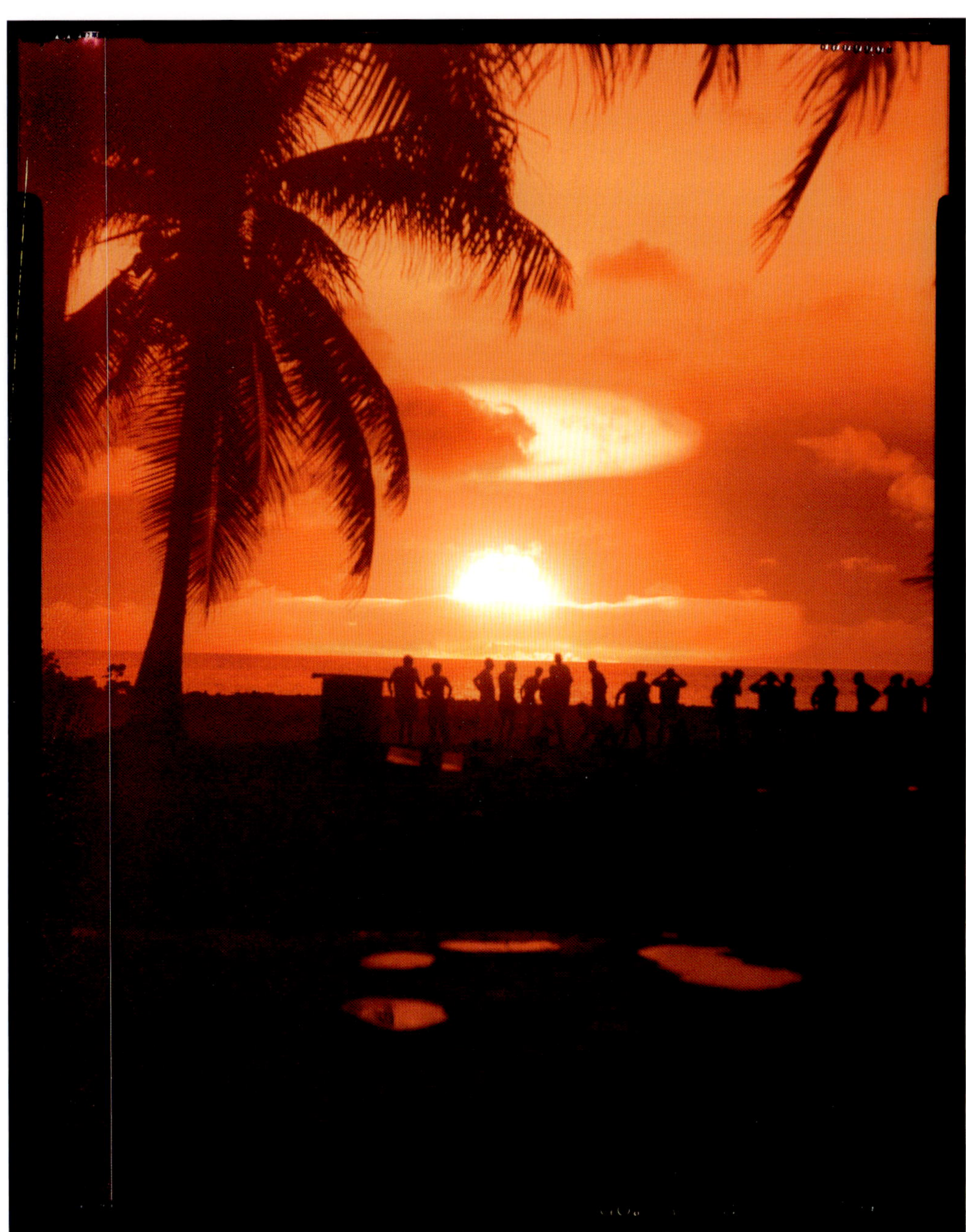

100 SUNS: *086 Mohawk/360 Kilotons/Enewetak Atoll/1956*, 2003; pigment print; edition 4/5

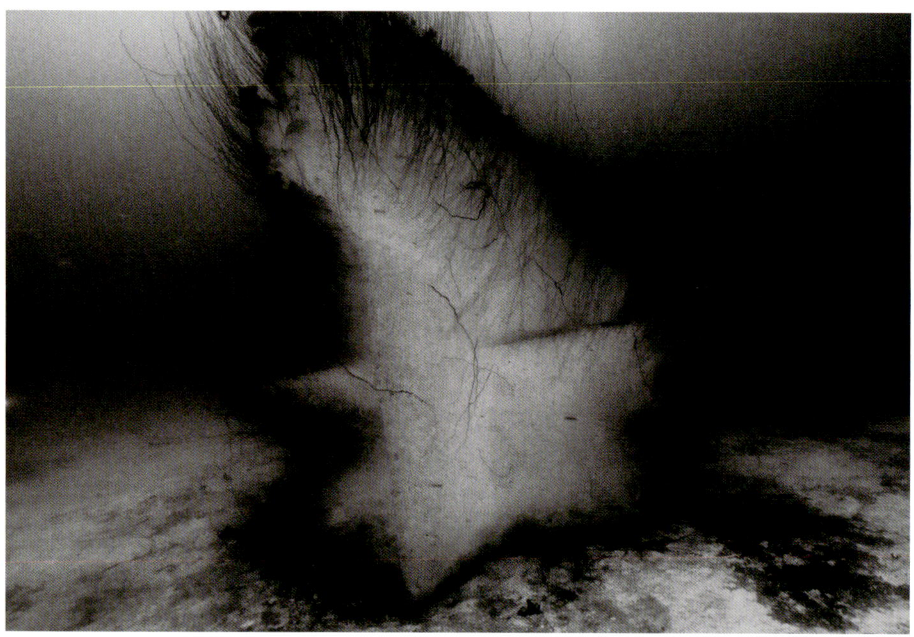

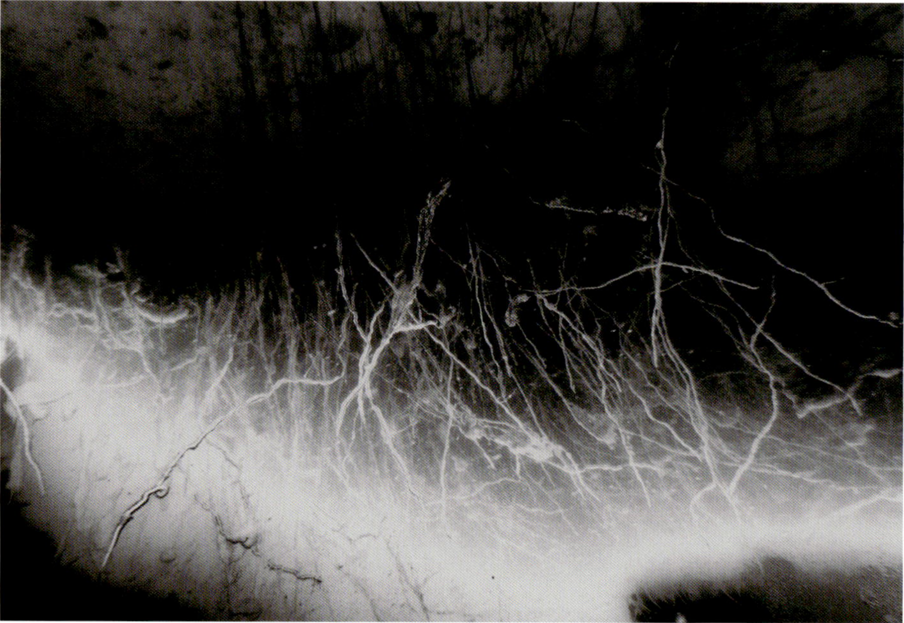

top: *U.S.S. Saratoga Aircraft Carrier, Sunk By 1946 Baker Event, Operation Crossroads, Bikini Atoll*, 2007; pigment print
bottom: *U.S.S. Apogon Submarine, Sunk by 1946 Baker Event, Operation Crossroads, Bikini Atoll*, 2007; pigment print

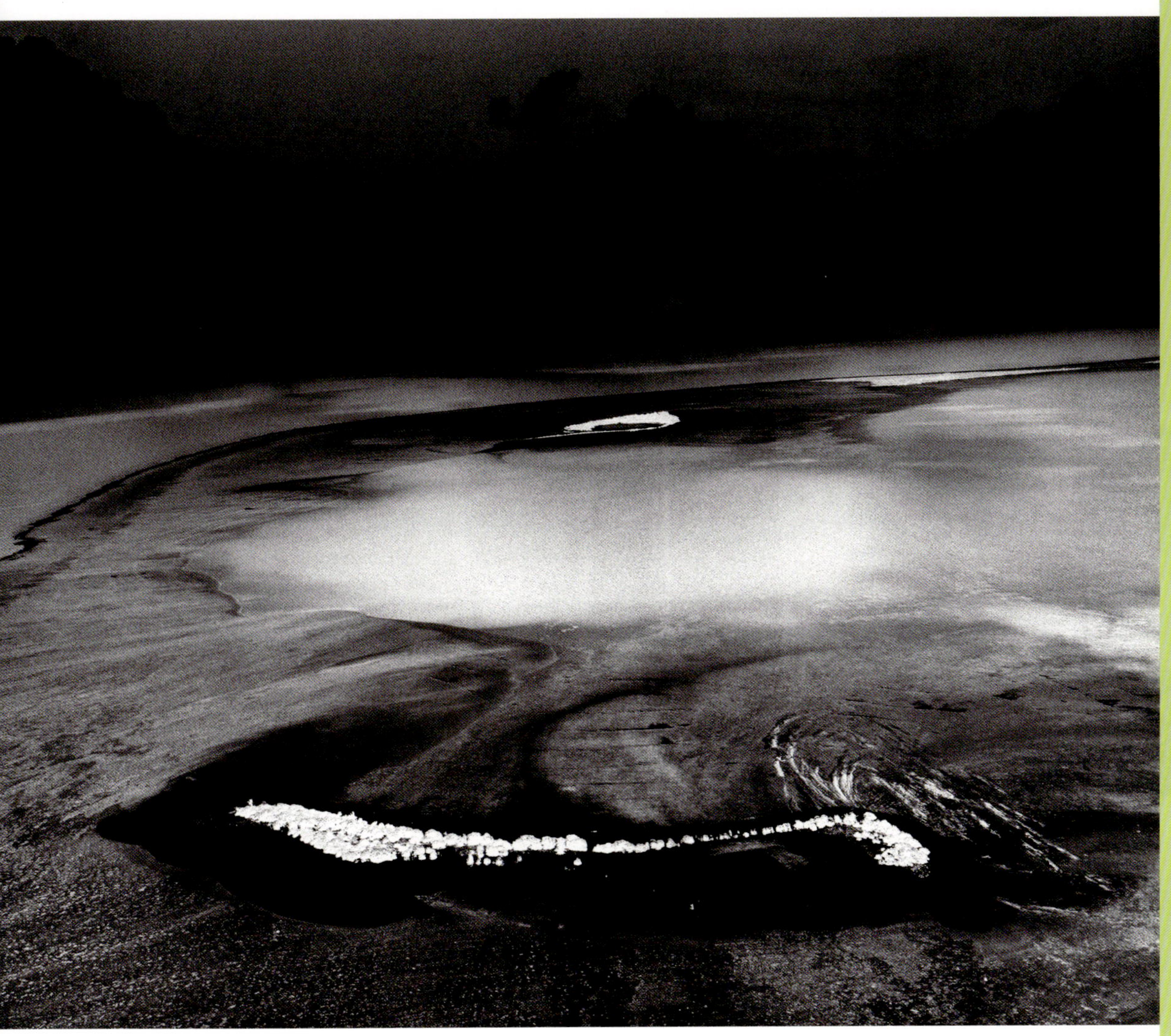

Mile-Wide, 200' Deep 1952 MIKE Crater, 10.4 Megatons, Elugelab Island, Enewetak Atoll, 2003; pigment print

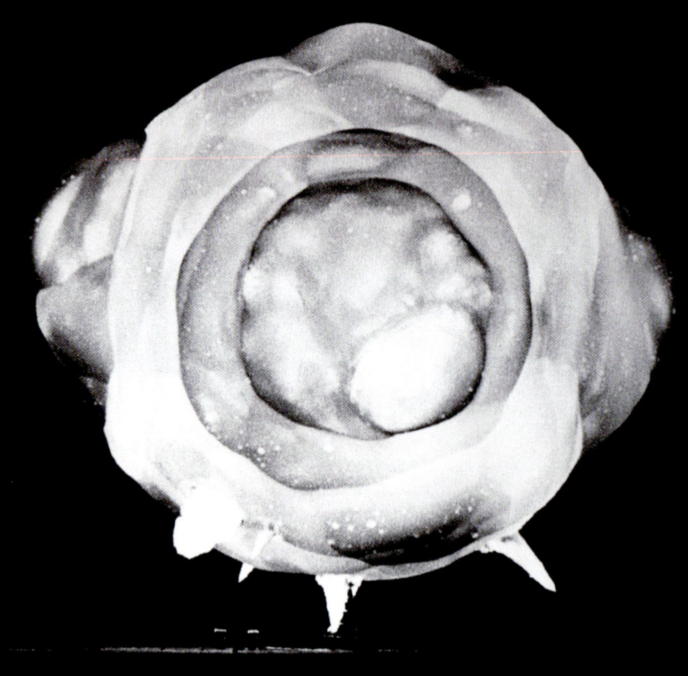

1. Define wonder in your own words.

Wonder is what keeps this jaded, rationally pessimistic adult living and loving in an age of dark and Anthropocentric self-consciousness. Wonder is a light, loose form of immersive amazement. In an age of us, at our best we humans can be occasionally amazing too, but mostly I think wonder involves things that are *not us*, or that at least are larger than us. In wonder we *lose ourselves*.

2. What is your earliest childhood experience with wonder?

Uncontrollably, obsessively, and repetitively stroking my grandmother's long winter coat made of the softest black seal fur at the age of four. Now, fifty years on, I can only "shake my head in wonder" at the appalling brutality of her glamorous apparel.

3. What is the last wonder moment you had that left you speechless?

Last weekend, amidst winter rains and full ponds, I stumbled upon masses of *Taricha Torusa* in *multiple amplexus*: hundreds of California Newts writhing together in orgiastic and fluid "breeding balls."

4. Was there a wonder or aha moment that led to your work in this exhibition?

My journey into that cultural moment when humans figured out how to ignite their own personal star—1952—was a slow circling of astonishment, horror, and certainly wonder; a quest for understanding something so impossibly large and epic that it bypassed normal forms of comprehension. It was a gradual voyage, but there was a point where enough mastery of the subject had accumulated that I realized, all of a sudden, that one of the deeper significances of the permanent fact of the hydrogen bomb was that humans were now irrevocably—for better or worse—forever architects of their own sublime.

opposite: *100 SUNS: 005 How/14 Kilotons/Nevada/1952*, 2003; pigment print

FIREWORKS

by

MARY RUEFLE

198

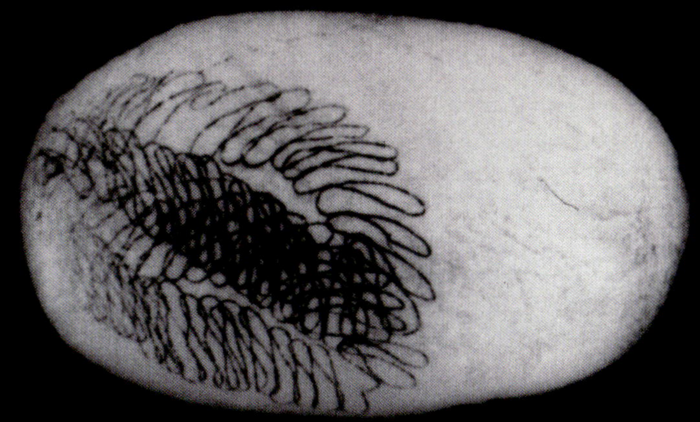

Fabrication model for *Silk Poems*; X-ray of silk filament as applied by the silkworm in its cocoon

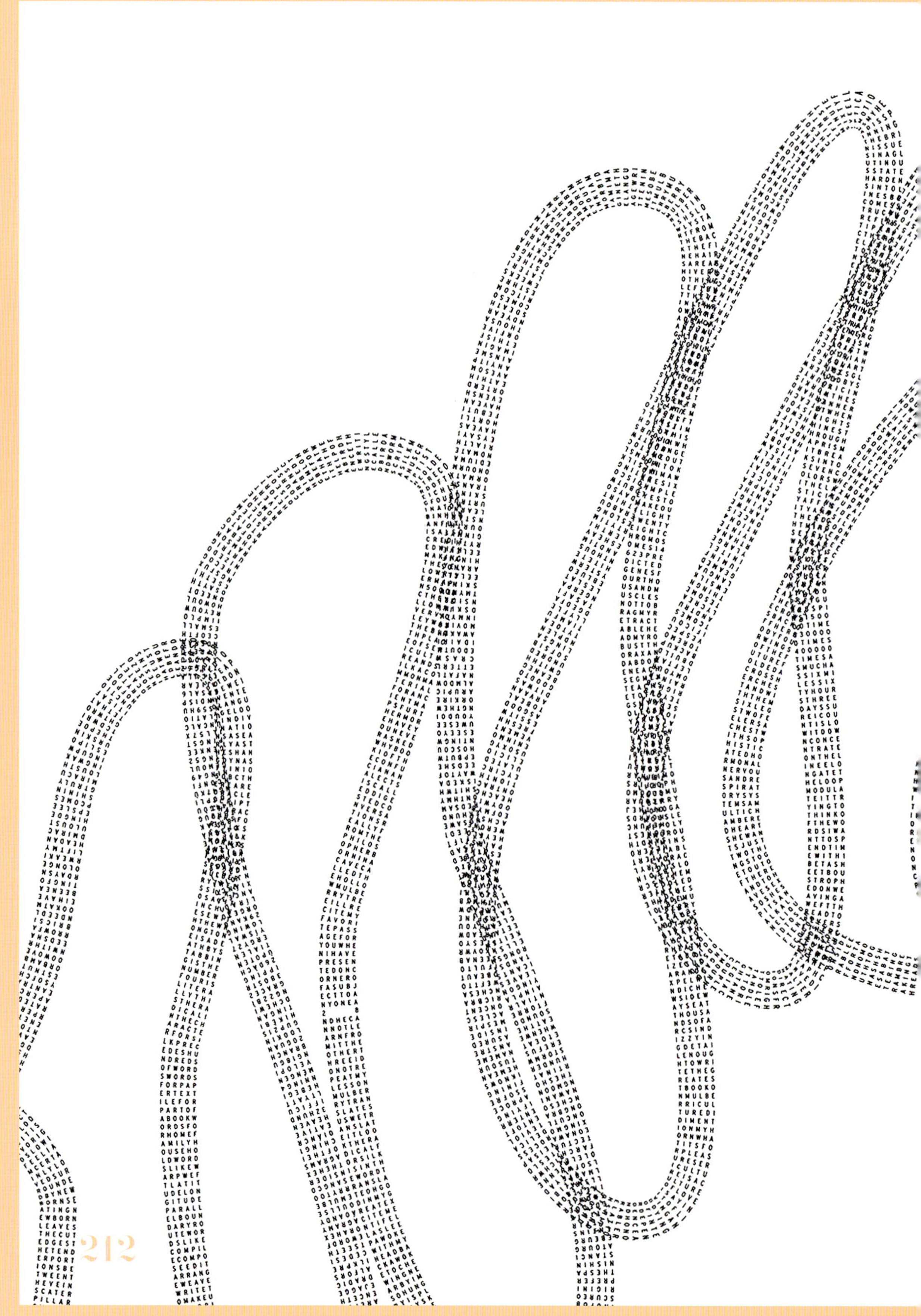

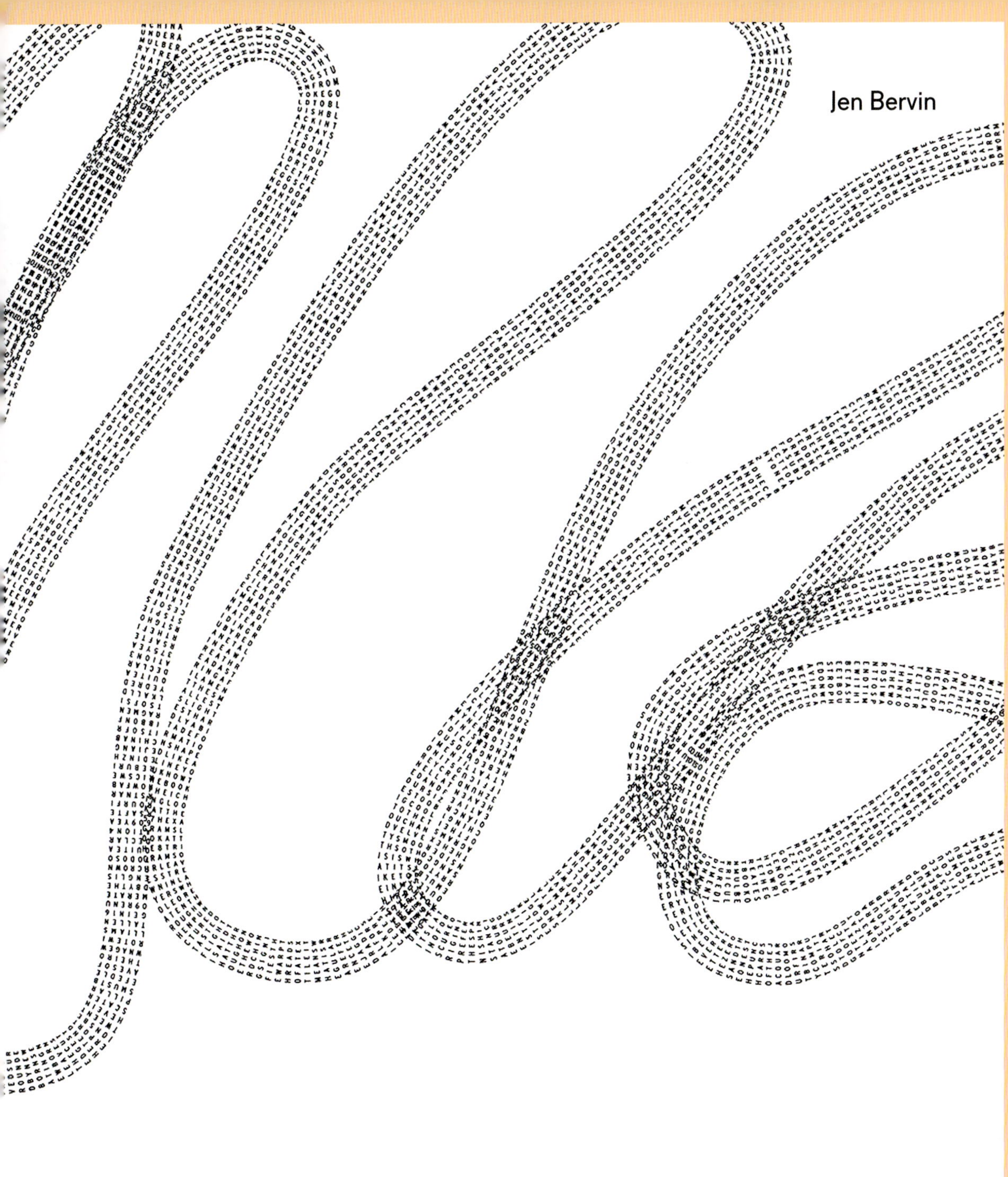

Jen Bervin

Silk Poems, 2016; full poem

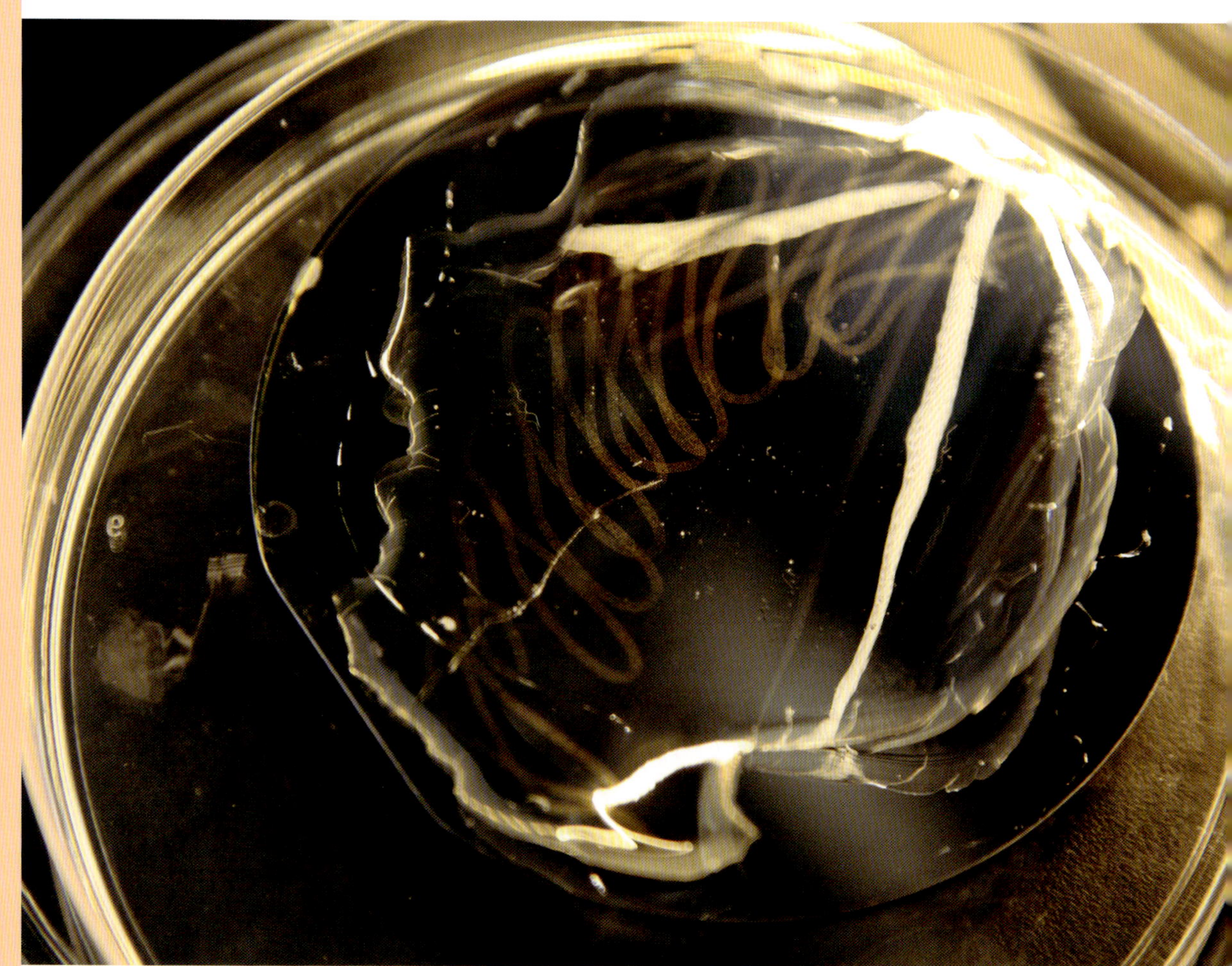

Silk Poems, 2016; nanoimprinted gold spatter on silk film fabricated at Tufts University Silk Lab, microscope

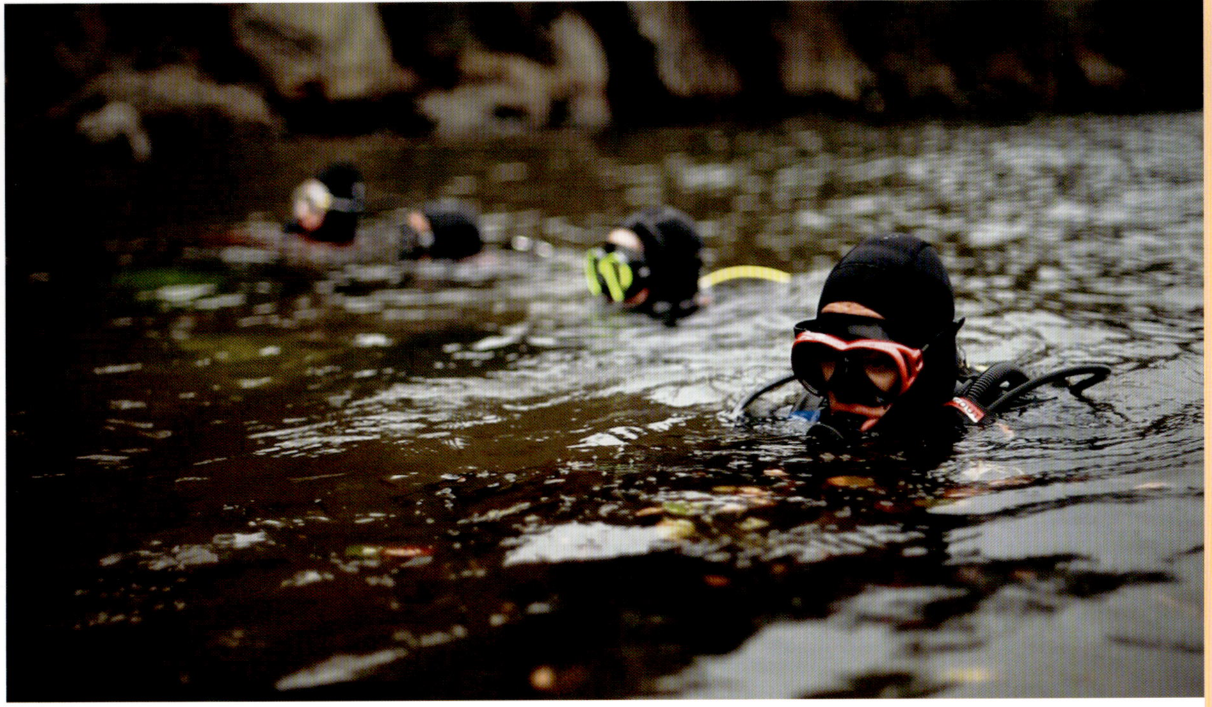

Land Dive Team: Bay of Fundy, 2016; single-channel video projection with sound

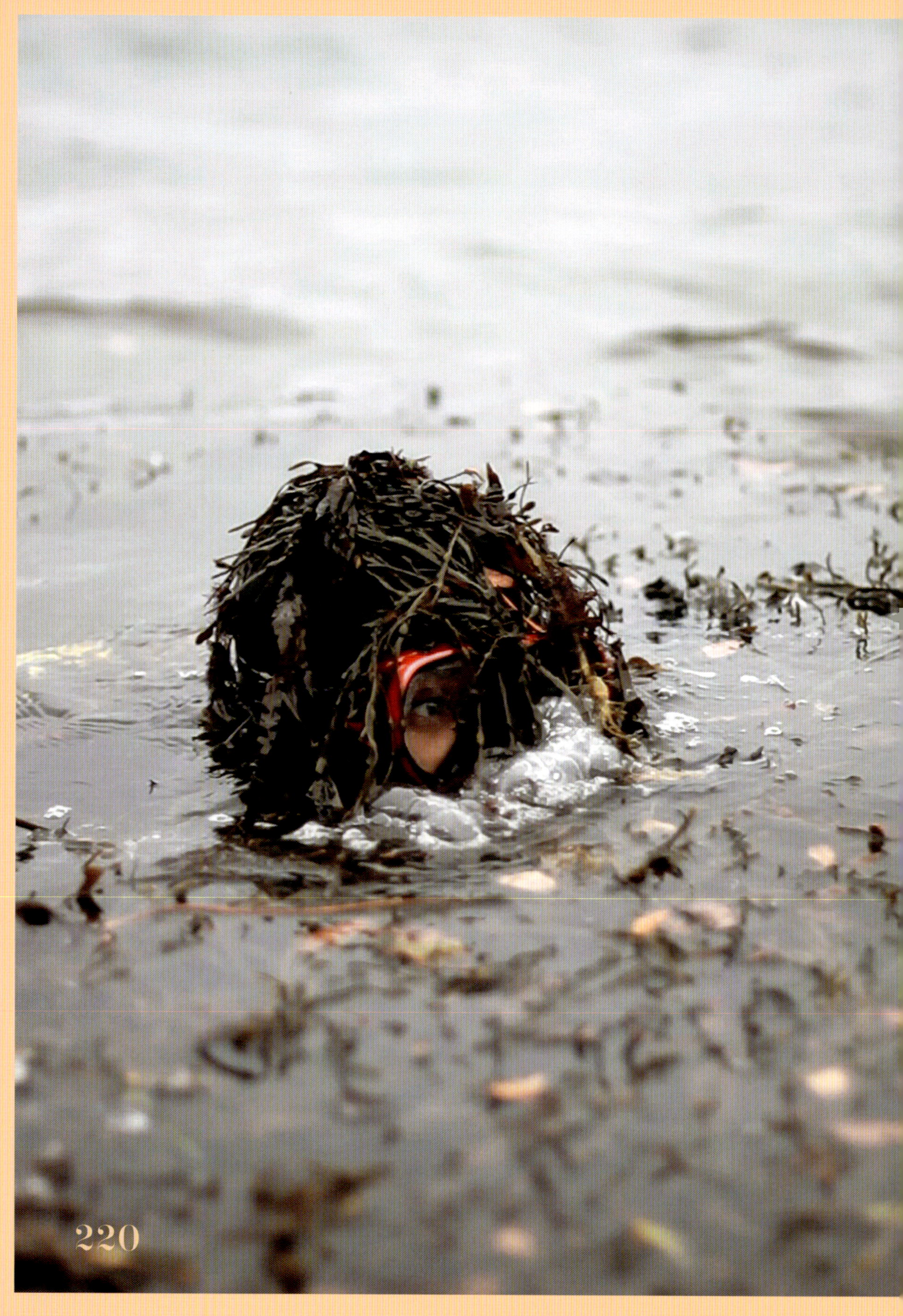

1. Define wonder in your own words.

On one of my earliest scuba dives, when that weightlessness was still new to me, I was drifting forward about thirty feet below the surface of the far water, away from the dock, when the "ground" dipped suddenly downward into darkness. Continuing forward, the wall of the reef dropping off, and blue turning to black below and in front of me, the sensation was utterly of flying. The wonder moment, and that surely was one, is thrilling, with a kind of electricity even, but in hindsight can seem terrifying. There's something of the sublime in wonder, but a choked-up, verklempt feeling, too.

2. What is your earliest childhood experience with wonder?

We called it "Adventure," or maybe "Great Adventure," under the spell of the nearby theme park with that name. It was an abandoned classroom in our kindergarten building, filled with tiers of children's chairs and desks stacked to the ceiling. The lights were always off and magically the door was kept unlocked. The room was large, or so it seemed, and totally full of old furniture. The possible routes for crawling under and climbing through the stacks felt infinite as we navigated, nearly breathless, in a silent row on our hands and knees.

3. What is the last wonder moment you had that left you speechless?

During the making of *Land Dive Team: Bay of Fundy*, I sat in meditation with three other divers as the Fundy tide rolled in and rose over our heads. There was wind that day, and the tide came in with waves in fits and starts. When the water was right at our sightline, it would rise over our eyes and then dip back below. It was like watching two movies at the same time. There was the landscape, the crew, our divemaster, the beach. But that alternated with a different movie, more of an animation really, of suspended rockweed dancing below the surface of the water. That game of trying to keep the same focal point as two different "landscapes" flickered before my eyes in real time was extraordinary. I'd like to go back and make the second movie, of everything we saw beneath the surface of the water.

4. Was there a wonder or aha moment that led to your work in this exhibition?

Yes, and it is also a scuba story. This memory is by contrast light-filled at shallow depth, but there was a lot of motion in the water. All of the plants on the reef were swaying one way and then bending backward in the other direction. It was all somehow exactly timed with the cycle of breath. Breathe in and the whole "field" of the sea floor is moving left. Breathe out and everything is moving right. I shot a clumsy video on that reef called *Guanica Breathing*; it was the next summer, while working on a new video project about breathing and healing, that the *Breathing on Land* and *Land Dive Team* projects began.

opposite: *Land Dive Team: Bay of Fundy*, 2016; single-channel video projection with sound

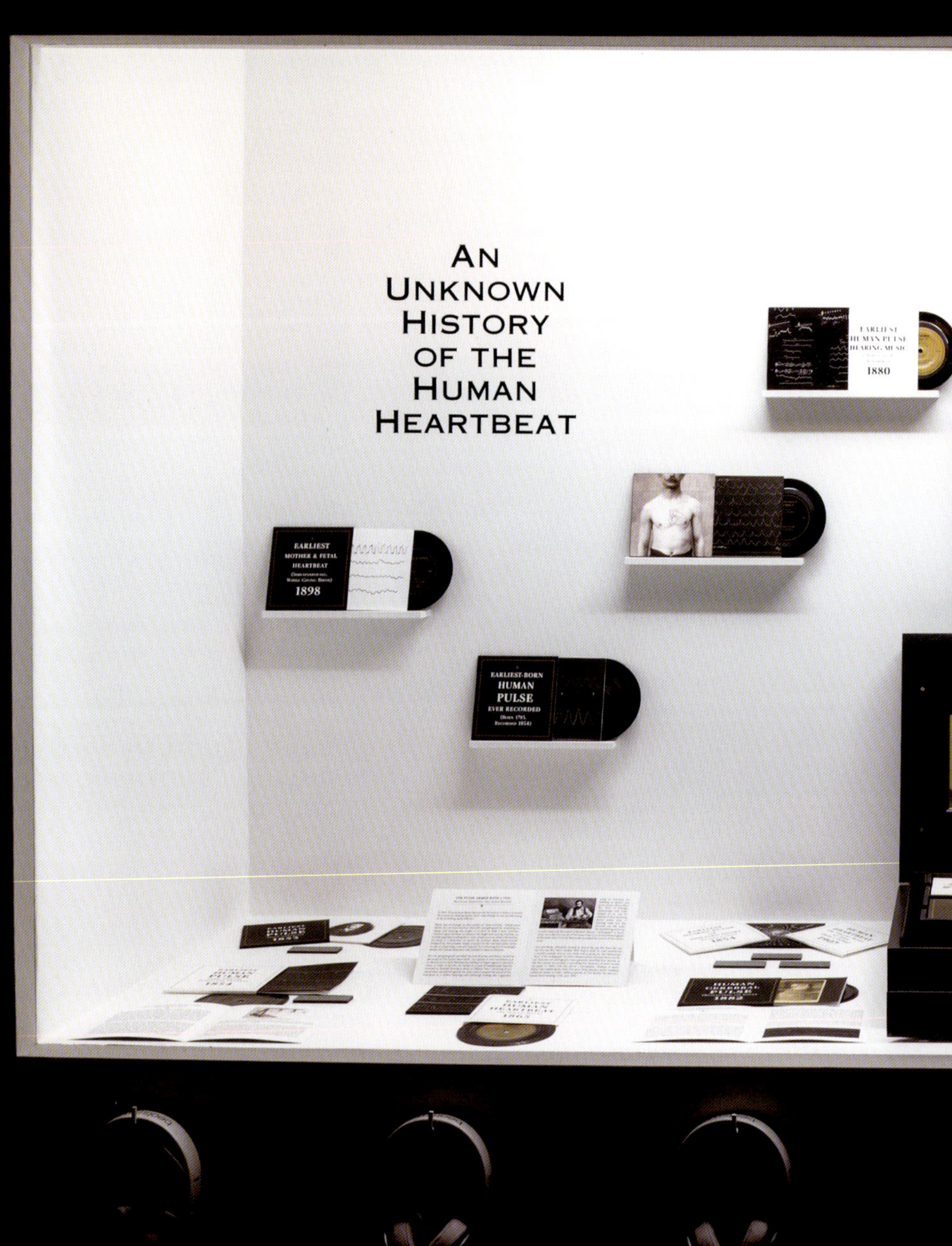
AN
UNKNOWN
HISTORY
OF THE
HUMAN
HEARTBEAT
EARLIEST
HUMAN PULSE
HEARING MUSIC
1880
EARLIEST
MOTHER & FETAL
HEARTBEAT
1898
EARLIEST-BORN
HUMAN
PULSE
EVER RECORDED

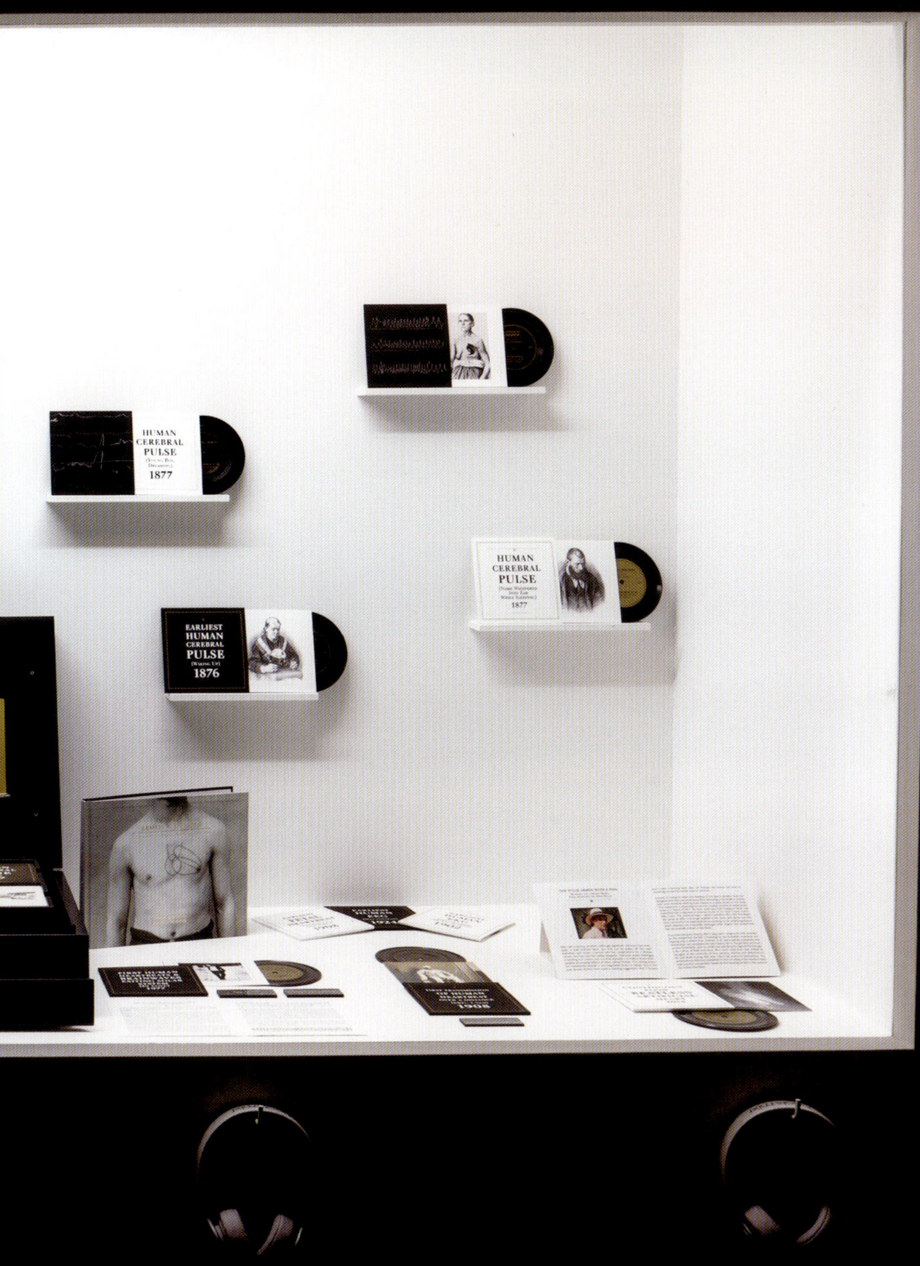

The Pulse Armed With a Pen (An Unknown History of the Human Heartbeat), 2014; 28 custom cut 5-inch vinyl records, audio recordings, archival digital prints (record sleeves, liner notes, labels, slides), three centuries of various human pulse and heartbeat tracings, glass slides, custom bound book, oak, silk, engraved gold mirror, brass, headphones, media players

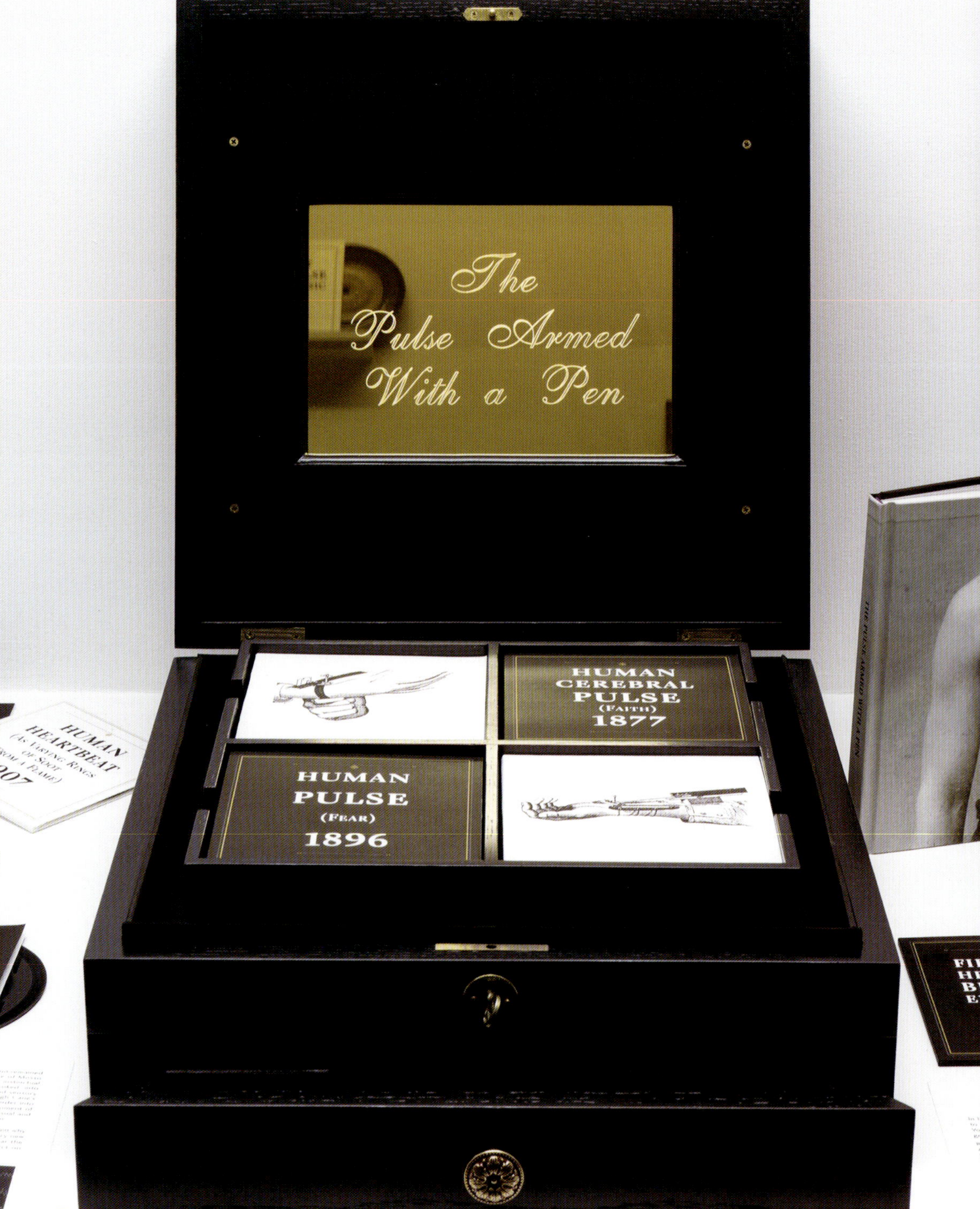
The Pulse Armed With a Pen
HUMAN CEREBRAL PULSE (FAITH) 1877
HUMAN PULSE (FEAR) 1896
HUMAN HEARTBEAT (AS VISING RINGS OF SMOT FROM A FLAME) 1907

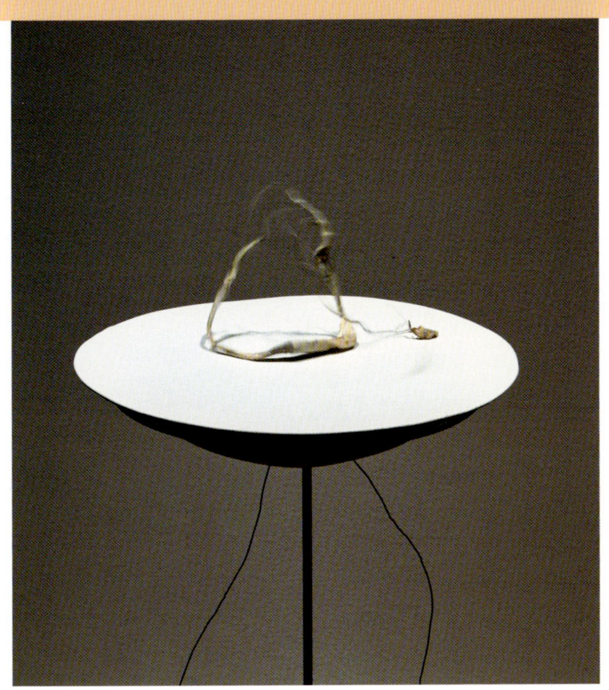

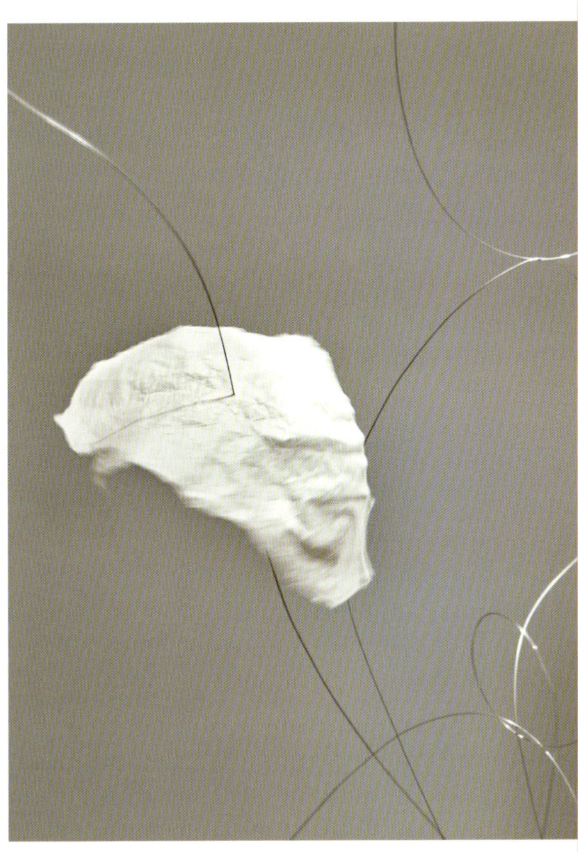

top: *Bone Score (Drum)*, 2016
bottom: *Bone Score (Tangle)*, 2016

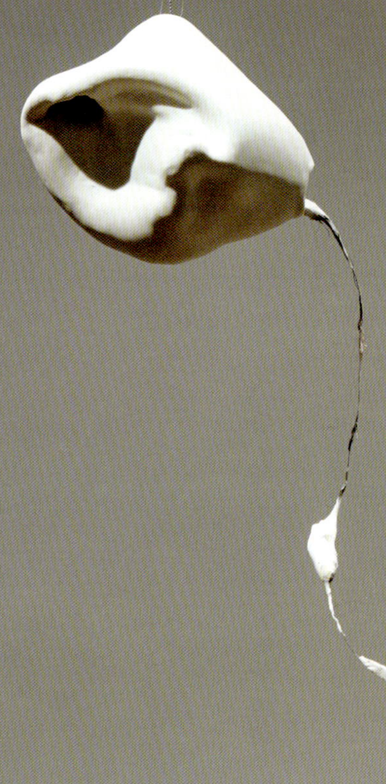

above: *Bone Score (Long Tail)*, 2016; unglazed porcelain, magnet wire, magnets, abaca paper, wire, amplifier, audio player, wood; sounds of breathing, a heart beating, fire, a Kepler star pulse, a children's song
opposite: *Lean*, 2012; steel, magnet, wall

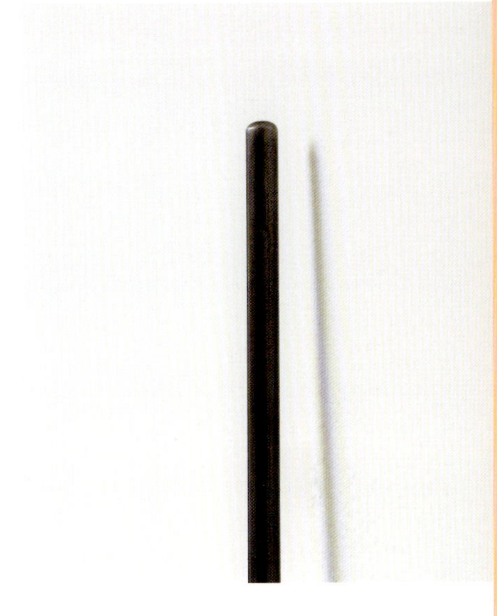

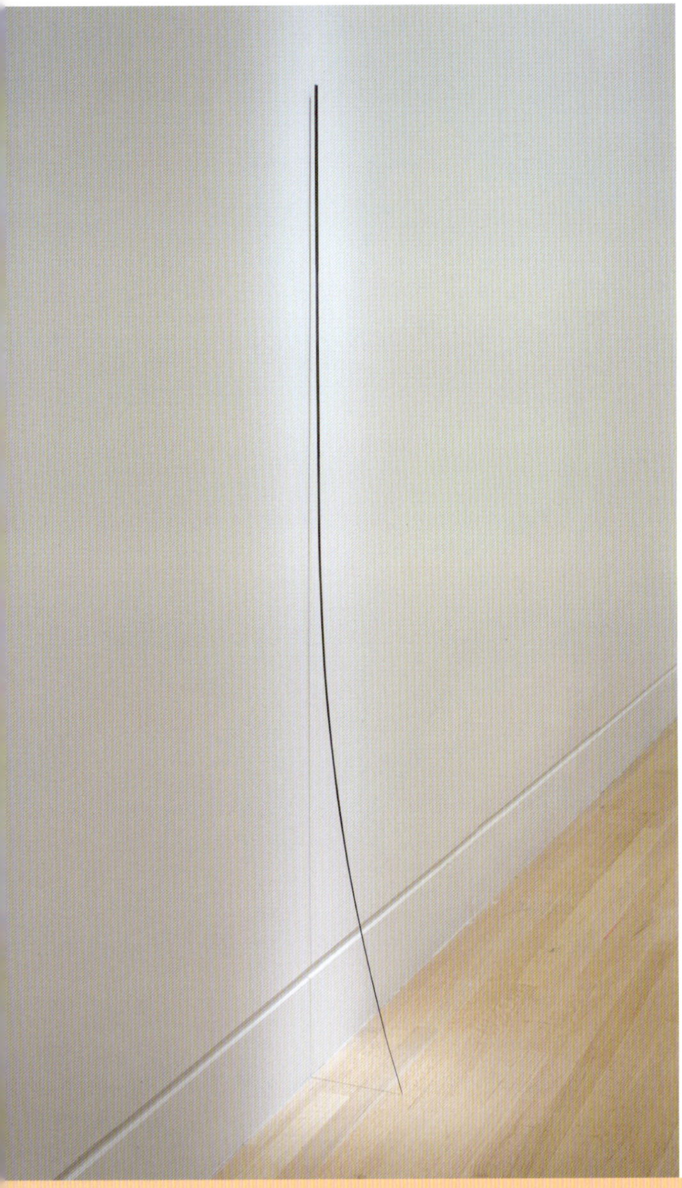

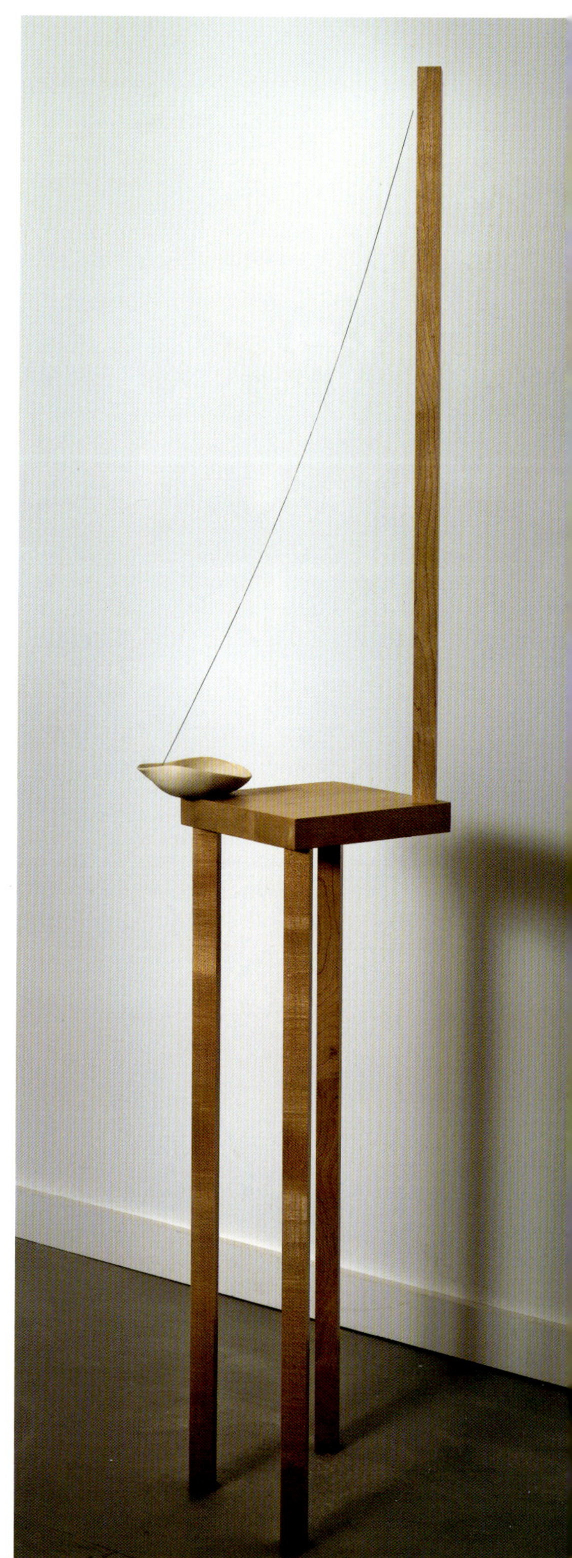

1. Define wonder in your own words.

Wonder reverberates. It contains an element of disbelief, but also confusion and perhaps disruption or pleasure. It takes me out of time. An experience of wonder activates my emotions, so it is more durable and complicated than an experience that is purely phenomenal or sensory. Wonder remains with me. After the experience is over, I continue to think about or feel it.

2. What is your earliest childhood experience with wonder?

I have a strong memory from when I was about eight years old, of visiting a science museum with my father. The museum was in a huge space, as big as a football field. At either end of the space, up high above the people and the exhibits, there were giant parabolic satellite dishes facing one another. You could walk up a tall staircase, speak into the parabola, and have a conversation with someone facing the parabola on the other side of the room.

I waited for my father to traverse the room, then climbed my staircase. I stood in front of that enormous dish, alone in that noisy place, and heard my father speaking to me with total clarity. He was hundreds of feet from me, on the other end of the huge room, but he was whispering in my ear. I felt a collapse of space and time, as well as an unfamiliar sense of this very familiar person.

At that time, I didn't comprehend why the experience was so powerful to me and why I could not forget it. It made an impression far beyond all of the other scientific spectacles in the museum. In retrospect, I think it was because it encapsulated a complex series of emotions that were beyond my understanding at the time. The simultaneity of intimacy and distance, presence and absence, made each more palpable.

3. What is the last wonder moment you had that left you speechless?

I recently visited a place called the Integratron in the desert near Joshua Tree, California. It's a wooden, parabolically shaped building, hand-built without nails or screws by an obsessed and brilliant man. You could stand in the center of the room, speak, and hear your voice "spoken" back to you. It was a completely strange sensation of feeling your own voice as extrinsic, as though it were coming from outside your body. This was extraordinary in itself, but it also brought me back to the experience I described above, poignantly, because I hadn't thought of it since I lost my father two years ago.

4. Was there a wonder or aha moment that led to your work in this exhibition?

A good friend died a few years ago. She was Buddhist, and part of her death ceremony included the playing of some singing bowls. Certainly, this was a situation where I was extra receptive, and I had a somatic impression of those sounds in a way that I had never experienced. The sounds were tactile; I felt them more than I heard them. For months afterwards, the clarity, potency, and corporality of those tones returned to me often. I generally think of sound as carrying content or emotion, but this was something quite different. It was not apparent intellectual or even emotional content that had affected me. It was the palpable physical energy in those tones that moved through me, and their vibrations seemed to reverberate within my body.

opposite: *Stability Study (bowl)*, 2015; wood, steel, magnet, ceramic

PERIDOT

by

MARY RUEFLE

I awoke in an ecstasy.
The sky was the color of a cut lime
that had sat in the refrigerator
in a plastic container
for thirty-two days.
Fact-checkers, check.
I am happy.
Notice I speak in complete sentences.
Something I have not done since birth.
And the sky responds.

The Thing Itself

by Maria Popova

One unusually chilly October, I found myself in the middle of a Southern nowhere, on a midwifery farm founded in the 1970s and practically unchanged since. A dear friend—a born-and-raised New Englander who had rebelled by becoming an artist and growing a large hippie heart—had journeyed there to give birth.

There was an eerie and exhilarating time-travel feeling to the farm—remote and rudimentary, it was a deliberate freeze-frame of civilization taken in a different era. When night fell, it fell completely. Darkness engulfed the land—the kind of darkness those of us nursed on urban over-illumination have forgotten exists, darkness punctuated only by glimmers of celestial light poking through the thinning autumn foliage.

One particularly starless night, Amanda and I ventured out of our cabin for a walk after dinner. We didn't take a flashlight, or even a phone. There was a single road backboning the farm and we had walked it many times in the daylight, so we decided to reverence the darkness and trust our creaturely spatial instincts. Unable to see more than five feet ahead, we discerned the general direction of the road from the clearing above the trees, where the cloudy nocturne seemed ever so slightly less dark than the heavy darkness surrounding us—darkness so thick that each stride seemed to slice the night air apart. We walked slowly yet assuredly, arm-in-arm, the newborn strapped to Amanda's chest.

Just as we were about to turn around, a most extraordinary sight arrested us: in the middle of the woods, a meadowy clearing revealed itself, sprinkled with what appeared to be a galaxy of tiny fallen stars. Mid-stride, I gasped—a radiant reflex, sparked by the recognition of a thoroughly unphotographable marvel, the kind that stuns you with the sheer astonishment of its unanticipated and unapologetic beauty.

It took me a moment and some deeply buried vestige of ninth-grade biology to realize that these were glowworms—hundreds, perhaps thousands of them, flickering gently in slow motion as they punctuated the darkness like a living constellation. But the most remarkable thing, the most poetic thing, was that they didn't glow to delight us—they glowed to find each other in the dark.

I stood there, held in the stillness of this unrepeatable moment of wonder—the blanket of darkness, the embroidery of light, the ancient ritual of love, the brand new life.

This is what wonder does—it arrests us and moves us at the same time. A moment of wonder is one of invigorating serenity—an encounter with something entirely new, and yet an encounter we recognize as an act of remembering.

Every artist can recount at least one such moment of wonder, or what Anthony Burgess called "an instant of recognition of verbally inexpressible spiritual realities"—discovery and remembrance folded into a single instant that crystallizes some essential facet of the creative impulse, be it microscopic or monumental, for the artist.

James Baldwin stands on a street corner waiting for the light to change, sees the city reflected in a puddle and sees the world as if for the first time. Patti Smith, a toddler in the park, watches a swan lift off from the lake and become one with the sky, illuminating the transcendent interconnectedness of all things revealed in beauty. Pablo Neruda reaches his hand through a hole in the backyard fence of his boyhood home, and another little boy's hand reaches back, passing him a small wooden toy, revealing for the future poet the wondrous feeling of connection that is the reason art exists. Virginia Woolf, astride in the garden, suddenly realizes that the flower and the earth are one and is astonished by an acute awareness that "behind the cotton wool is hidden a pattern," that "the whole world is a work of art ... there is no Shakespeare ... no Beethoven," that "we are the words; we are the music; we are the thing itself."

Wonder is the cotton wool lifted, the hand through the fence, the swan in the sky, the world in the puddle, the bioluminescent constellation in the middle of the forest. Wonder is what reveals to us—what makes us—the thing itself.

Sharon Ellis

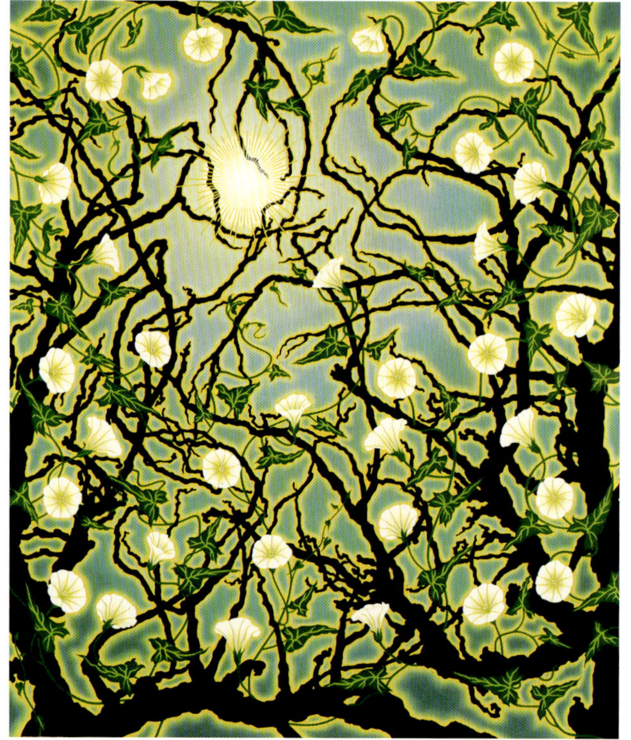

 After the Fire, 2010; alkyd on canvas

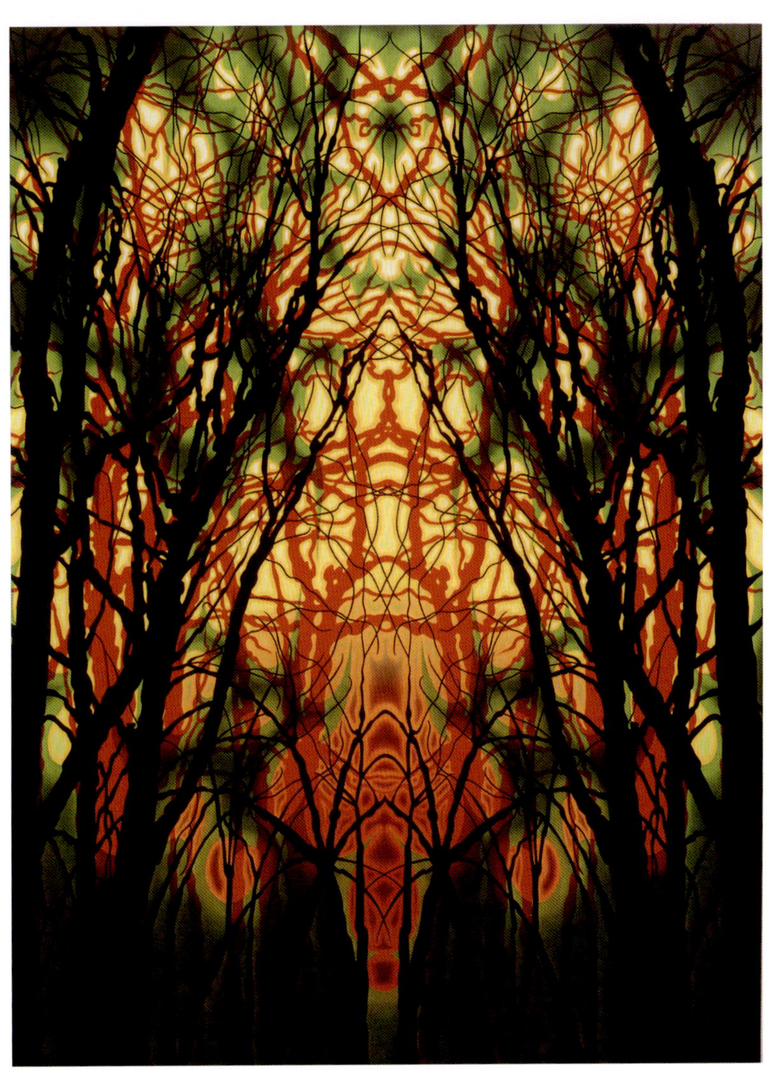

Afternoon, 1998; alkyd on canvas

241

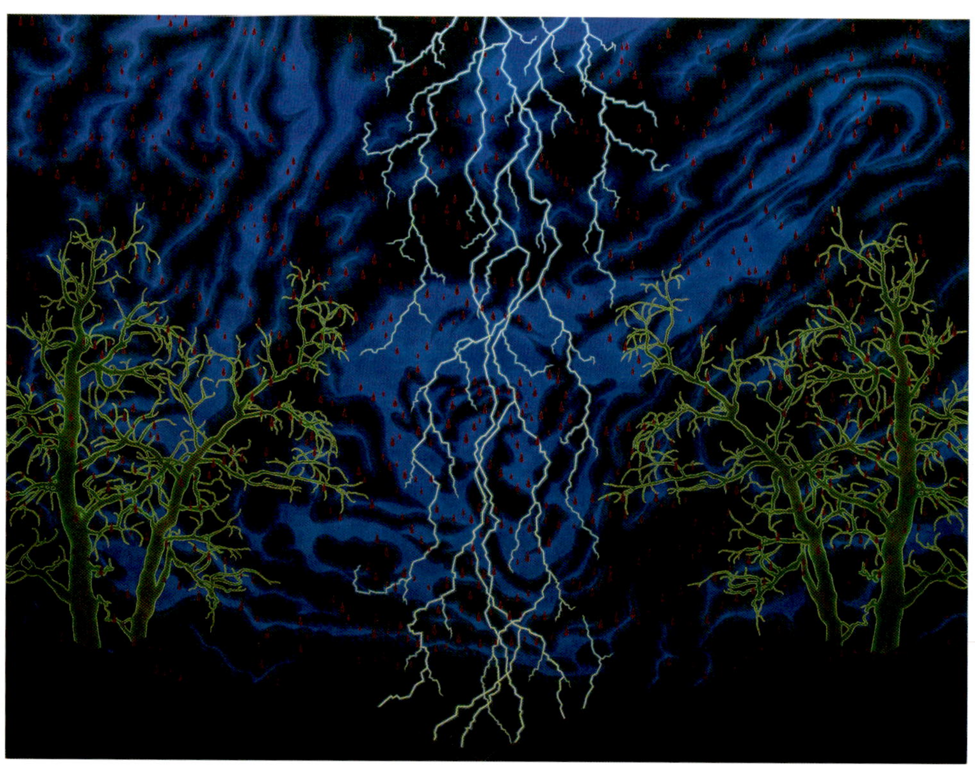

 Night Storm, 2013; alkyd on canvas

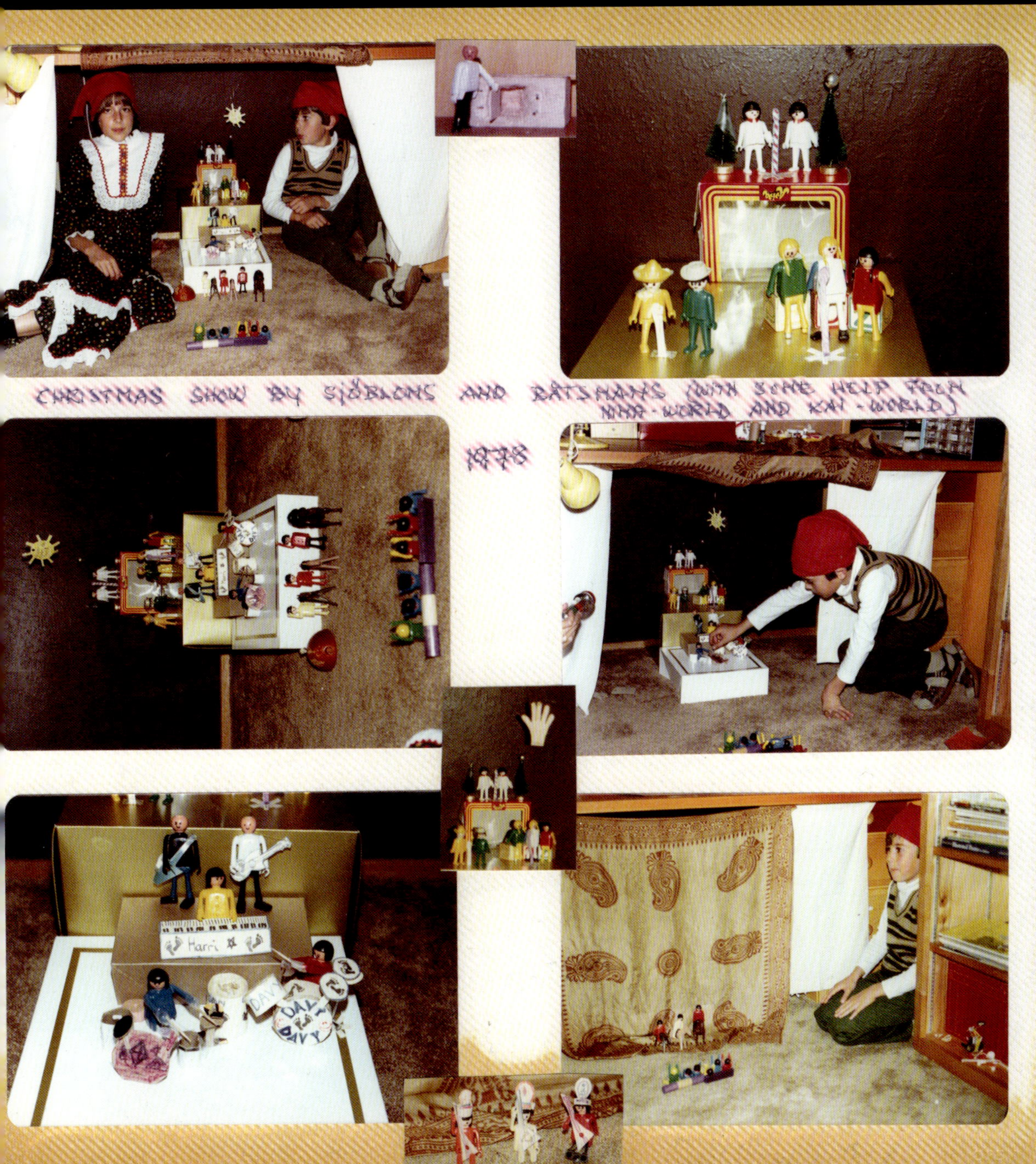

CHRISTMAS SHOW BY SJÖBLOMS AND BATEMANS (WITH SOME HELP FROM MAR-WORLD AND KAY-WORLD)
1978

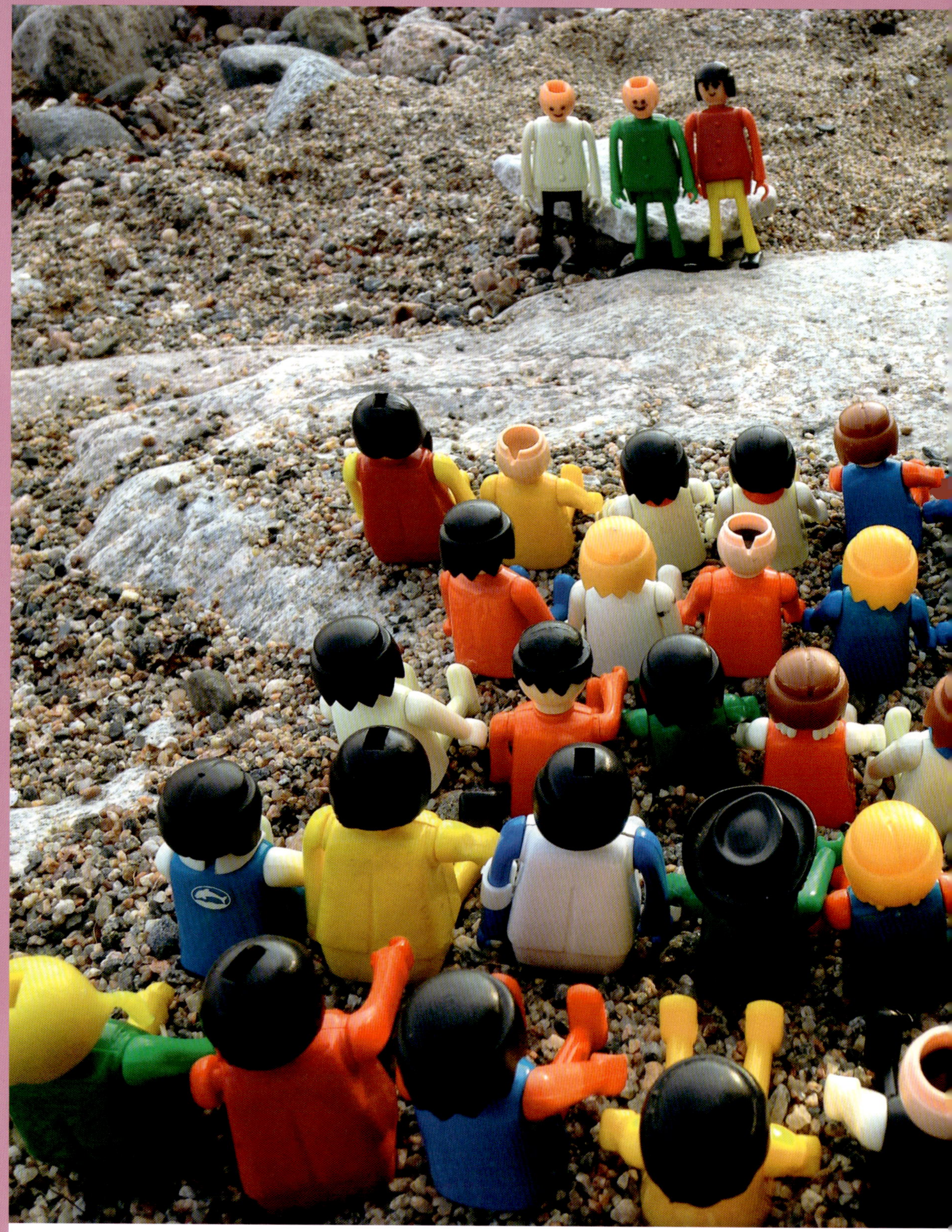

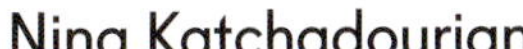

Nina Katchadourian

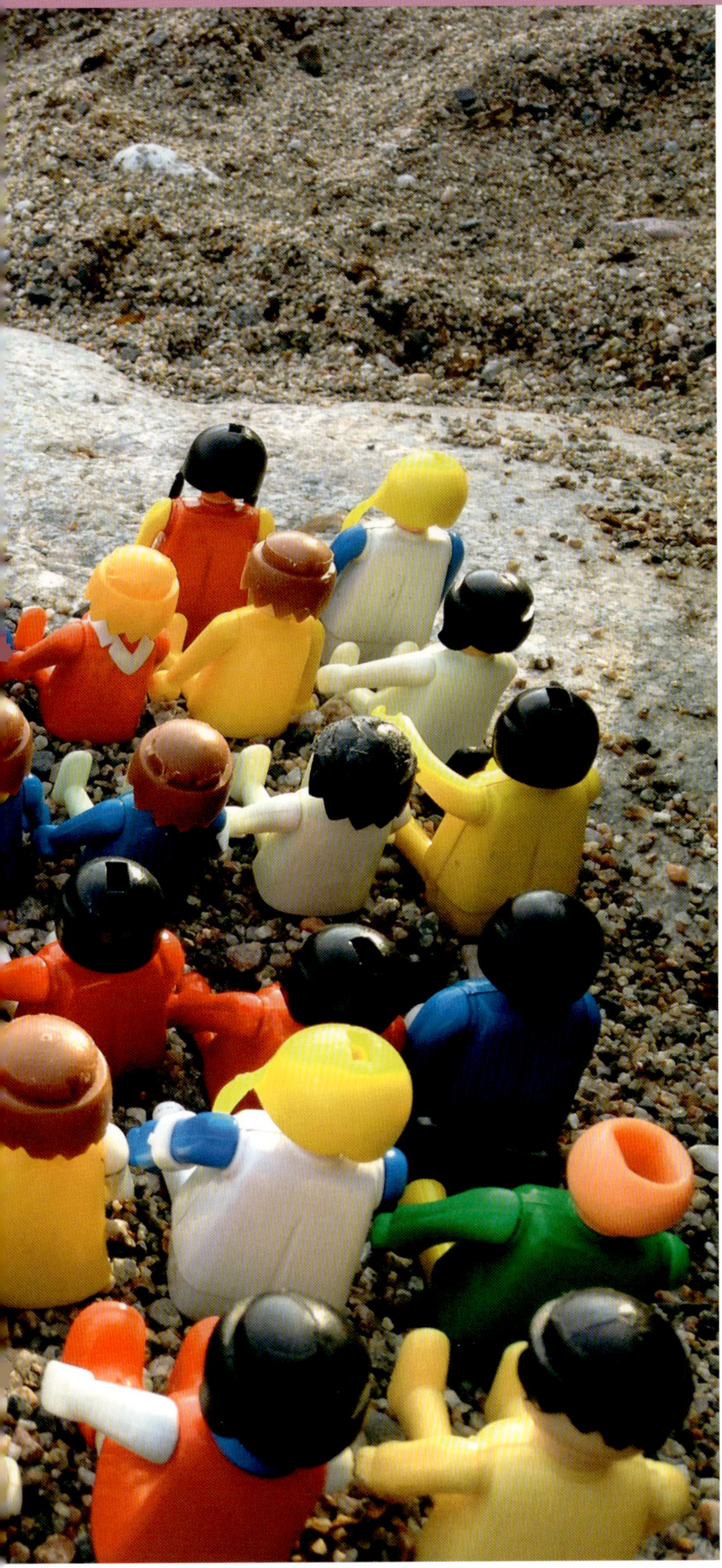

production still from *The Recarcassing Ceremony*, 2016

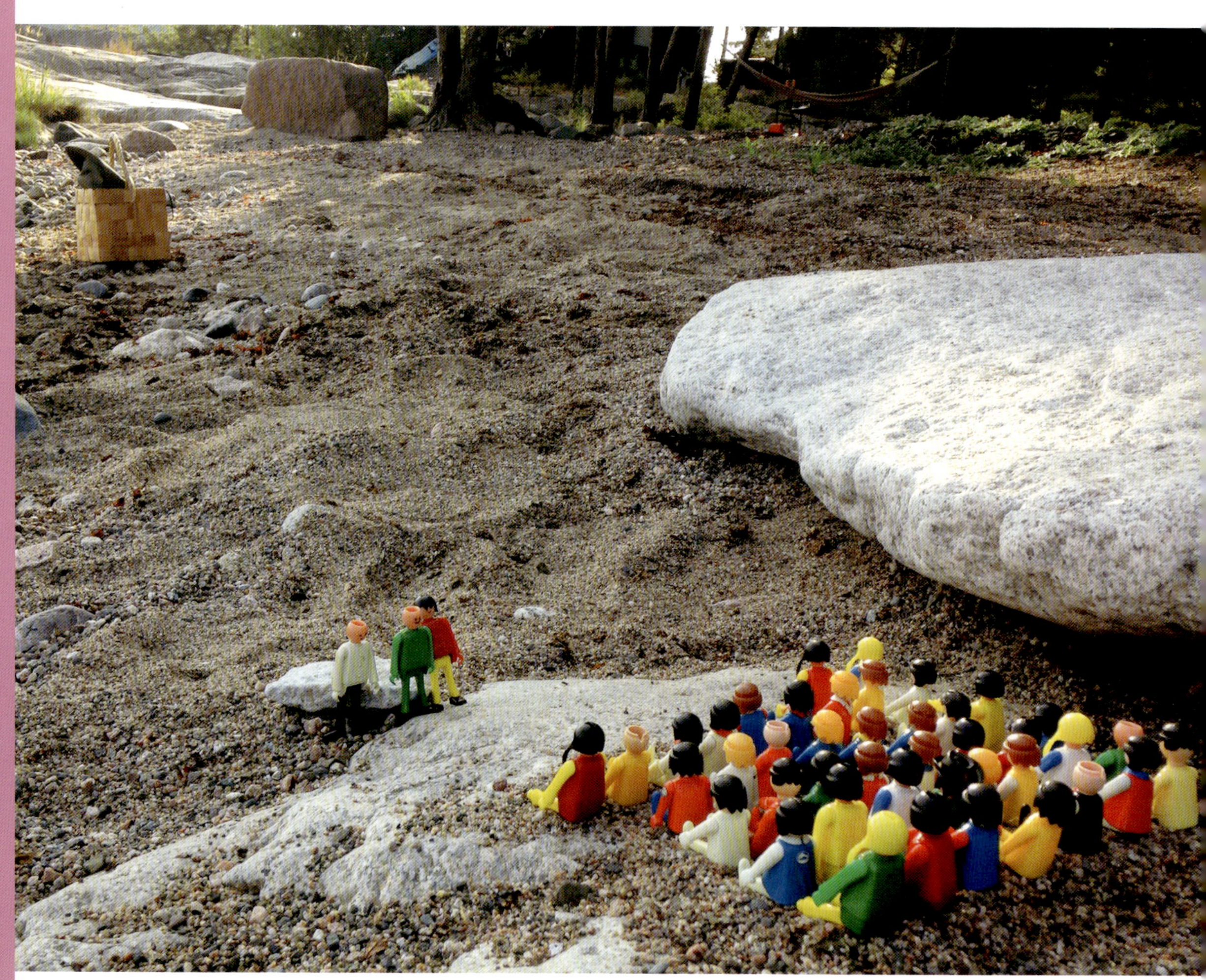

  production still from *The Recarcassing Ceremony*, 2016

1. Define wonder in your own words.

When the fly that you hear in the room turns out to be inside your own mouth.

2. What is your earliest childhood experience with wonder?

My grandmother's ability to use her thumbnail as a screwdriver.

3. What is the last wonder moment you had that left you speechless?

Reading "It is soft, white, and as wholesome as childhood itself" as the description for a familiar bread-like product on the company's website.

4. Was there a wonder or aha moment that led to your work in this exhibition?

After years of searching, finally locating the cassette tape from 1980 that had the recording my parents made of the Recarcassing Ceremony.

Megan and Murray McMillan

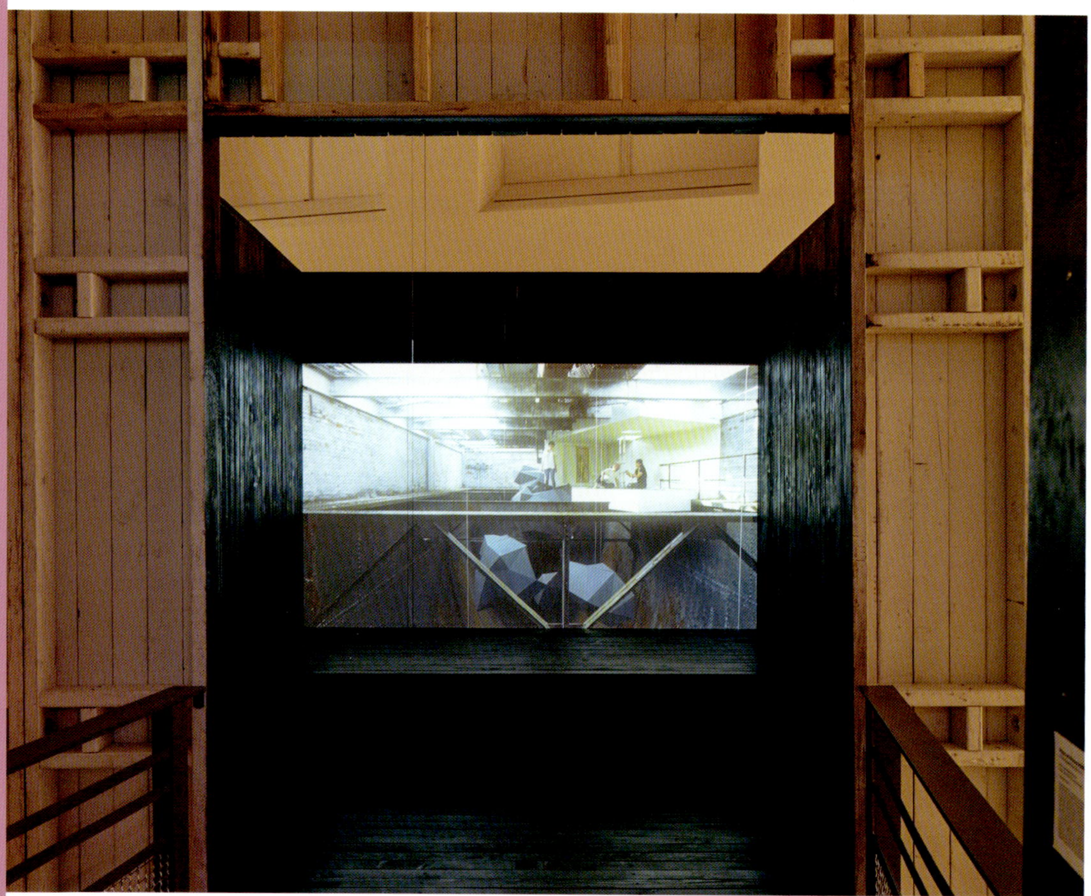

 In What Distant Sky, 2013–16; video in purpose-built room

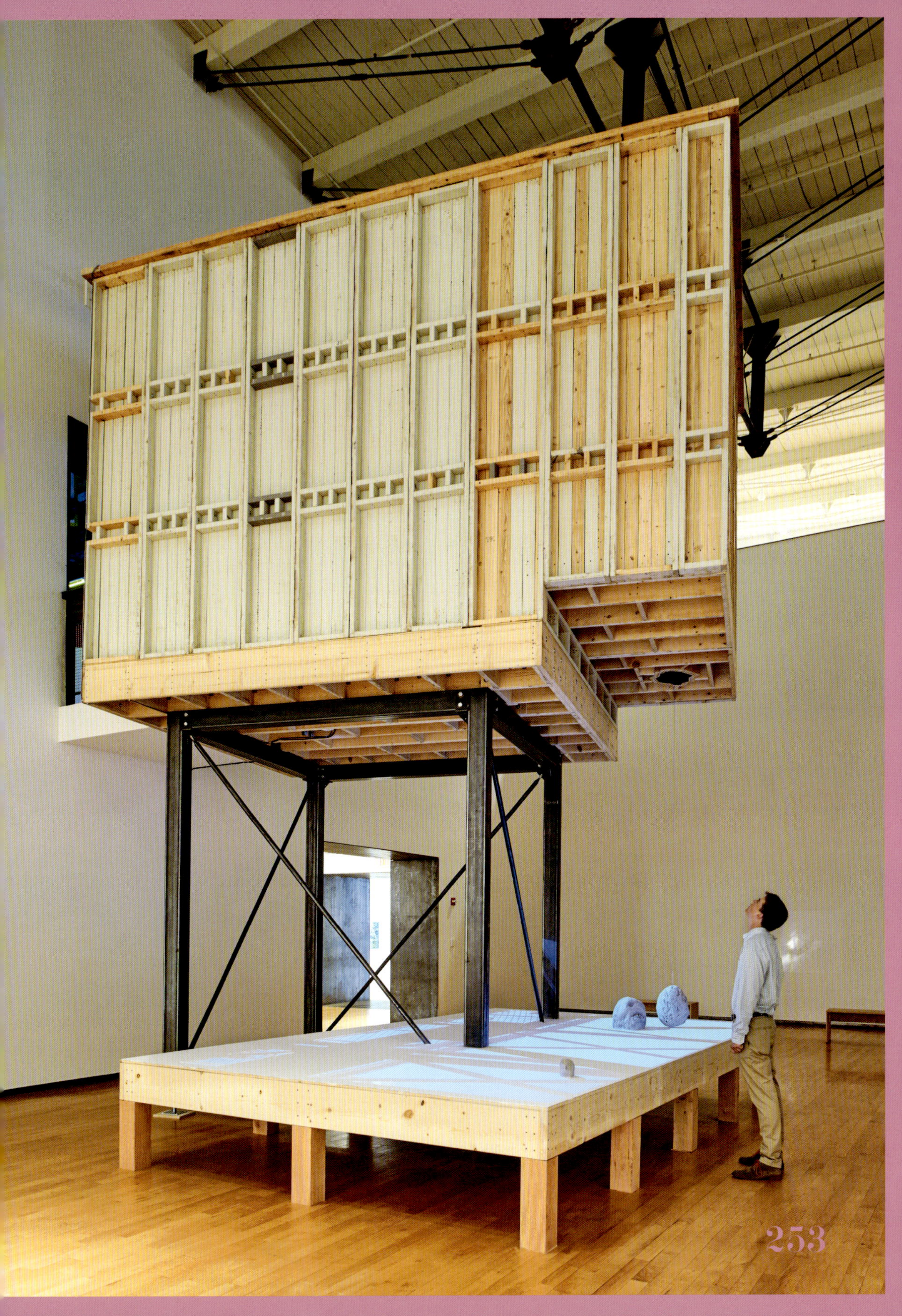

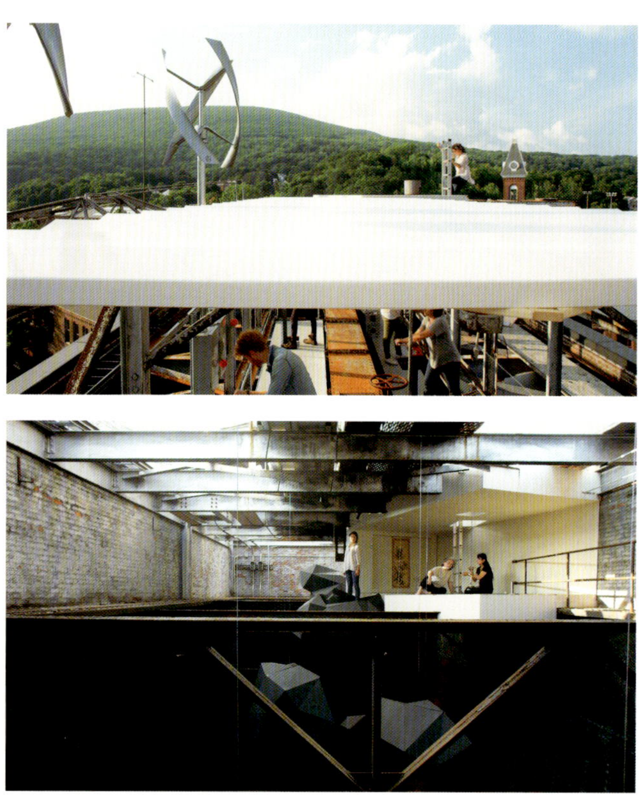

top: *In What Distant Sky (Photograph 3)*, 2013; digital still
bottom: *In What Distant Sky (Photograph 2)*, 2013; digital still

Paul's Fish Fry in Bennington, Vermont, is no longer
Closed For The Season Reason Freezin. The umbrellas
have opened over the picnic tables and the bees are
beginning to annoy the french fries, the thick shakes
and the real malts of my past:

I am thirteen thousand miles removed, on the delta
of the Pearl River, eating a litchi. Its translucent flesh just
burst in my mouth; shreds of it glitter between my teeth.
I smile but the fruit seller is sour. In fact, he is so sour
the only man on earth he resembles is Paul. But the litchi…

Actually none of this has happened yet. I am nineteen
years old. I am riding in the boxcar of a freight train
hurtling toward Pocatello, Idaho. In a very dangerous move
I maneuver my way back to the car behind me, an open gondola
carrying two tons of timberland eastward out of Oregon:

it is here I will lie all night, my head against the logs,
watching the stars. No one knows where I am. My mother thinks
I am asleep in my bed. My friends, having heard of a derailment
at ninety miles an hour on the eastbound freight, think I am
dead. But I'm *here*, hurtling across the continent with unbelievable speed. We are red-hot and we go, the steel track
with its imperceptible bounce allows us to go, our circuitous
silhouette against the great Blue Mountains and my head in a
thrill watching the stars: I am not yet at a point in my life
where I am able to name them, but there are so many and they are

so white! I'm hurtling toward work at Paul's toward the litchi-
bite in Guangzhou, toward the day of my death all right, but all
I can say is I am *happyhappyhappy* to be here with the stars and
the logs, with my head thrown back and then pitched forward
in tears. And the litchi! it's like swallowing a pearl.

Exuberance: The Passion for Life[1]

by Kay Redfield Jamison

It is a curious request to make of God. <u>Shield your joyous ones</u>, asks the Anglican prayer: <u>Shield your joyous ones</u>. God more usually is asked to watch over those who are ill or in despair, as indeed the rest of the prayer makes clear: "Watch now those who weep this day," it goes. "Rest your weary ones: soothe your suffering ones." The joyous tend to be left to their own devices, the exuberant even more so.

Perhaps this is just as well. Those inclined toward exuberance have enjoyed the benign neglect of my field. Psychologists, for reasons of clinical necessity or vagaries of temperament, have chosen to dissect and catalogue the morbid emotions—depression, anger, anxiety—and to leave largely unexamined the more vital, positive ones. Not unlike God, if only in this one regard, my colleagues and I have tended more to those in the darkness than to those in the light. We have given sorrow many words, but a passion for life few.

Yet it is the infectious energies of exuberance that proclaim and disperse much of what is marvelous in life. Exuberance carries us places we would not otherwise go—across the savanna, to the moon, into the imagination—and if we ourselves are not so exuberant we will, caught up in the contagious joy of those who are, be inclined collectively to go yonder. By its pleasures, exuberance lures us from our common places and quieter moods; and—after the victory, the harvest, the discovery of a new idea or an unfamiliar place—it gives ascendant reason to venture forth all over again. Delight is its own regard, adventure its own pleasure.

Exuberance is an abounding, ebullient, effervescent emotion. It is kinetic and unrestrained, joyful, irrepressible. It is not happiness, although they share a border. It is instead, at its core, a more restless, billowing state. Certainly it is no lulling sense of contentment: exuberance leaps, bubbles, and overflows, propels its energy through troop and tribe. It spreads upward and outward, like pollen toted by dancing bees, and in this carrying ideas are moved and actions taken. Yet exuberance and joy are fragile matter. Bubbles burst; a wince of disapproval can cut dead a whistle or abort a cartwheel. The exuberant move above the horizon, exposed and vulnerable....

Exuberance is a vital emotion; it demands not only defense but exposure, for despair far more than joy has found sympathy with poets and scholars. Joy lacks the <u>gravitas</u> that suffering so effortlessly commands. Joy without reflection is evanescent; without counterweight, it has no weight at all. Or so one would think.

Yet joy is essential to our existence. Exuberance, joy's more energetic relation, occupies an ancient region of our mammalian selves, and one to which we owe in no small measure our survival and triumphs. It is a material part of our pursuits—love, games, hunting and war, exploration—and it is a vibrant force to signal victory, proclaim a time to quicken, to draw together, to exult, to celebrate. Exuberance is ancient, material, and profound. "The Greeks understood the mysterious power of the hidden side of things," wrote Louis Pasteur. "They bequeathed to us one of the most beautiful words in our language—the word 'enthusiasm'—<u>entheos</u>—a god within. The grandeur of human actions is measured by the inspiration from which they spring. Happy is he who bears a god within, and who obeys it."

Like many essential human traits, exuberance is teeming in some and not to be caught sight of in others. For a few, exuberance is in the blood, an irrepressible life force. It may ebb and flow, but the underlying capacity for joy is as much a part of the person as having green eyes or a long waist. For them, as the psalm promises, a full joy cometh in the morning. Not so for most others. Exuberance is a more occasional thing, something to be experienced only as splendid moments of love or attainment, or known in youth but lost with time. The nonexuberant lack fizz and risibility: they need to be lifted up on the enthusiasm of others; roused by dance or drug; impelled by music. They do not kindle of their own accord.

Variation in temperament is necessary. Exuberance, indiscriminately appointed, is anarchical. If all were effervescent, the world would be an exhausting and chaotic place, driven to incoherence by competing enthusiasms or becalmed by indifference to the day-to-day requirements of life. Our species, like most, is well served by a diversity of temperaments, a variety of energies and moods. Exuberance is a fermenting, pushing-upward-and-forward force, but sometimes its fixity is critical to survival. The joyous, and the not so, need one another in order to survive.

I believe that exuberance is incomparably more important than we acknowledge. If, as it has been claimed, enthusiasm finds the opportunities and energy makes the most of them, a mood of mind that yokes the two is formidable indeed. Exuberant people take in the world and act upon it differently than those who are less lively and less energetically engaged. They hold their ideas with passion and delight, and they act upon them with dispatch.

Their love of life and of adventure is palpable. Exuberance is a peculiarly pleasurable state, and in that pleasure is power....

Psychologists, who in recent years have taken up the study of positive emotions, find that joy widens one's view of the world and expands imaginative thought. It activates. It makes both physical and intellectual exploration more likely, and it provides regard for problems solved or risks taken. Through its positive energies, it heals as well. One joy, the Chinese believe, scatters a hundred griefs, and certainly it can be an antidote to fatigue and discouragement. Into those set back by failure, joy transfuses hope.

Exuberance is also, at its quick, contagious. As it spreads pell-mell through a group, exuberance excites, it delights, and it dispels tension. It alerts the group to change and possibility. Ted Turner, who would know, believes a leader is someone with the ability to "create infectious enthusiasm."[2] This is a defining quality of great teachers, statesmen, and adventurers. Put to good use, infectious enthusiasm is a wonderful thing; used badly, it is calamitous.

Mostly, exuberance is a bounty and a blessing. It has its dangers... but it is, all told, an amazing thing.

...

1. This is an excerpt from the work originally published by Alfred A. Knopf in 2004, pp. 3–7.

2. Appears to come from Ken Auletta, *Media Man: Ted Turner's Improbable Empire* (Atlas Books/W. W. Norton & Company, 2004).

Tom Friedman

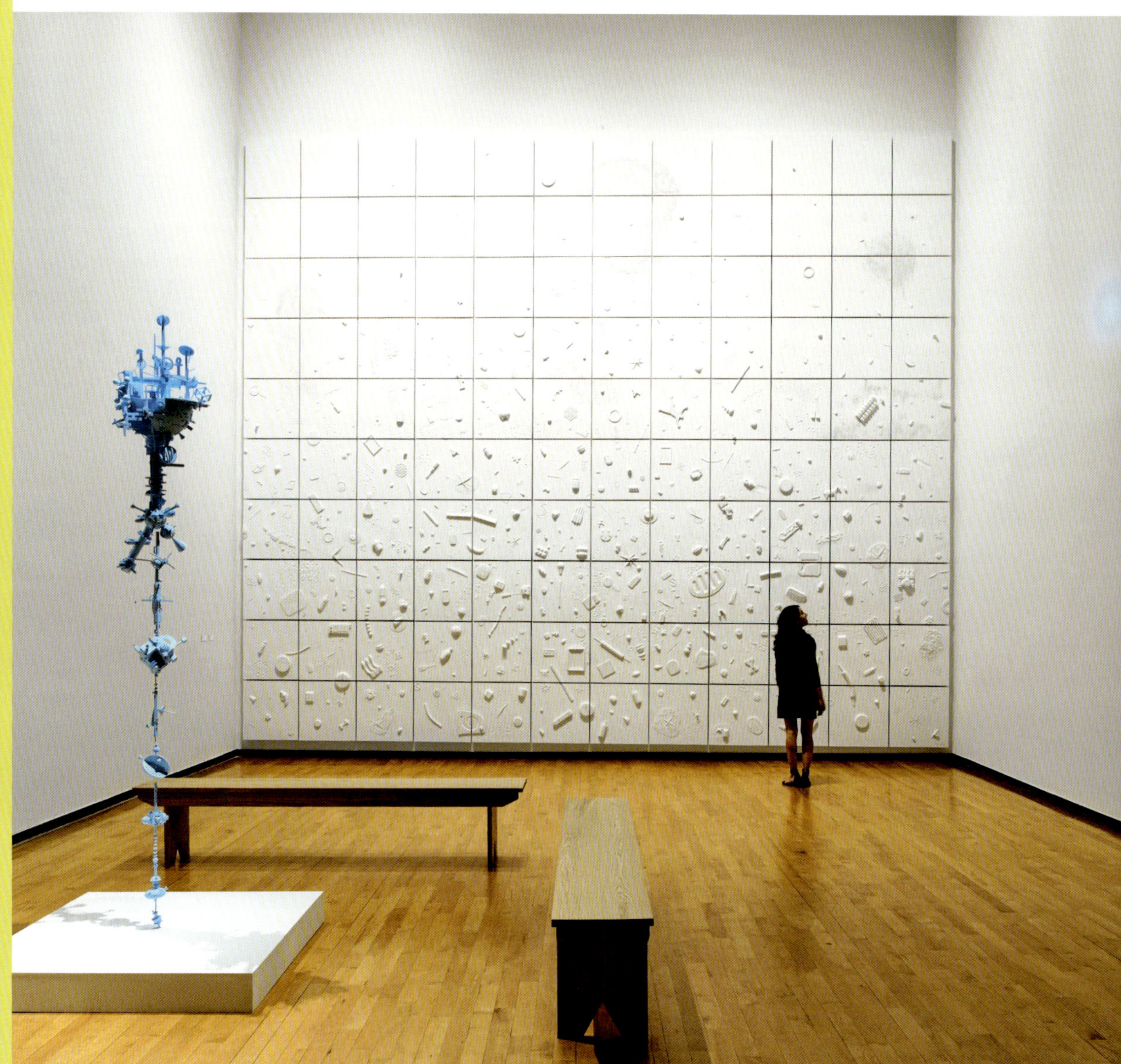

The Wall, 2016; plaster
Flashlight on Wall (UFO), 2016; video

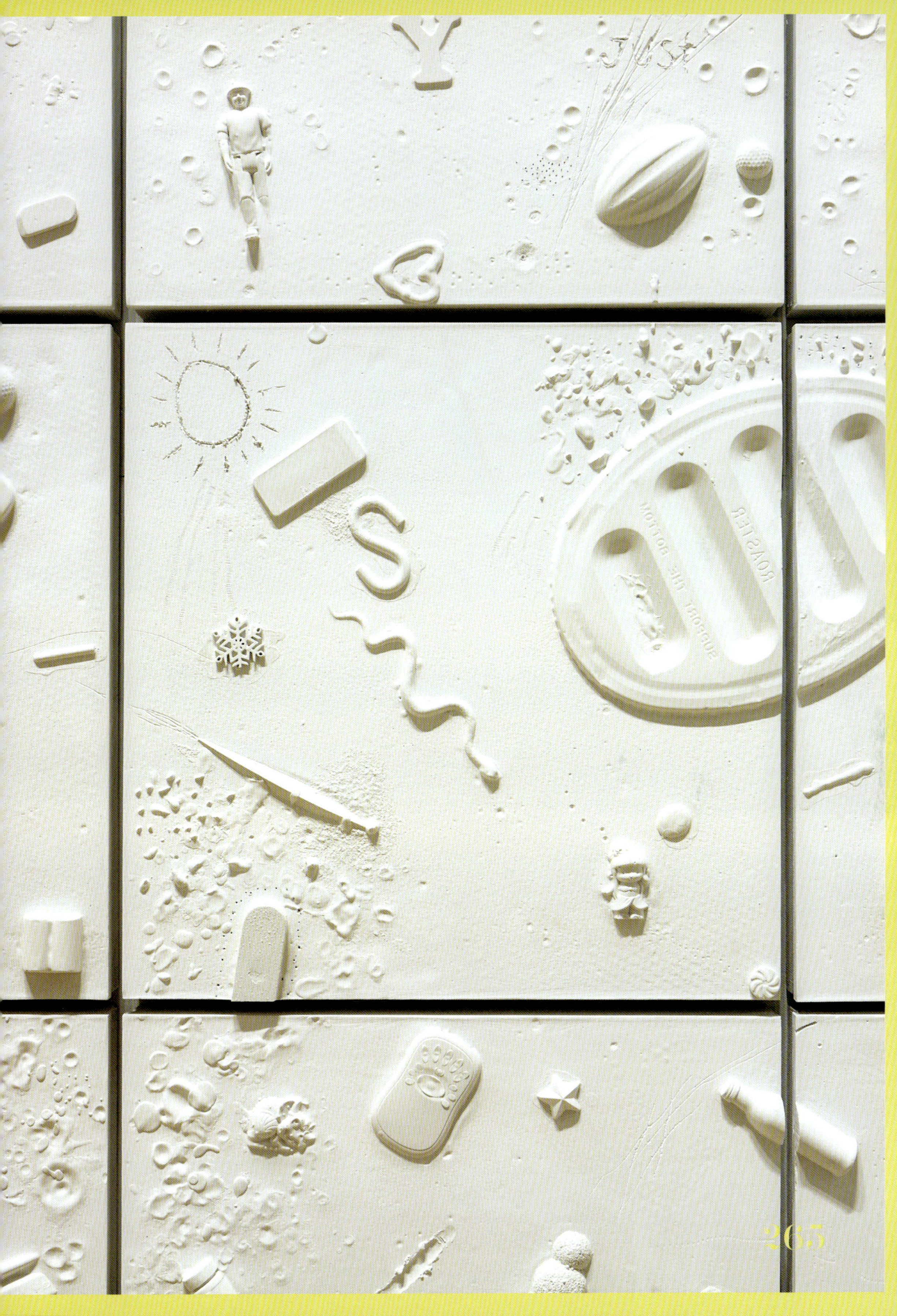

S
ROASTER
THE BOTTOM

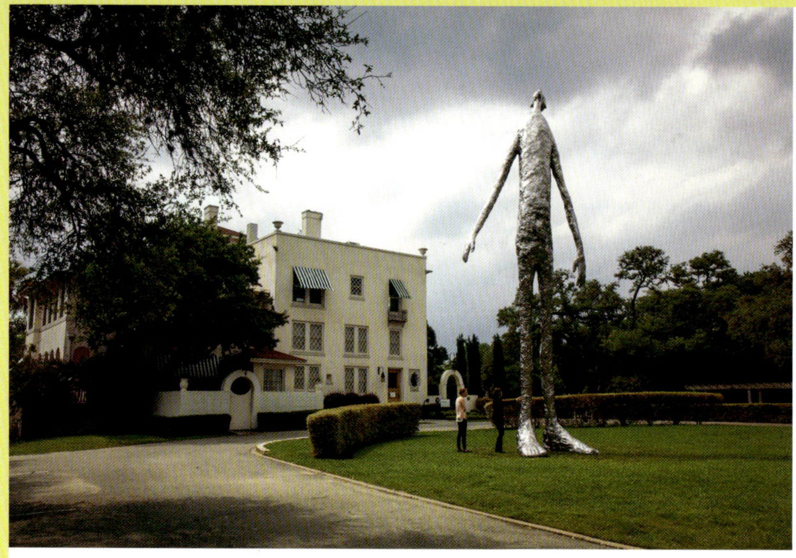

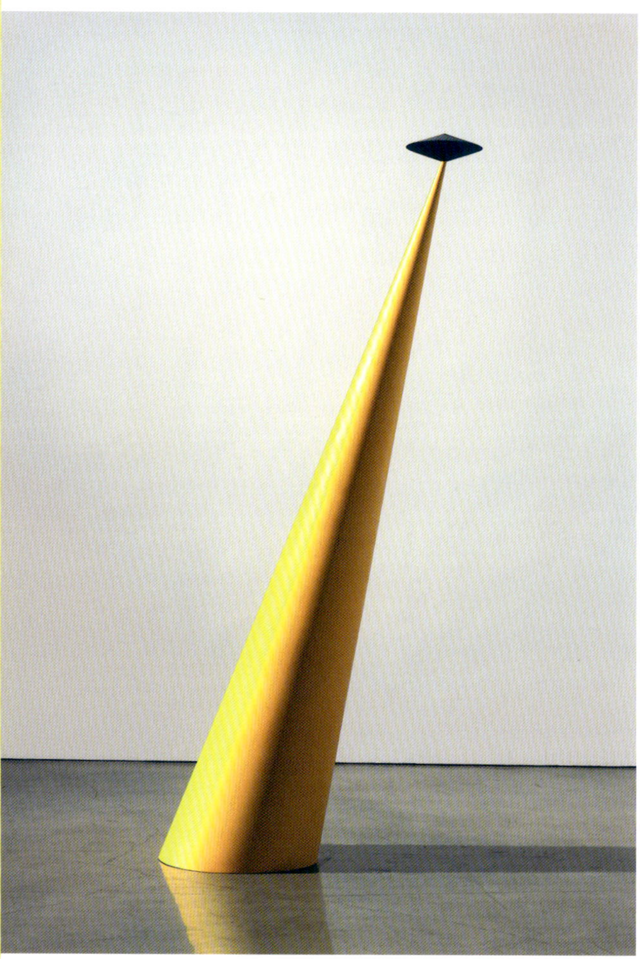

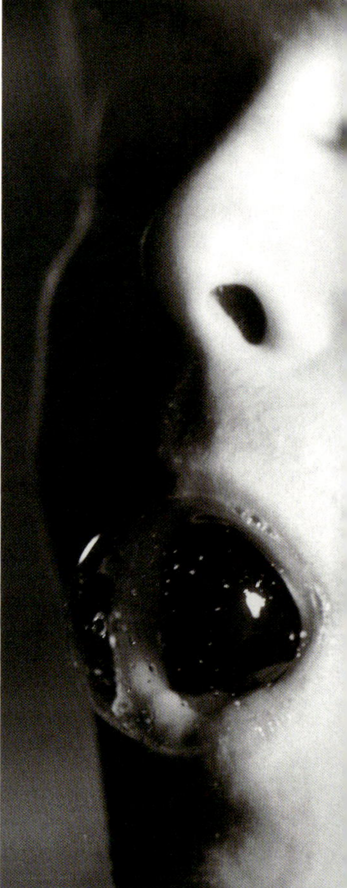

top: *Looking Up*, 2015; stainless steel
middle: *Untitled*, 1900; black and white photograph
bottom: *UFO*, 2006; wood
opposite: *Untitled (blue space station)*, 2012; Styrofoam, paint

266

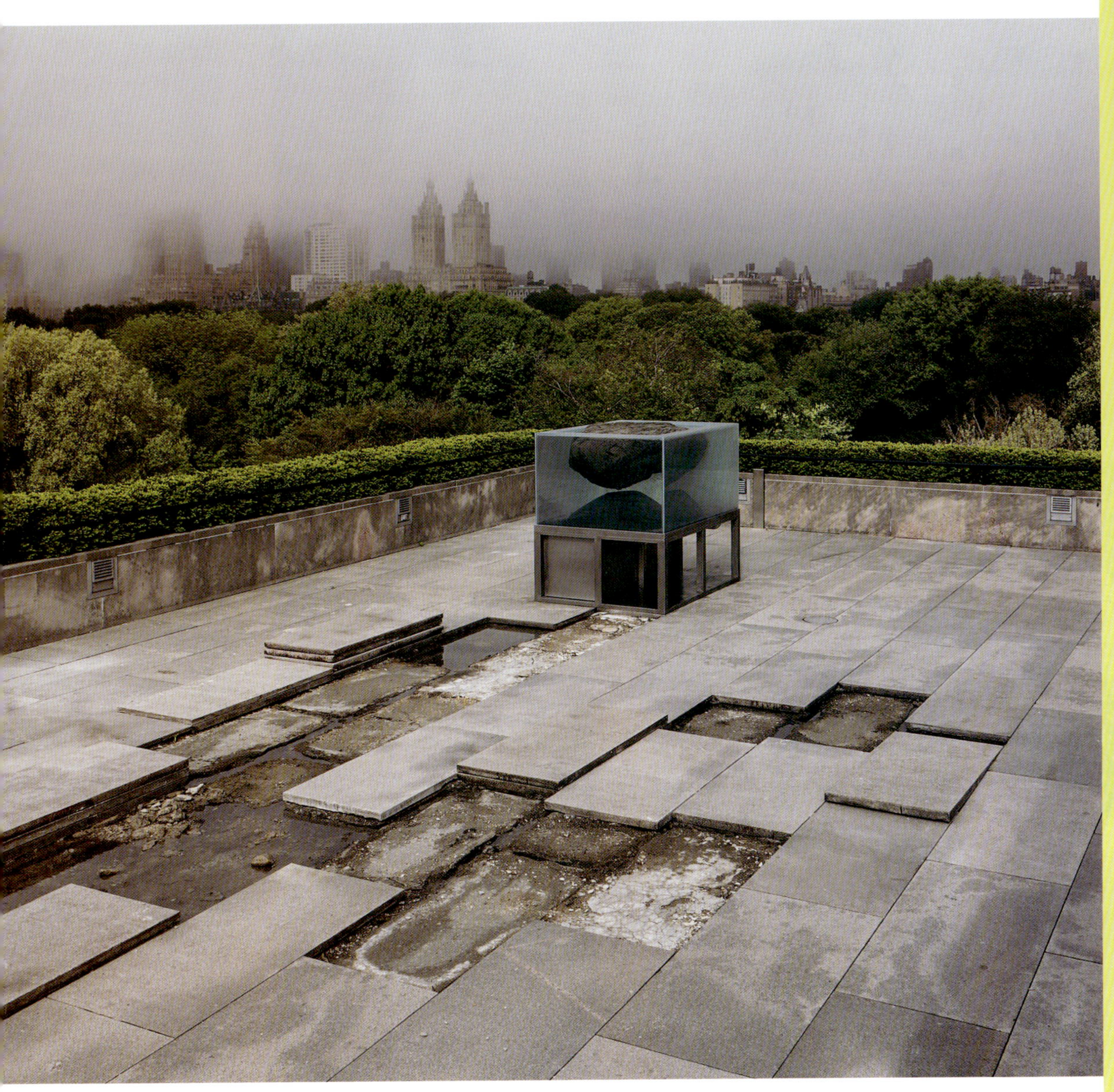

installation view of *The Roof Garden Commission: Pierre Huyghe* at The Metropolitan Museum of Art, 2015

C.C. Spider, 2011; spiders in corner of the wall

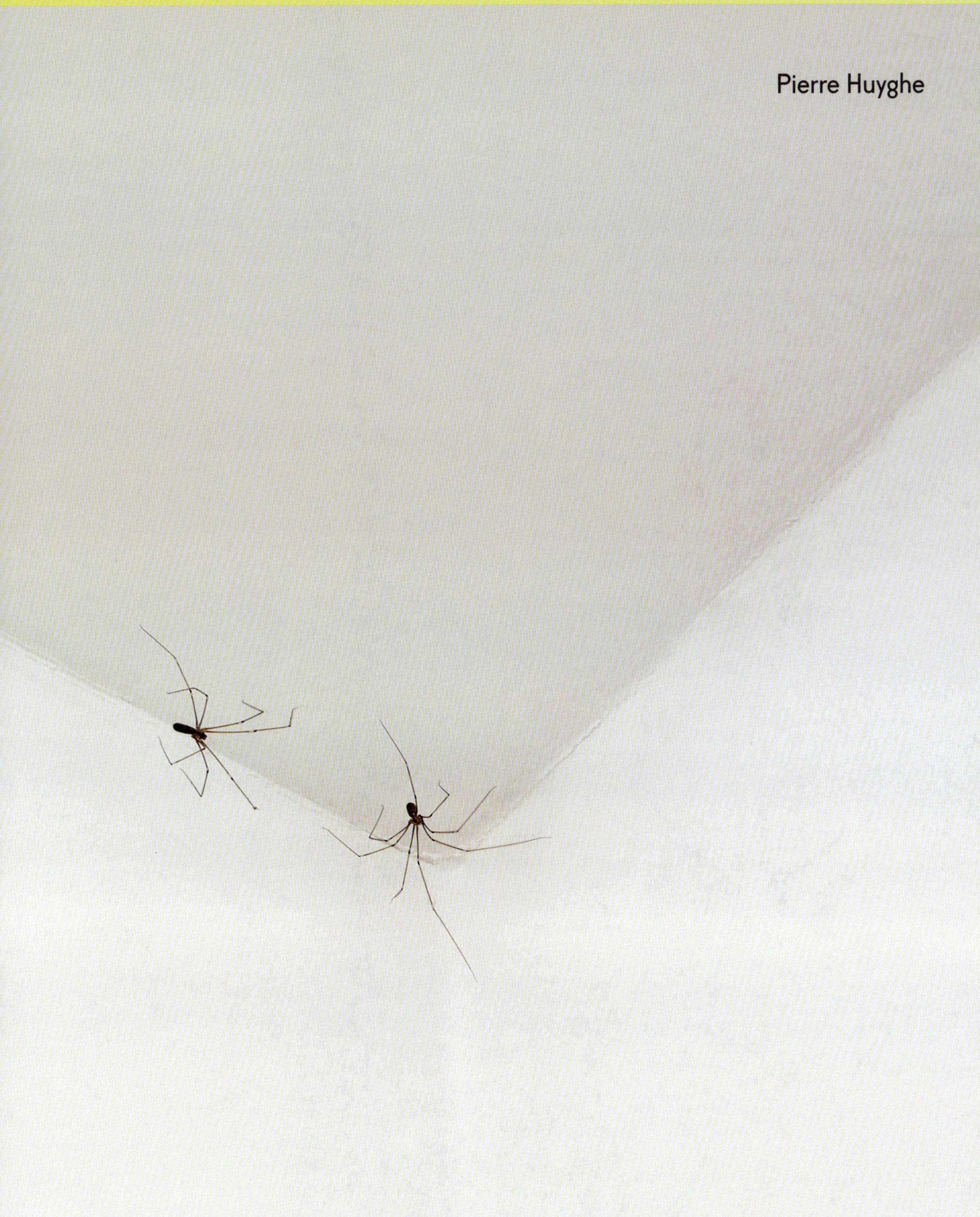

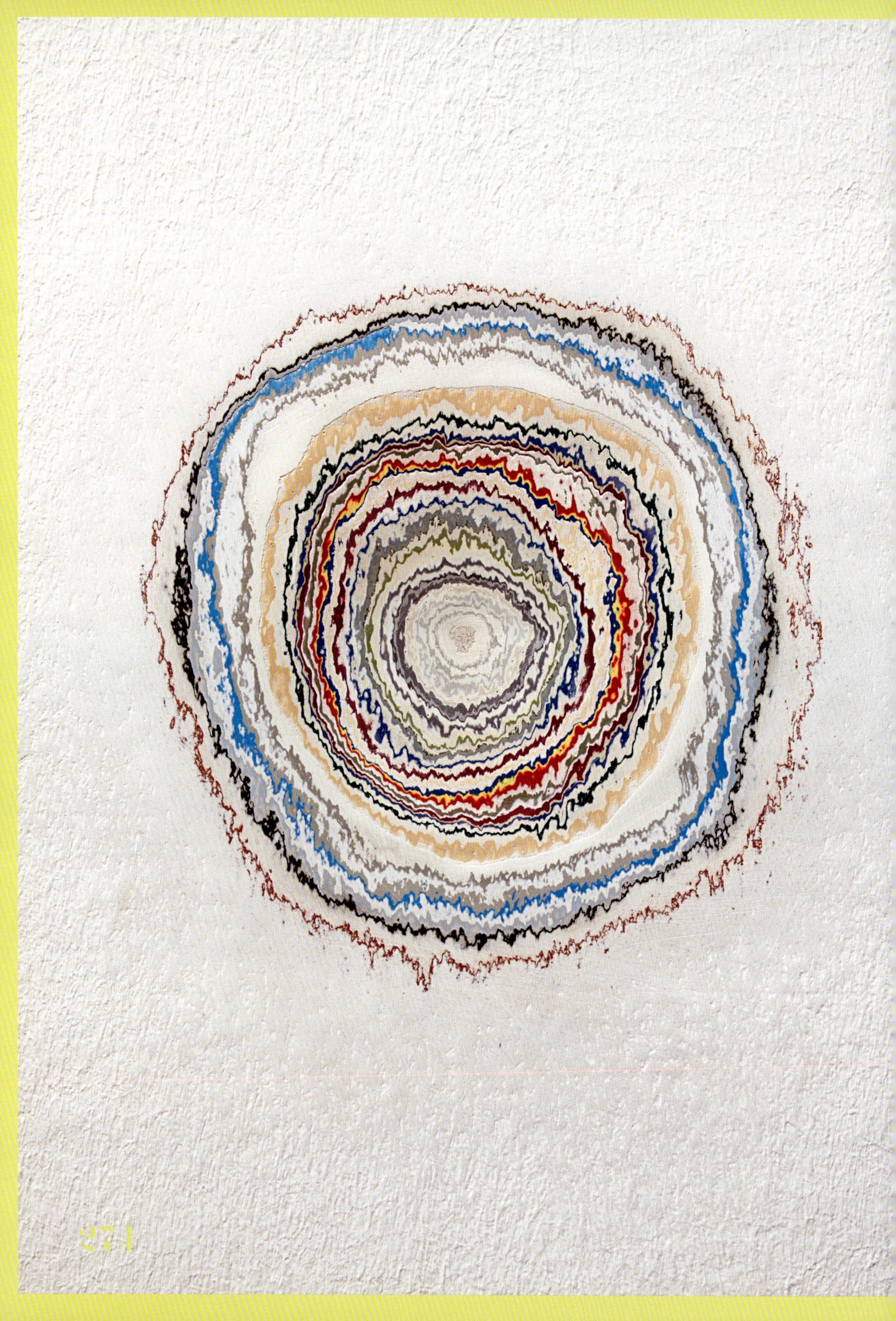

1. Define wonder in your own words.
A state of joy; discovering something unknown, unexpected, or that goes beyond the absurdity of existence; being open to the world.

2. What is your earliest childhood experience with wonder?
My mother.

3. What is the last wonder moment you had that left you speechless?
My daughter's birth.

4. Was there a wonder or aha moment that led to your work in this exhibition?
The curiosity in living activity.

opposite: *Timekeeper*, 1999; architectural intervention, succession of exhibition layers; exhibition view from Museum Ludwig; Cologne, Germany; April–July 2014

Chris Taylor

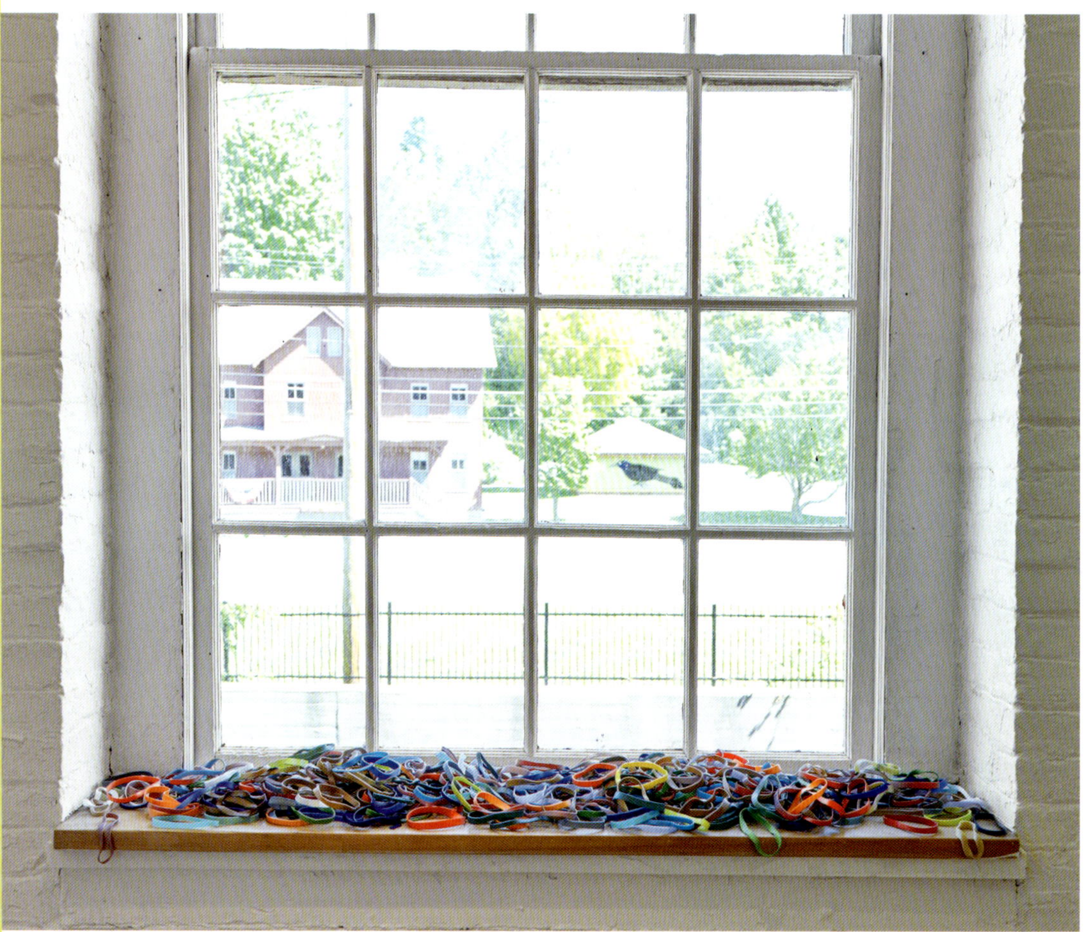

 Assorted, 2016; blown glass

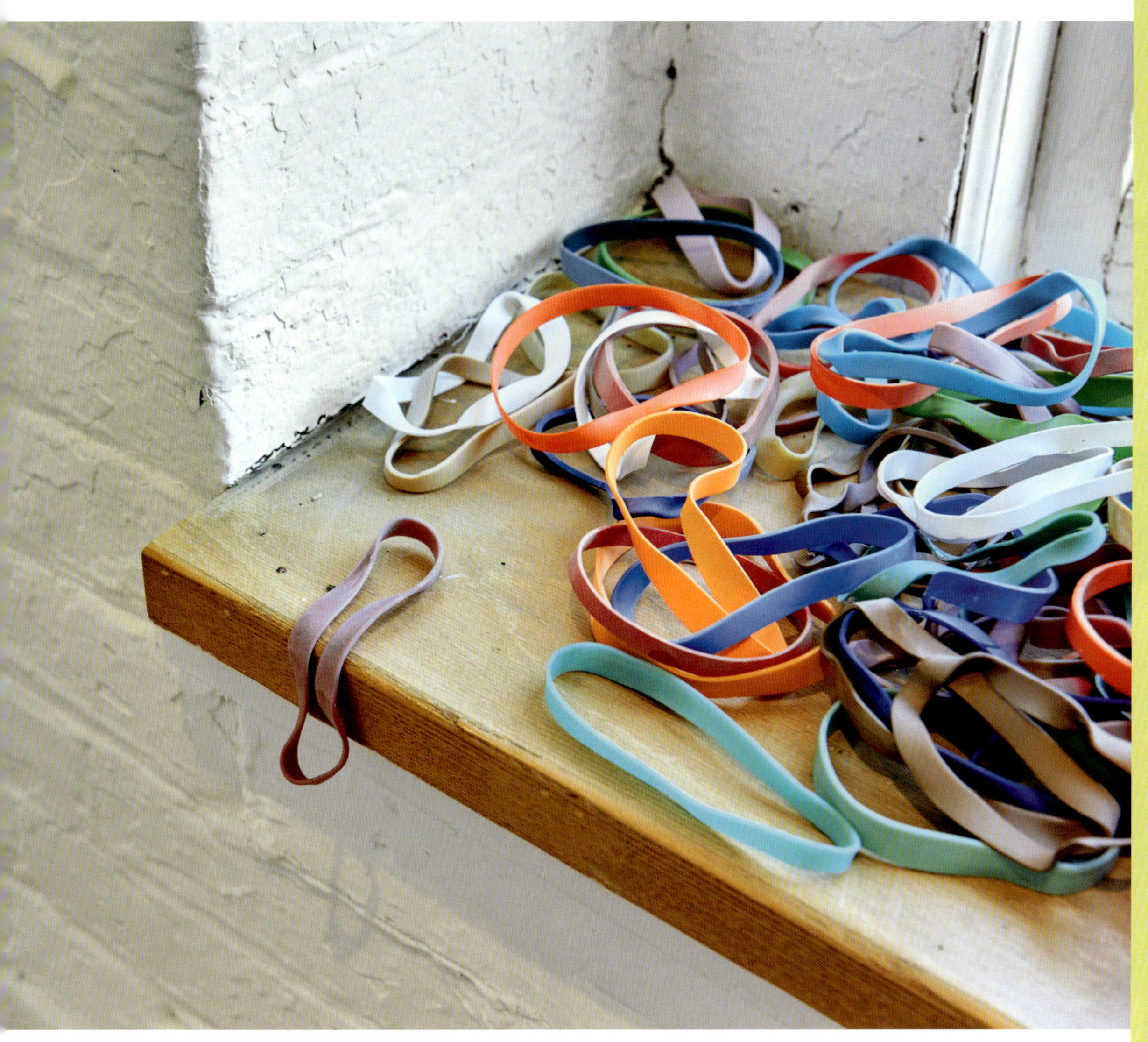

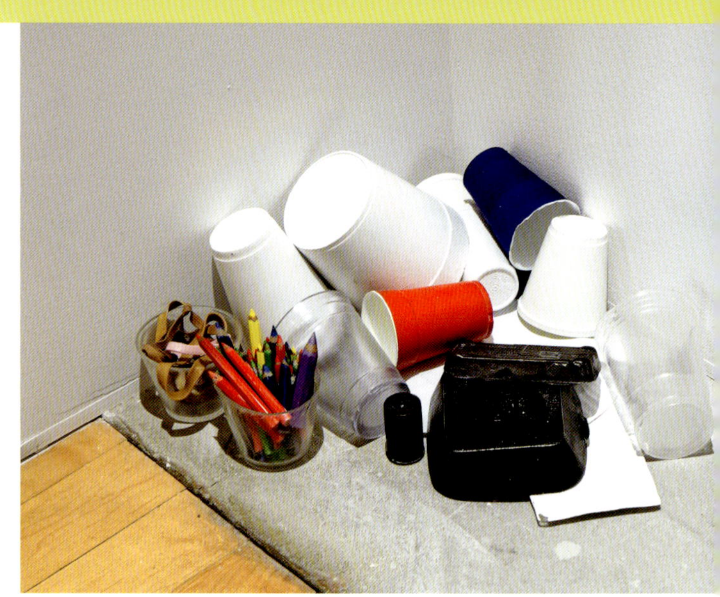

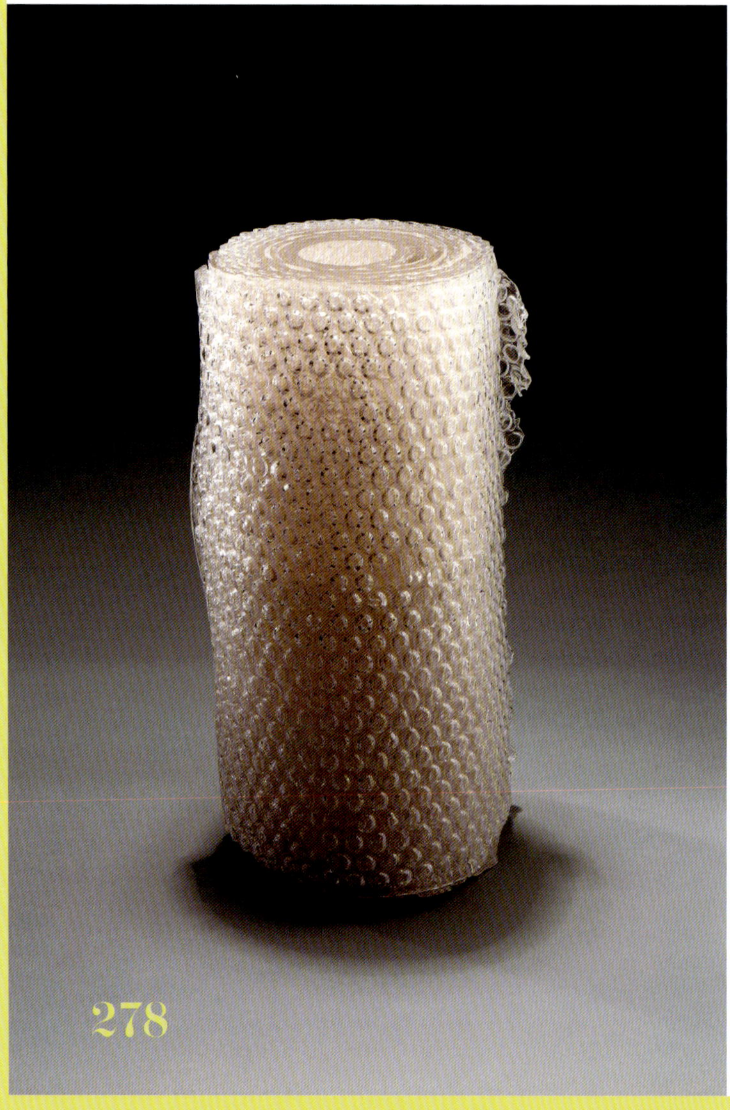

A boy from Brooklyn used to cruise on summer nights.
As soon as he'd hit sixty he'd hold his hand out the window,
cupping it around the wind. He'd been assured
this is exactly how a woman's breast feels when you put
your hand around it and apply a little pressure. Now he knew,
and he loved it. Night after night, again and again, until
the weather grew cold and he had to roll the window up.
For many years afterward he was perpetually attempting
to soar. One winter's night, holding his wife's breast
in his hand, he closed his eyes and wanted to weep.
He loved her, but it was the wind he imagined now.
As he grew older, he loved the word *etcetera* and refused
to abbreviate it. He loved sweet white butter. He often
pretended to be playing the organ. One of his last mornings,
he noticed the shape of his face molded in the pillow.
He shook it out, but the next morning it reappeared.

In Conversation with Lawrence Weschler

by Denise Markonish and Sean Foley

Denise Markonish: Wonder is personal, it's also ineffable, and exists in a place where language stops, which makes even trying to define it really absurd. To do an exhibition about it is just as crazy and something that Sean and I have struggled with; how do you pin down this amorphous and slippery thing—or do you even try to? Sean and I have always defined wonder as the moment when you stop and enter a liminal space between knowing and not knowing, what you call the "pillow of air." Can you explain your concept?

Lawrence Weschler: The pillow of air basically connotes that moment when, facing the object of marvel, you suddenly notice that a pillow of air has become lodged in your mouth and that you haven't even breathed in ten seconds, and you have to remind yourself to take a breath.

Sean Foley: You find yourself possessed.

DM: It also relates to the fact that wonder is such a felt thing that language inevitably fails it. Yet, as a writer, <u>your</u> job, of course, is to put language to things.

LW: Yeah, but I think you have to earn your silence. People say, "Oh you can't talk about the Holocaust," or "You can't talk about this other thing, whatever it is"—but that's just not true. Rather, you have to come up to the limits of language by way of language, and only then let go. One way to approach wonder, for example, is to do so historically, and tie it back to wonder cabinets.

Or, conversely, one could look toward the future: indeed, present-day wonder is so interesting because we're at a moment when machines are being taught to do more and more. Arthur C. Clarke, when faced with images from Michael Benson's book <u>Beyond: Visions of the Interplanetary Probes</u>, which were just astonishingly gorgeous images made by space probes, made the argument that these were the first instances of art created by an entirely new species, machino-sapiens. Clarke felt that, while it is true that mere matter on Earth could not self-create space probes—you needed something in between, which would still be human life—once the organic strata had run its course, you could then transfer everything onto machines.

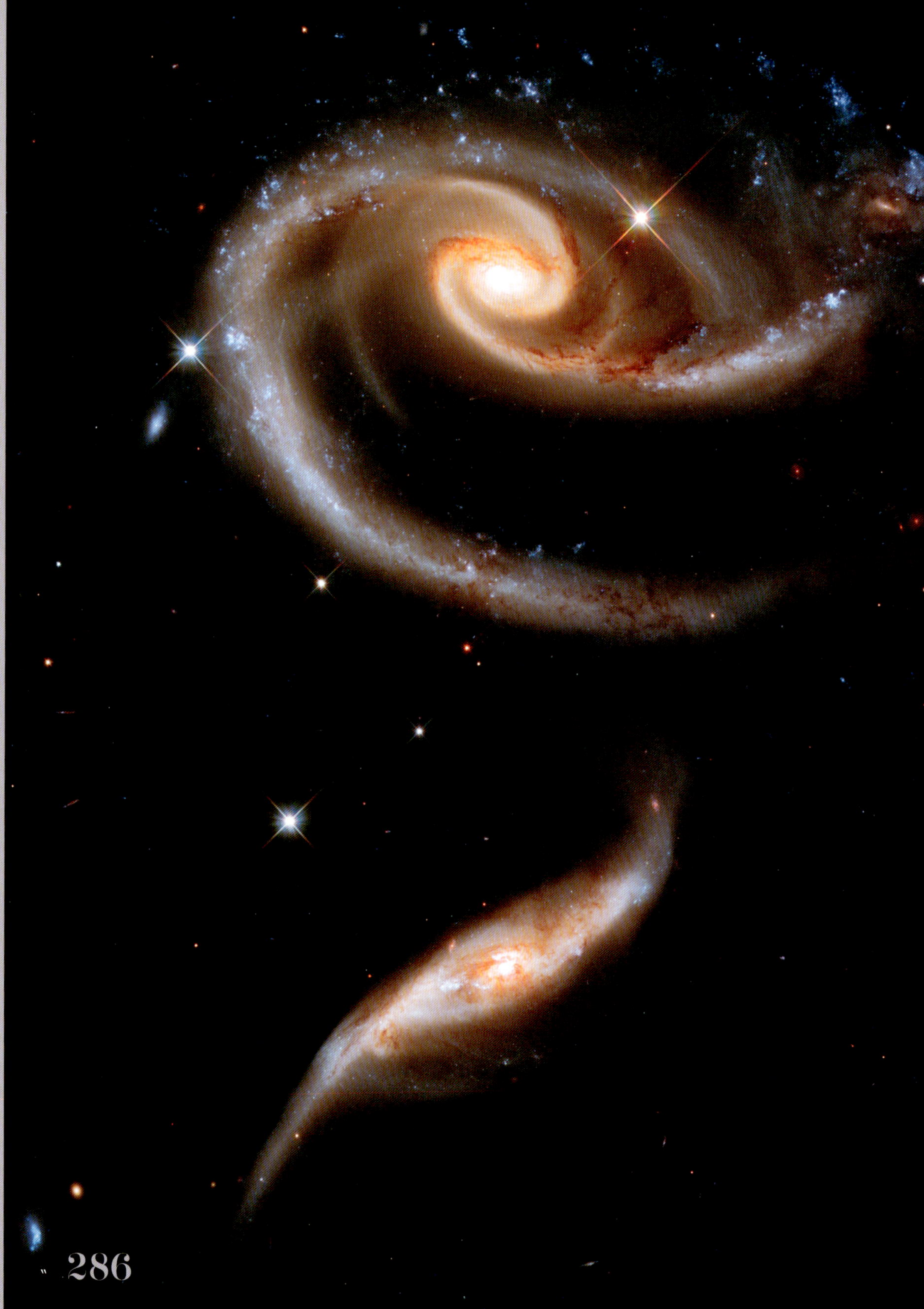

DM: Essentially, you could get rid of the middleman.

LW: But beyond that, the purpose of the middleman on Earth, according
to Clarke, was to create the very machines that would transcend himself.
And, to hear Clarke tell it, Benson's collection of photographs illustrated the
first instance of that. In an afterword I wrote to the same book, I disagreed,
for it seemed to me, looking at those images, that the one thing a machine
cannot, and, by definition, will never be able to do, is to experience wonder,
to experience awe. In order to experience wonder or awe or the sublime, you,
by definition, have to be contingent, puny, unnecessary; and what awe—what
wonder—addresses is your finitude and ... your smallness. That's part of
what the experience of awe is about: how could a human being do this?
This is unbelievable. Unbelievable is not a category a machine can relate to.
All of which might also account for the current upsurge of interest in awe.

The other thing that's happening at the present moment—and this was
in part what my book Mr. Wilson's Cabinet of Wonders was about—is that we
seem to be experiencing a throwback to a particular earlier moment historically,
when there was a debauched taste for wonder. That was roughly after 1492,
when all this stuff from the intersections with incredible other worlds started
flooding into Europe. In his book Marvelous Possessions, Stephen Greenblatt
posits that in order to go to all of these new places, there had to have been an
incredible increase in the amount of positivist knowledge about stars and tides,
about sailing techniques and engineering: all the surges in science, or what we
now call science, and technology that preceded 1492. The increases in those
sorts of knowledge had to have been incredible. But, as Greenblatt observes,
once people actually got to those places, all manner of weird objects started
showing up—moose antlers, purple parrot feathers, and sacrificial urns along
with reports of tribal custom and human sacrifice. All of that in turn sanctioned
belief in all sorts of earlier marvels: people started thinking, Wait a second, if
moose antlers are possible, why aren't unicorn horns possible? Which in turn led to
travelers finding sea unicorn horns—narwhal tusks—bringing them back home,
and suddenly sanctioning all sorts of beliefs they thought they'd gotten past.

SF: It's like when kids test their own belief in Santa Claus and how that wavers
over the years. They believe, they stop believing, and then they believe all the
more fervently.

LW: Indeed, going from belief to non-belief is not a sudden thing. It's just that
kids (or explorers) gather more and more knowledge about things that blow

their minds, which in turn has them reconsidering what they had previously
dismissed as fraud. So, historically, what Greenblatt and others call the
Age of the Marvelous, stretching from about 1492 to about 1650 or 1700,
disappears slowly. But the reason it disappears is it just turns into shtick
at a certain point. The more wonder cabinets that exist, the less rare they
become, the more subject to self-evident fraudulence, and soon you even
get Shakespeare calling the whole endeavor gullible, at best.

SF: It turns into an art fair.

LW: Yeah. But it also reifies, for when everybody has a piece of the cross you
start getting very strong critiques of the whole practice: you get Descartes who
says "Whoa, wait, let's sort this all out with some scientific rigor." Which in turn
leads to the Age of Science, the pendulum swinging far the other way, with less
and less patience for indeterminacy and marvel and drop-jawed pillow-of-air
wonder. In that sense, one might talk about the way that the post-modern, if
you want to call it that, has roots in the pre-modern; they are both critiquing
the same countervailing scientistic tenor. It's like the old question, why are
grandparents and grandchildren so happy with one another?

SF: Common enemies.

LW: Right, precisely. In the same way that scientism and positivism had a vogue
from roughly 1700 to 1950; that, in turn, has a tidal feeling to it. The scientific-
positivist hegemony had created some pretty scary things: atomic bombs,
ecological devastation, etc. And suddenly you had a hankering for things that
positivism wasn't addressing. I don't want to make too much of this because it
seems to me that you find some of the most extraordinary senses of wonder at
the edge of science.

SF: Can you talk more about the alignment of science and wonder that occurs
at the edge?

LW: Scientific advancement itself—Einstein insisted—must always start in
wonder. The late great entomologist Tom Eisner talked about the moment
just after you'd made an observation and you let your mind roam free with
hypotheses. That's the fun moment; sure, afterwards you needed to batten
things down. But actually the whole process needs to start with drop-jawed
astonishment and free-reeling reverie. In that sense, there are moments in
doing science that are not only susceptible to, but actually require, ecstasies
of wonder.

There's a great Carl Sagan quote I have up on the wall there. David Hockney originally took this quote and did a drawing of a sort of monolith onto which the passage was inscribed—an image that later suggested a sort of tombstone for Sagan after he died. The Sagan quote reads: "In some respects, science has far surpassed religion in delivering awe. How is it that hardly any major religion has looked at science and concluded, 'This is better than we thought! The Universe is much bigger than our prophets said, grander, more subtle, more elegant. God must be even greater than we dreamed'? Instead they say, 'No, no, no! My god is a little god, and I want him to stay that way.' A religion, old or new, that stressed the magnificence of the Universe, as revealed by modern science, might be able to draw forth reserves of reverence and awe [or, for our purposes, wonder] hardly tapped by conventional faiths. Sooner or later such a religion will emerge."[1] But that's a particular non-bureaucratic way of doing science.

DM: That is what made Sagan so unique; he had a vision for science being so much bigger than us, for it being based in fact and finding, but also in awe and emotion. It makes me think of his other quote about us all being made from "star stuff"; that realization is true wonder.

SF: It also reminds me of the idea of the natural philosophers and their Pre-Enlightenment methods of studying nature and the physical universe.

LW: Yeah, that's a way to put it. And that's in turn why Sagan was disdained by many people in his own professional tribe as a "mere showman."

DM: Well, it's emotive, too, and people don't often like to think of science being entangled with emotion; but it is clear that science, for Sagan and others, contains the multitude of wonder from experience and emotion to empirical fact.

LW: I just remembered that I sent the same Sagan drawing back to David [Hockney] when Stephen Jay Gould died and added one of Gould's quotes from <u>The Structure of Evolutionary Theory</u> on the back. It says: "Something almost unspeakably holy—I don't know how else to say this—underlies our discovery and confirmation of the actual details that made our world and also, in realms of contingency, assured the minutiae of its construction in the manner we know, and not in any one of a trillion other ways, nearly all of which would not have included the evolution of a scribe to record the beauty, the cruelty, the fascination, and the mystery."[2]

DM: What a great quote! It gets back to that very idea of how to put these big moments of wonder into language; both Sagan and Gould excelled at that. But if I remember correctly, so did your own daughter at the age of twelve. Can you tell that story?

LW: Well, one day I got a call from my daughter Sara's school and they said "You'd better come in here." Apparently, they'd had a pop quiz in which the kids were asked to answer some question like: "Why are human beings on earth?" And given fifteen minutes to do so. Sara had responded—let's see, wait a second, here it is—"I believe that there is, despite the fact that we humans have done so much damage to the world, a reason for our existence on this planet. I think we are here because the universe, with all its wonder and balance and logic, needs to be marveled at, and we are the only species (to our knowledge) that has the ability to do so. We are the one species that does not simply except [sic] what is around us, but also asks why it is around us, and how it works. We are here because without us here to study it, the amazing complexity of the world would be wasted. And finally, we are here because the universe needs an entity to ask why it is here."

DM: Wow, that is just so incredible. That she was thinking like that at twelve is extraordinary.

LW: It took Kant three volumes to get there.

DM: Carl Sagan, Stephen Jay Gould, and Sara Weschler ... what a trio!

LW: But having said that, I do think many twelve year olds approach the world that way, though she may be more articulate than some. Another way of putting it is that there is a longing to get back to first things, and that's part of what the taste for wonder is.

SF: I think adults crave those wonder years of youth, but we're unable to slow down our lives enough to be lost in anything that's not task-oriented or constructive. That's a problem if you're looking for a taste of wonder. A. O. Scott recently wrote in the <u>The New York Times Magazine</u> that "we live in the grip of a technological paradox in which the proliferation of wonders dilutes the possibility of wonder. This partly has to do with marketing and mass consumption, with the democratization of the special and the rare. More of us can now see more of the world than ever before, whether literally through travel or virtually through images. Some of the mystery, the frisson of discovery, is lost because of that."[3] He goes on to say how experiences a century ago were unprecedented in

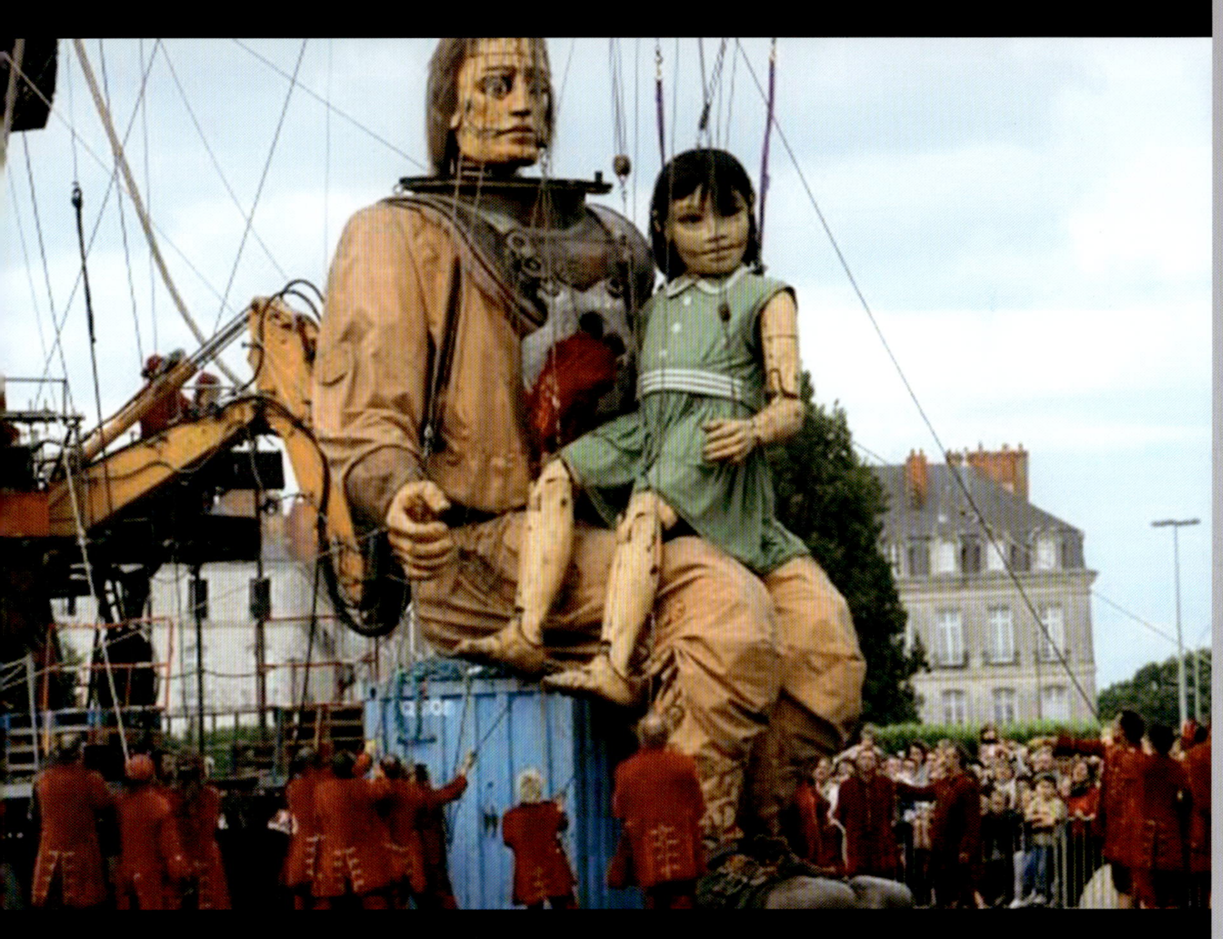

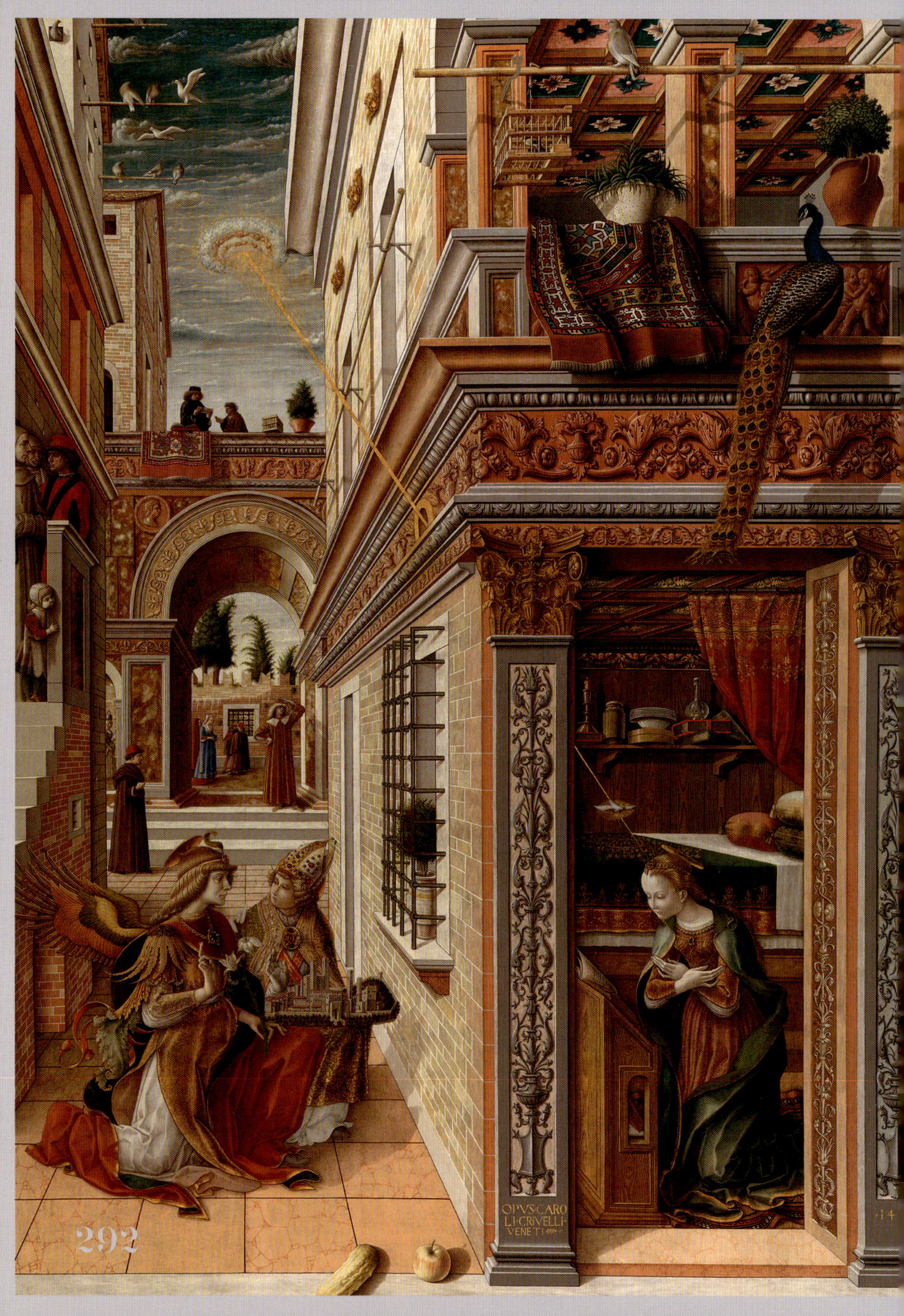

292
OPVS CARO
LI CRIVELLI
VENETI

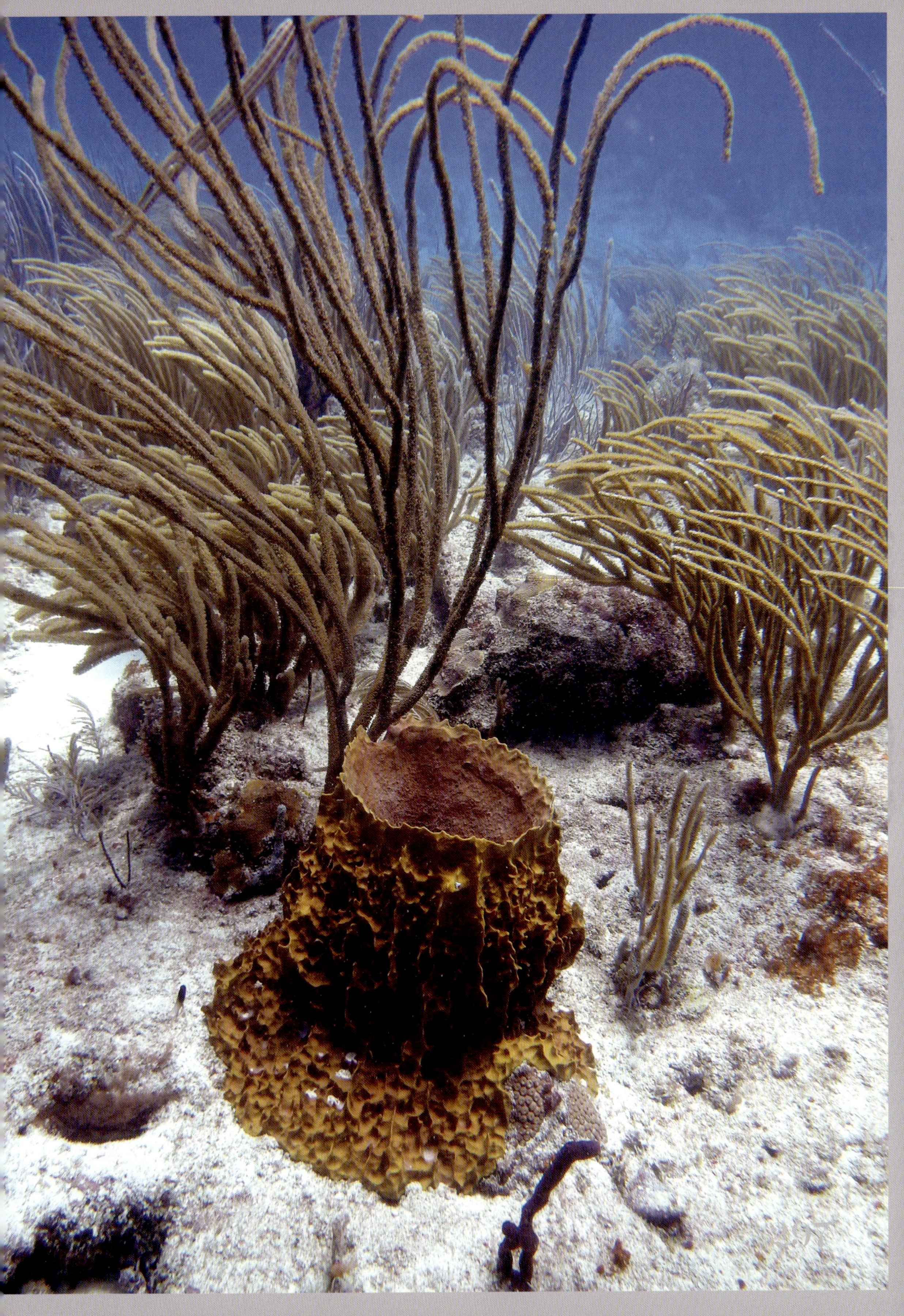

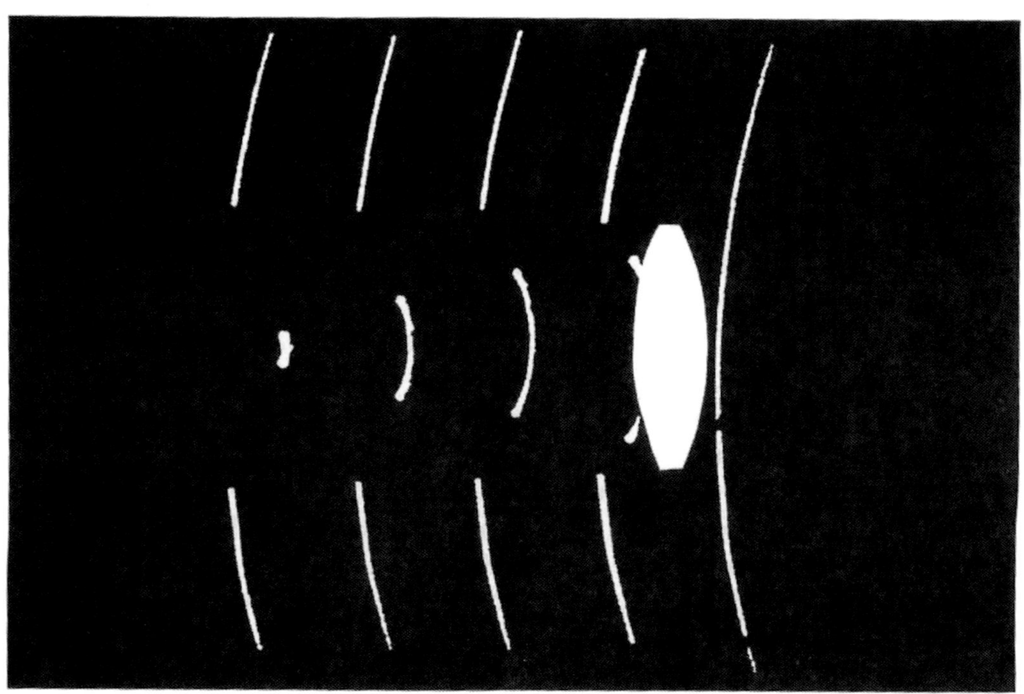

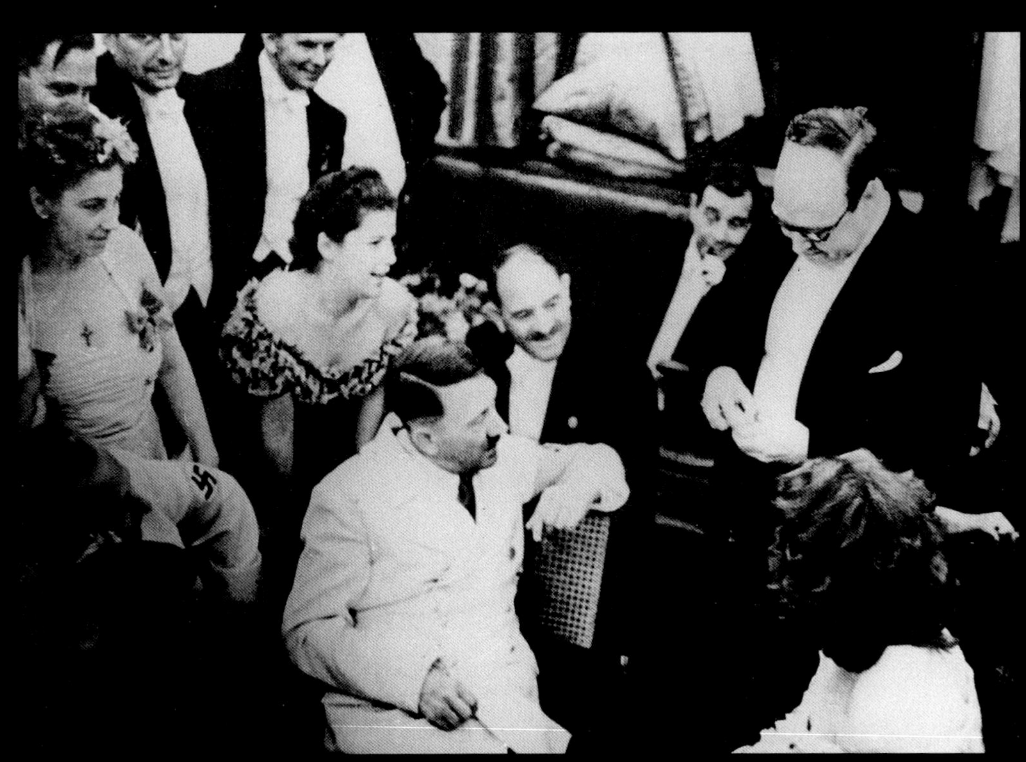

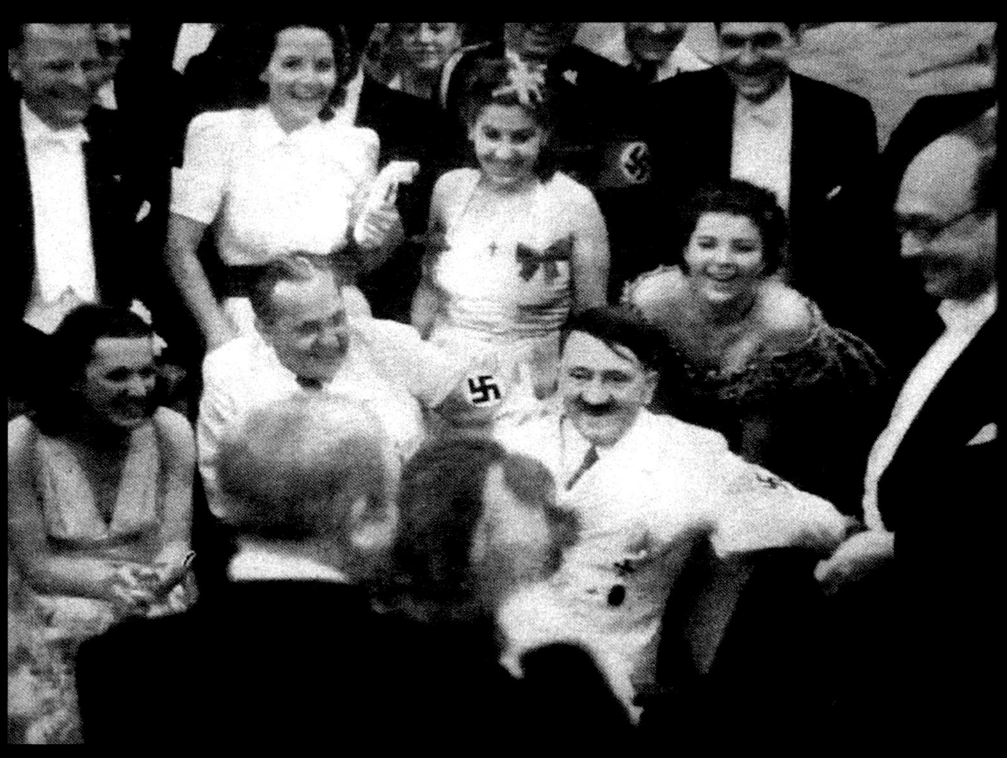

DM: That poem is beautiful. I remember early on, when Sean and I were talking about wonder, he said to me, "You're not thinking about doing an exhibition about this?" and I said, "Well, no, I thought we would." He responded, "But it's impossible!" to which I countered, "Well, that just makes me want to do it even more." My boss once called me a natural contrarian, and I've never been one to shy away from a challenge! And here we are, five years later, and we are still puzzling over what it means to tackle wonder as an exhibition and in writing. I think what we've come to realize is you can't prescribe wonder, so instead we decided to work with artists who are intimately engaged with wonder as part of their practice (and life, I would add) and who might provoke wonder in visitors to the exhibition. I think we will succeed if this show makes people more attuned, so when they go on with their lives they can encounter moments that will blow their hearts open.

SF: In that sense, the exhibition becomes propositional.

DM: Yes, exactly. And in choosing artists it was very important for us that this sense of mindful wonder is ingrained in how they function. The contributors all approach the challenge from different perspectives, but the thing that links them all is a philosophy of wonder. It's a strange but inspiring problem, though, how to have it coalesce into an exhibition.

SF: I think you have to upset the expectations of the viewer. As an artist, whenever I have a show, the fear is that I have worked in the messy studio environment surrounded by other things and then I have to take the work out of the space of creation and hang it up in a neutral setting. What happens to the translation of the work when that shift takes place? It's unsettling. Yet museum audiences are conditioned to shift into a different mindset and behavior. So, then, how can we introduce the unfamiliar so that the audience doesn't just shift into autopilot? How do we create an environment that gives permission to let go?

DM: I think we're conscious of that balance. We don't want the show to be one heart explosion after the next, because then it starts…

LW: You become dulled to it.

DM: Exactly, you become dulled to it. So I think that idea of invitation and provocation, fertile confusion, those are the things that…

LW: Allow for the re-enchantment of the world.

DM: I think this gets at the fact that there is something about wonder that it is both immediate and slow. It is a thing that hits you, but the way it stays with you is lifelong. So to be able to play with that is really important, we want there to be moments in this show that people really remember and that they excitedly want to share with others. This can then become a collective wonder.

LW: This makes me think that the problem of the curator trying to evoke wonder is an issue of precision.

DM: Yes, even though precision within something so amorphous feels counterintuitive.

LW: There's a great poem on that by Linda Gregg called "The Precision," from her book <u>Things and Flesh</u>[7]:

> There is a modesty in nature. In the small
> of it and in the strongest. The leaf moves
> just the amount the breeze indicates
> and nothing more. In the power of lust, too,
> there can be a quiet and clarity, a fusion
> of exact moments. There is a silence of it
> inside the thundering. And when the body swoons,
> it is because the heart knows its truth.
> There is directness and equipoise in the fervor,
> just as the greatest turmoil has precision.
> Like the discretion a tornado has when it tears
> down building after building, house by house.
> It is enough, Kafka said, that the arrow fit
> exactly into the wound that it makes. I think
> about my body in love as I look down on these
> lavish apple trees and the workers moving
> with skill from one to the next, singing.

What's funny about that poem is the way the word "singing" has been placed there with such precision. The whole poem is a setting, kind of as if you have this great diamond with all these wonderful facets and you have to get the exact setting for it.

DM: I love that line, "when the body swoons, it is because the heart knows its truth." It makes me want to go back to Descartes. He has this whole passage about fainting. He writes: "Fainting is not very far from dying: a person dies when the fire in his heart is completely extinguished, and he merely faints when it is smothered in such a way that traces of the heart are left that afterwards rekindle it. Many bodily indispositions can cause us to faint; but the only passion that we observe doing this is extreme joy."[8] It's melodramatic, but again, he is getting at how the passions affect the whole body.

LW: But Descartes is making fun of that, too, distaining the excess.

DM: Absolutely...

LW: "Enough with the fainting already!"

DM: But he doesn't align fainting with wonder.

LW: Well, it's complicated, what he's trying to do. And Shakespeare, too, is making fun [swooning noises], just as Stephen Colbert does in his over-the-top imitations of Lindsey Graham.

DM: Thinking about those last few poems reminds me of the title for this exhibition: Explode Every Day. This comes from a great Ray Bradbury quote, where he said; "You remain invested in your inner child by exploding every day. You don't worry about the future, you don't worry about the past—you just explode."[9] So much of the writing around wonder talks about it as such a rare experience, but those poems are very much in the everyday and in the small moment. Personally, I think it's more interesting to think about how you find wonder in the everyday rather than in the extraordinary.

LW: It comes back to this business about autopilot that Sean mentioned. David Hockney speaks wonderfully about how when driving you are alert in a passive way—you're making sure nothing has entered into your field of vision that's a danger—but you can go for minutes on end without actually noticing anything. This is the exact opposite of a pillow of air—the two minutes at the end of which you suddenly realize you can't actually remember anything you've seen. They are both about gazing—looking and seeing—but there is a distinction between the two. This reminds me in turn of R. B. Onians...

DM: What's the title of that book again?

LW: [gets up to grab the book off his shelf] The Origins of European Thought: About the Body, the Mind, the Soul, the World, Time and Fate.

DM: Best book title ever! The title alone needs its own bookshelf.

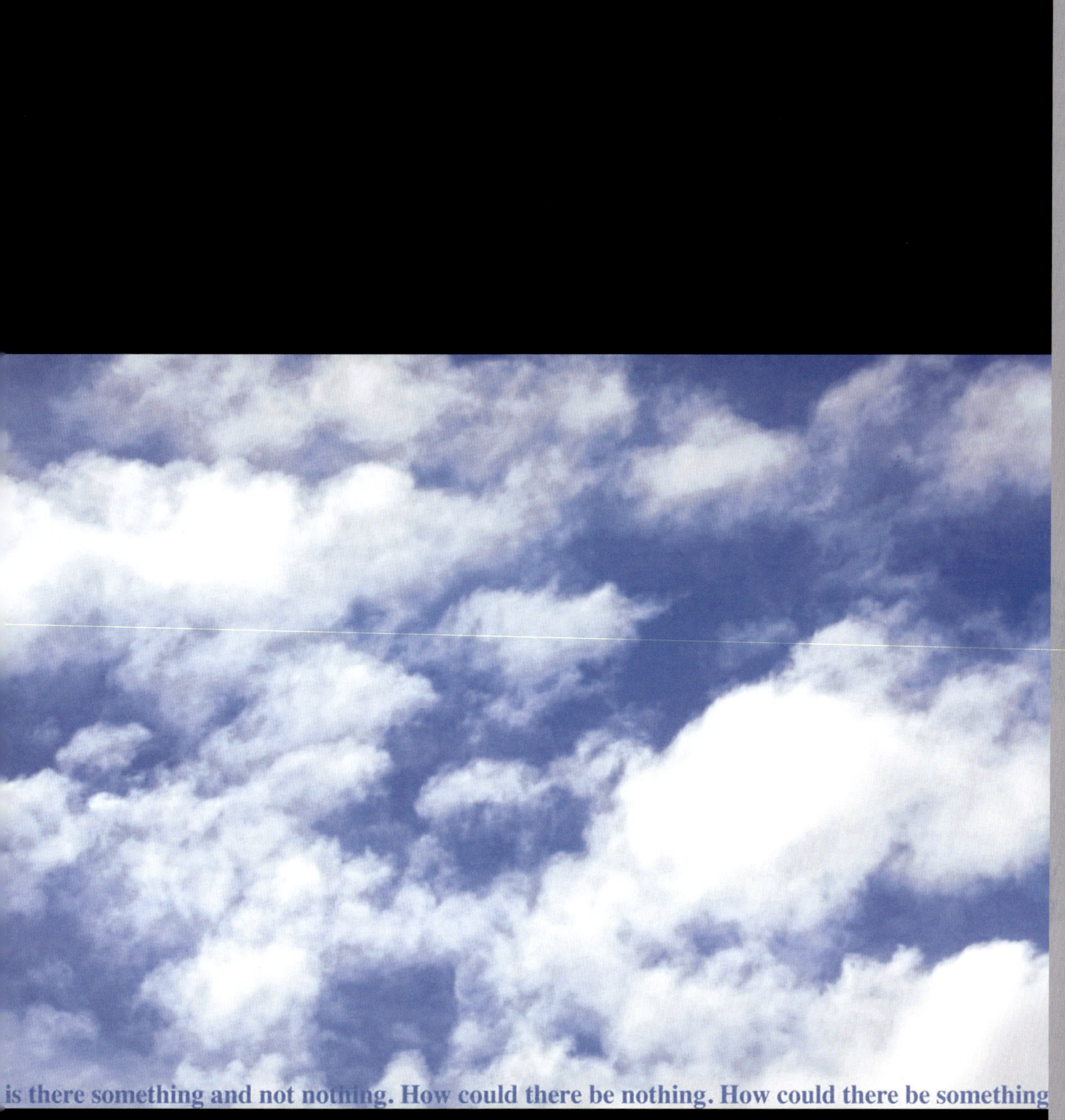

is there something and not nothing. How could there be nothing. How could there be something

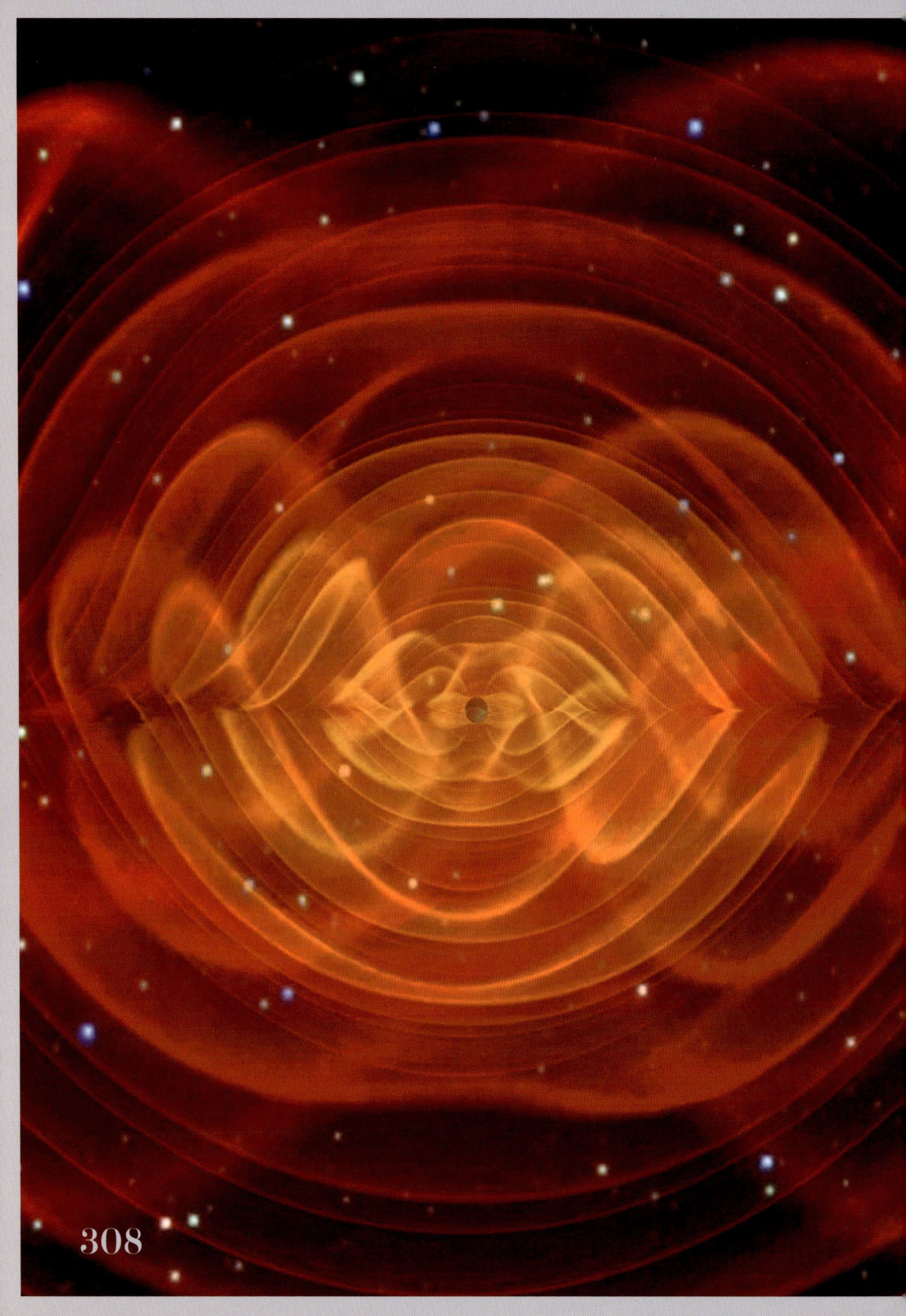

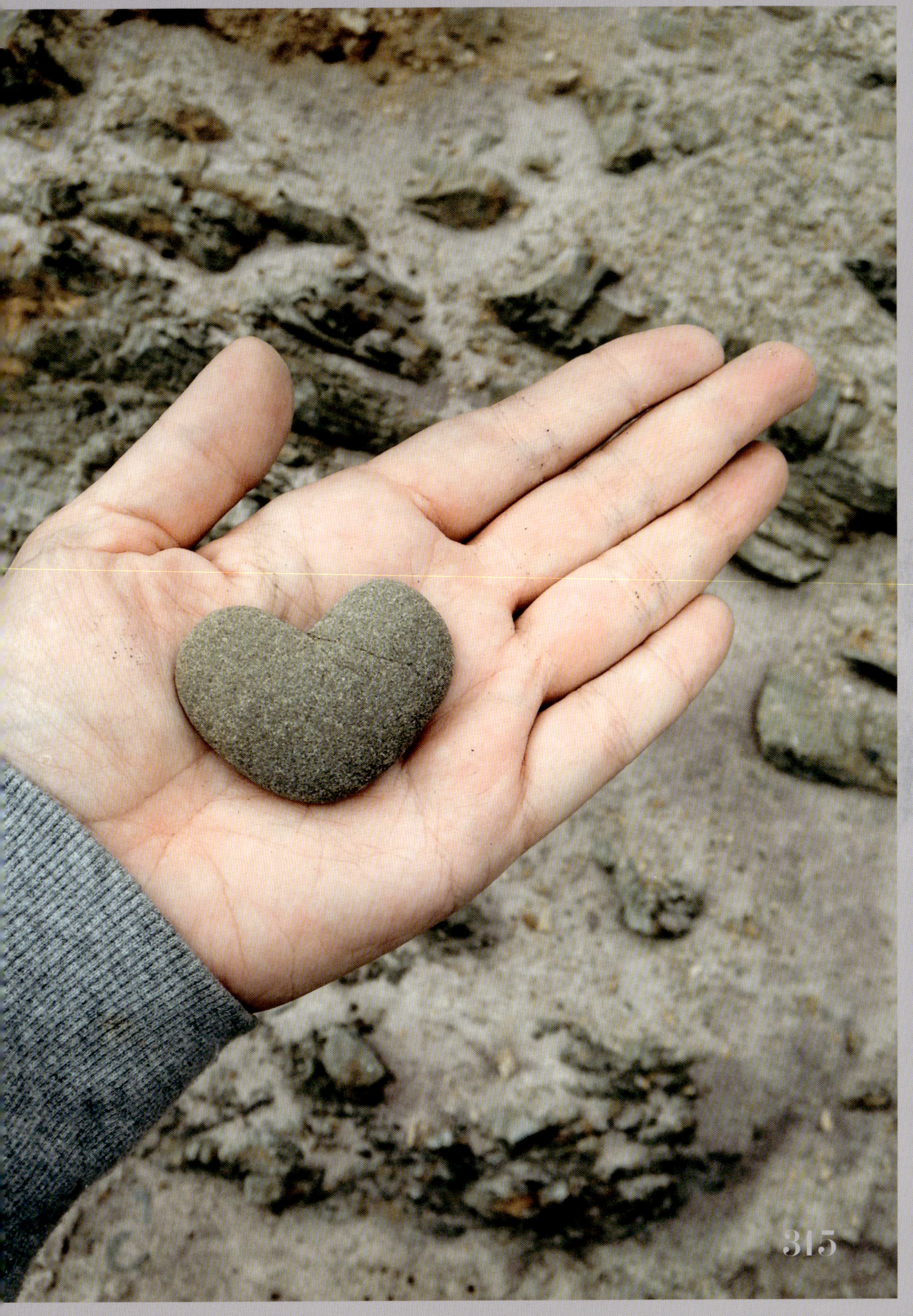

All dimensions height x width x depth
unless otherwise indicated

Jonathan Allen
Twenty-First-Century Silks, 2016
2-channel video
total running time: 20-minute loop
courtesy of the artist

Jen Bervin
Silk Poems, 2016
nanoimprinted gold spatter on silk film fabricated
at Tufts University Silk Lab, microscope
3.5 inches diameter

Charlotte Lagarde
Jen Bervin's Silk Poems, 2016
video
total running time: 10 minutes

Silk Poems is a project of Creative Capital
courtesy of the artists

Jason de Haan
Future Age, 2009–present
gold ring placed in tree
dimensions variable

Proposed Mt Greylock Blowhole, 2016
core samples, wood
dimensions variable

Swallow All the Brain, 2016
ammonite, brachiopod, clam and turtle fossils,
humidifiers, concrete
dimensions variable

all courtesy of the artist and Clint Roenisch
Gallery, Toronto

Tristan Duke
Cube (above/below)
Dodecahedron (above/below)
Icosahedron (above/below)
Octahedron (above/below)
Tetrahedron (above/below)
all 2016
hand-drawn holograms on metal plates with
rotating turntables
each .875 x 10 x 10 inches
courtesy of the artist

Sharon Ellis
Afternoon, 1998
alkyd on canvas
40 x 30 inches
collection of Tom Peters

Four Seasons, 1999
alkyd on canvas
38 x 30 inches
collection of Christopher Grimes

Summer, 2004
alkyd on canvas
28 x 40 inches
collection of Bronya and Andrew Galef

After the Fire, 2010
alkyd on canvas
28 x 24 inches
collection of Robert and Anne Conn

Night Storm, 2013
alkyd on canvas
30 x 40 inches

Beltane, 2014
alkyd on canvas
34 x 42 inches

all courtesy of the artist and Christopher Grimes
Gallery, Santa Monica

Tom Friedman
Untitled (blue space station), 2012
Styrofoam, paint
106 x 20 inches
courtesy of the artist and Luhring Augustine,
New York

Flashlight on Wall (UFO), 2016
video
total running time: 2:52 minutes

Small Black Ball, 2016
Styrofoam, flock
.38 x .38 x .38 inches

The Wall, 2016
plaster
241.5 x 290 inches

all courtesy of the artist

Christopher Gausby
Summa Imaginis Beatitudinis Mentis, 1990
artist's book: ink, paint, gold leaf, collage on paper
9 x 7 inches (approximate)
courtesy of Newberry Public Library, Chicago

Notebook IV, June 1990–April 15, 1991, 1991
manuscript and collage on paper: gold leaf, gouache,
ink, pencil, shell gold
8.875 x 11.875 inches
courtesy of the Spencer Collection, New York Public
Library, Astor, Lenox and Tilden Foundations

Notebook V, 1993
artist's book: ink, paint, gold leaf, collage on paper
9 x 7 inches (approximate)

De Trinitate, 1996
artist's book: ink, paint, gold leaf, collage on paper
9 x 7 inches (approximate)

Egaugnal, 2006
artist's book: ink, paint, gold leaf, collage on paper
9 x 7 inches (approximate)

all courtesy of Newberry Public Library, Chicago

Philosophy Kit, 2006–10
Mixed media
20 x 30 x 17 inches
courtesy of the artist

Hope Ginsberg
Breath Portrait I-VII, 2016
All archival inkjet prints, edition 1/3
each 10 x 14 inches

Land Dive Team: Bay of Fundy, 2016
Single-channel video projection with sound,
edition 1/3
total running time: 7:09 minutes
featuring: Jessica Bradford, Rachel Barrett, Richelle
Martin, Hope Ginsburg
camera: Matt Flowers, Jessica Carey
sound: Joshua Quarles
editing: Mike Olenick
support provided by the Film/Video Studio
Program at the Wexner Center for the Arts

both courtesy of the artist

Laurent Grasso
Soleil Double, 2014
16mm film digitized
total running time: 11 minute loop
dimensions variable
courtesy of Galerie Perrotin, Paris, and Sean Kelly
Gallery, New York

Studies into the Past
oil on wood
35 x 45.5 inches
courtesy of Sean Kelly Gallery, New York

*79, Pompeii Eruption, head of the God Harpocrate
combed by the crown, Ptolemaic period, Egypt*
cabinet in walnut wood, oil on wood, bronze, neon
17.5 x 43 x 12 inches
courtesy of Sean Kelly Gallery, New York

Pierre Huyghe
C.C. Spider, 2011
spider, protocol
dimensions variable
courtesy of the artist and Esther Schipper, Berlin

Institute For Figuring and Margaret Wertheim
Business Card Wall Frieze, 2016
folded business cards
180 x 72 x 2 inches

Fractal Ruin, 2016
folded business cards, using business card origami
techniques by Dr. Jeannine Mosely
56 x 19 x 19 inches

*Topographical Layers of a Level Two Mosely
Snowflake Sponge Business Card Fractal*, 2016
folded business cards
72 x 72 x 2 inches

all courtesy of Institute For Figuring

Business Card Wall Frieze and *Fractal Ruin* were
constructed with folding assistance from Christina
Simons and Jacob Dotson. Business card design by
Cindi Kusuda and Margaret Wertheim. Curatorial
consulting by Christine Wertheim.

Nina Katchadourian
The Recarcassing Ceremony, 2016
video with sound
total running time: 25 minutes
courtesy of the artist and Catharine Clark Gallery,
San Francisco

Michael Light
100 SUNS: 005 How/14 Kilotons/Nevada/1952, 2003
framed pigment print, glazed with u/v blocking
non-reflective glass, edition 4/5
20.3125 x 16.3125 x 1.5 inches

100 SUNS: 027 Shasta/17 Kilotons/Nevada/1957, 2003
framed pigment print, glazed with u/v blocking
non-reflective glass, edition 4/5
16.3125 x 20.3125 x 1.5 inches

*100 SUNS: 054 Erie/14.9 Kilotons/Enewetak
Atoll/1956*, 2003
framed pigment print, glazed with u/v blocking
non-reflective glass, edition 4/5
16.3125 x 20.3125 x 1.5 inches

100 SUNS: 057 Baker/21 Kilotons/Bikini Atoll/1946,
2003
framed pigment print, glazed with u/v blocking
non-reflective glass, edition 4/5
16.3125 x 20.3125 x 1.5 inches

100 SUNS: 058 Baker/21 Kilotons/Bikini Atoll/1946,
2003
framed pigment print, glazed with u/v blocking
non-reflective glass, edition 4/5
20.3125 x 20.3125 x 1.5 inches

100 SUNS: 062 Sequoia/5.2 Kilotons/Enewetak
Atoll/1958, 2003
framed pigment print, glazed with u/v blocking
non-reflective glass, edition 4/5
11.3125 x 14.3125 x 1.5 inches

100 SUNS: 063 King/500 Kilotons/Enewetak
Atoll/1952, 2003
framed pigment print, glazed with u/v blocking
non-reflective glass, edition 4/5
16.3125 x 20.3125 x 1.5 inches

100 SUNS: 064 Dog/81 Kilotons/Enewetak
Atoll/1951, 2003
framed pigment print, glazed with u/v blocking
non-reflective glass, edition 4/5
20.3125 x 24.3125 x 1.5 inches

100 SUNS: 066 Mike/10.4 Megatons/Enewetak
Atoll/1952, 2003
framed pigment print, glazed with u/v blocking
non-reflective glass, edition 4/5
16.3125 x 20.3125 x 1.5 inches

100 SUNS: 070 Mike/10.4 Megatons/Enewetak
Atoll/1952, 2003
framed pigment print, glazed with u/v blocking
non-reflective glass, edition 4/5
16.3125 x 16.3125 x 1.5 inches

100 SUNS: 071 Oak/8.9 Megatons/Enewetak
Atoll/1958, 2003
framed pigment print, glazed with u/v blocking
non-reflective glass, edition 4/5
16.3125 x 16.3125 x 1.5 inches

100 SUNS: 072 Oak/8.9 Megatons/Enewetak
Atoll/1958, 2003
framed pigment print, glazed with u/v blocking
non-reflective glass, edition 4/5
16.3125 x 16.3125 x 1.5 inches

100 SUNS: 073 Magnolia/57 Kilotons/Enewetak
Atoll/1958, 2003
framed pigment print, glazed with u/v blocking
non-reflective glass, edition 4/5
16.3125 x 20.3125 x 1.5 inches

100 SUNS: 076 Wahoo/9 Kilotons/Enewetak
Atoll/1958, 2003
framed pigment print, glazed with u/v blocking
non-reflective glass, edition 4/5
11.3125 x 14.3125 x 1.5 inches

100 SUNS: 081 Truckee/210 Kilotons/Christmas
Island/1962, 2003
framed pigment print, glazed with u/v blocking
non-reflective glass, edition 4/5
20.3125 x 24.3125 x 1.5 inches

100 SUNS: 084 Yellowwood/330 Kilotons/Enewetak
Atoll/1958, 2003
framed pigment print, glazed with u/v blocking
non-reflective glass, edition 4/5
20.3125 x 16.3125 x 1.5 inches

100 SUNS: 085 Frigatebird/600 Kilotons/Christmas
Island/1962, 2003
framed pigment print, glazed with u/v blocking
non-reflective glass, edition 4/5
14.3125 x 11.3125 x 1.5 inches

100 SUNS: 086 Mohawk/360 Kilotons/Enewetak
Atoll/1956, 2003
framed pigment print, glazed with u/v blocking
non-reflective glass, edition 4/5
11.3125 x 14.3125 x 1.5 inches

100 SUNS: 091 Apache/1.85 Megatons/Enewetak
Atoll/1956, 2003
framed pigment print, glazed with u/v blocking
non-reflective glass, edition 4/5
24.3125 x 30.3125 x 1.5 inches

100 SUNS: 093 Bravo/15 Megatons/Bikini Atoll/1954,
2003
framed pigment print, glazed with u/v blocking
non-reflective glass, edition 4/5
16.3125 x 20.3125 x 1.5 inches

100 SUNS: 094 Sunset/1 Megaton/Christmas
Island/1962, 2003
framed pigment print, glazed with u/v blocking
non-reflective glass, edition 4/5
16.3125 x 20.3125 x 1.5 inches

100 SUNS: 096 Romeo/11 Megatons/Bikini
Atoll/1954, 2003
framed pigment print, glazed with u/v blocking
non-reflective glass, edition 4/5
20.3125 x 16.3125 x 1.5 inches

100 SUNS: 098 Apache/1.85 Megatons/Enewetak
Atoll/1956, 2003
framed pigment print, glazed with u/v blocking
nonreflective glass, edition 4/5
32.3125 x 40.3125 x 1.5 inches

100 SUNS: 100 Yankee/13.5 Megatons/Bikini
Atoll/1954, 2003
framed pigment print, glazed with u/v blocking
nonreflective glass, edition 4/5
24.3125 x 20.3125 x 1.5 inches

*Crater from 1952 MIKE Device, Elugelab Island,
Enewetak Atoll*, 2003
framed pigment print, glazed with u/v blocking
non-reflective glass, edition 4/5
40 x 50 inches

*Radioactive Bunker Facing BRAVO Crater, Nam
Island, Bikini Atoll*, 2003
pigment print, edition 5
24 x 30 inches

*U.S.S. Saratoga Aircraft Carrier, Sunk By 1946 Baker
Event, Operation Crossroads, Bikini Atoll*, 2007
pigment print
16 x 22 inches

*U.S.S. Saratoga Aircraft Carrier, Sunk By 1946 Baker
Event, Operation Crossroads, Bikini Atoll*, 2007
pigment print
16 x 22 inches

*U.S.S. Apogon Submarine, Sunk by 1946 Baker Event,
Operation Crossroads, Bikini Atoll*, 2007
pigment print
16 x 22 inches

*U.S.S. Apogon Submarine, Sunk By 1946 Baker
Event, Operation Crossroads, Bikini Atoll*, 2007
pigment print
16 x 22 inches

Black Bravo, 2007/2016
underwater video
total running time: 4:23 minutes

all courtesy of the artist and Hosfelt Gallery,
San Francisco

Charles Lindsay
FIELD STATION, 2016
fragile equipment cases from US Naval, Marine,
and military missions to the Gulf States, Iraq, and
Afghanistan, African slave idol, F-16 fighter circuit
board, stone age axe head, Japanese black bear penis,
golf balls, 24 karat golden beer can, play-pause-stop
controls, aluminum aerospace tape, convex lenses,
miscellaneous microscopic devices
dimensions variable

additional components:
CARBON, 2009
pigment print from unique carbon emulsion negative
64.5 x 46.5 x 2 inches

Rocket Brain, 2012/2016
salvaged 1970s missile guidance system built for
NASA and acquired on eBay, gyroscope, proximity
sensors, Raspberry pi and Arduino circuit boards with
custom coded behavior, fiber-optic cables directed
by random pattern generator, custom Pyrex cone,
aluminum, bulletproof Plexiglass, video screen (comb
jelly video captured at Hope Island, British Columbia)
93 x 18.5 x 18.5 inches

Code Humpback, 2014
steel cowls, field recordings, video, audio players, fans
90 inches high; width and depth variable

Brain Coral / Deep Time Machine, 2015
brain coral cast, kick drum kick, Soviet main frame
parts and wires, Raspberry pi video player and screen,
video (British Columbia and Pt. Reyes, California)
wooden shipping case, aluminum box, casters
26 x 26 x 16 inches

Crab Cage, 2015/2016
aluminum, glass, 24 karat gold leafed horseshoe crab
molts (Captiva, Florida), custom audio processor,
speaker, and LED patterned behavior, surveillance
cameras, monitor
62 x 20 x 78 inches

EMO Aluminum Works, 2015/2016
Aluminum aerospace tape, plaster, fiber optic cables,
Israeli military laser optics, scientific mirrors,
emergency off switch, plywood
72 x 48 x 6 inches

Fukking with Nature, 2016
Jeffrey Pine sap, fake diamonds, gold leaf, magnetic
heater/stirrer, flask, H2O, soil sampler, artificial
pine tree
30 x 26 x 21 inches

Light Table, 2016
aluminum, glass, LED lights, photo-multiplier tubes,
expanding foam, cloud computer, chromatography
column, "Floater" golf ball, vice, golden horseshoe
crab resuscitator, robotic conveyor belt, 24 karat
gold beer cans, Israeli military laser optics, syringe,
wires, loose screws, nuts, blades, flotsam, coconut,
Mr. Potato Head, Korean War era field radar unit,
miniature humans, beer coaster
33 x 40 x 100 inches

Sloths Dividing, 2016
glass, aluminum, fiber-optic cables, Arduino
circuit and custom LED programming (three-
toed sloth heart rates and bioluminescent oceanic
creature signaling)
100 x 44 inches (each of 3)

all courtesy of the artist

In What Distant Sky, 2013–16
video in purpose-built room
total running time: 5:14 minute loop
22 x 16 x 24 feet
courtesy of the artists

Ryan and Trevor Oakes
Map Tack (Lightfoam Sample), 2002
readymade map tack
.1875 x .1875 x .5 inches

Matchstick Dome, 2002
wooden kitchen matchsticks, acrylic glue
6 x 11 x 11 inches

Cardboard Sculpture, 2003
corrugated cardboard, paper shims, glue
21 x 70 x 10 inches

Have No Narrow Perspectives, 2009
stainless steel, enamel, epoxy
102 x 72 x 48 inches

Have No Narrow Perspectives: Field Museum, 2009
pigment inkjet, cotton paper, linen tape,
museum board
4x enlargement; print edition 3/5, 2011; drawn
March to April, 2009
40 x 42 x 20 inches

Ocean Horizon Line 1: Santa Monica Pier, 2010
watercolor, cotton paper, gummed linen tape,
museum board
40 x 25 x 11 inches

The Getty's Central Garden in Winter, 2011
pigment inkjet, cotton paper, linen tape,
museum board
4x enlargement; print edition 1/5, 2012; drawn
November to December, 2011
40 x 42 x 20 inches

Schulte Home in Early Spring Fog, 2011
Pigment inkjet, cotton paper, linen tape,
museum board
4x enlargement; print edition 2/5, 2012; drawn
April to May, 2011
40 x 42 x 20 inches

The Periphery of Perception: EMPAC, 2012
pigmented black ink pen, cotton paper, linen tape,
museum board
26 x 34 x 22 inches

Bond Street Terrace, October 2014
pigmented color markers, cotton tape, linen tape,
museum board
16 x 18 x 7 inches

Skillman Studio View, 2013
pigment inkjet, cotton paper, linen tape,
museum board
4x enlargement; AP print, 2016; drawn 2013
20 x 22 x 6 inches

The Getty's Central Garden in Winter 2, 2014–15
pigment inkjet, cotton paper, linen tape,
museum board
4x enlargement; print edition 1/5, 2016; drawn
October 2014 to January 2015
40 x 42 x 20 inches
all courtesy of the artists

Demetrius Oliver
Aerolite, 2011–16
digital c-print mounted on Sintra, edition 1/3
40 x 60 inches

Bolide II, III, IV, 2016
glass and melted metal whistles
7 inches diameter
both courtesy of the artist and Inman
Gallery, Houston

Véréna Paravel and Lucien Castaing-Taylor
Spirits Still, 2013
transparencies
dimensions variable
courtesy of the artists

Dario Robleto
*The Pulse Armed With a Pen (An Unknown History
of the Human Heartbeat)*, 2014
28 custom cut 5-inch vinyl records, audio
recordings, archival digital prints (record sleeves,
liner notes, labels, slides), three centuries of various
human pulse and heartbeat tracings, glass slides,
custom bound book, oak, silk, engraved gold mirror,
brass, headphones, media players
18 x 14.5 x 21 inches (box overall, open); installed in
variable dimensions
courtesy of the artist and Inman Gallery, Houston

Rachel Sussman
Krypton Relativity, 2015
Glass tubing, electric voltage, krypton gas,
backing board
15 x 74 x 4 inches

[Selected] History of the Spacetime Continuum, 2016
paint, chalk marker, glitter
dimensions variable
both courtesy of the artist

Julianne Swartz
Lean, 2012
steel, magnet, wall
edition 3/3
69 x .25 x .25 inches
courtesy of the artist and Josee Bienvenu Gallery

Bone Score (Air), 2016
steel, balloon, magnet wire, magnet, amplifier,
audio player, wood; sounds of voices humming,
voices speaking, prayers, chants, a baby's voice,
glass resonating, water dripping
22 x 21 x 130 inches

Bone Score (Drum), 2016
unglazed porcelain, stainless steel, magnet wire,
magnets, abaca paper, wire, amplifier, audio player,
wood; sounds of breathing, swallowing, metal flexing,
an MRI, rain on a metal roof, a Beatles song, a heart
beating, a man's last breaths on an oxygen machine
11 x 8 x 50 inches

Bone Score (Long Tail), 2016
unglazed porcelain, magnet wire, magnets, abaca
paper, wire, amplifier, audio player, wood; sounds
of breathing, a heart beating, fire, a Kepler star pulse,
a children's song
8 x 12 x 102 inches

Bone Score (Paper Zero), 2016
stainless steel wire, magnet wire, magnet, abaca
paper, amplifier, audio player, wood; sounds of
breathing, a whispered conversation, a timpani
drum, rustling paper, a child's laugh, a rain
storm, thunder
26 x 22 x 125 inches

Bone Score (Tangle), 2016
stainless steel wire, magnet wire, magnets, abaca
paper, amplifier, audio player, wood; sounds of
breathing, a geiger counter, fireworks, electrical
current, a windy night, a flock of birds
32 x 22 x 93 inches

In Harmonicity, the Tonal Walkway, 2016
site-specific sound installation with speakers and
20-channel sound track
152 x 5 x 8 feet
The soundtrack was made entirely of singing,
spoken word, and sustained microtones of voice.
Swartz recorded people individually and then
spatially harmonized their voices using chords
of thirds and fifths. Featuring the voices of Estelí
Gomez, Cameron Beauchamp, Dashon Burton
Eric Dudley, Martha Cluver, Thann Scoggin,
Elisa Sutherland, Eliza Bagg, Stella Prince, José
Chardiet, Nicolas S. Eugst Mathews, Isabel Vazquez,
Lulu Hart, Maria Sonevytsky, Edwina Unrath,
David Moss, Sue LaRocca, Jennifer Odlum, Molly
Odlum, Frida Balloghi-Smith, Marshall McConville,
Jenny Monick, Junah Sibony, and Elodie Sibony.
Special thanks to Brad Wells, Director, Roomful
of Teeth; and Ben Senterfit, Director, Community
Music Space, Red Hook, New York.
all courtesy of the artist

Chris Taylor
Apparent, 2016
blown glass
dimensions variable

Assorted, 2016
blown glass
dimensions variable

Miscellaneous, 2016
blown glass
dimensions variable
all courtesy of the artist

Fred Tomaselli
CUBIC SKY, 1988
Plexiglas, enamel paint, fluorescent lighting, wood,
electrical wires
9 x 10 feet (approximate)
courtesy of the artist and James Cohan, New York

All the Bands I Can Remember Seeing, 1990
Prismacolor on paper
9 x 24 inches
private collection

BOX FOR YOUR HEAD, 1990
Ailanthus leaves, resin, wood, Plexiglas, fluorescent
light, enamel paint, t-shirt
29 x 25.75 x 20 inches
courtesy of the artist and James Cohan, New York

Portrait of John, 1995
Prismacolor on unique photogram
16 x 20 inches
private collection

Portrait of Laura, 1995
unique photogram
10.875 x 13.875 inches
collection of James Keith Brown and Eric Diefenbach

Portrait of Jim, 2012
Prismacolor on unique photogram
16 x 20 inches
private collection, New York

Alighieri, Dante. *Paradiso*. Translated by Robert and Jean Hollander. New York: Anchor Books, 2008.

Allen, Jonathan. "Deceptionists at War." *Cabinet Magazine: A Quarterly of Art and Culture*. Issue 26: Magic (Summer 2007).

Allen, Jonathan, and Sally O'Reilly. *Magic Show*. London: Hayward Publishing, 2009.

Aristotle. Metaphysics, Book 1, Section 982b. In *Aristotle in 23 Volumes*, Vols.17, 18. Translated by Hugh Tredennick. Cambridge: Harvard University Press; London: William Heinemann Ltd. 1933, 1989.

Armitt, Lucie. *Theorising the Fantastic*. London: Arnold/St. Martin's, 1996.

Bachelard, Gaston. *The Poetics of Reverie: Childhood, Language, and the Cosmos*. Boston: Beacon Press, 1969.

Barikin, Amelia. *Parallel Presents: The Art of Pierre Huyghe*. Cambridge: MIT Press, 2012.

Bellows, Andy Masaki, and Marina McDougall. *Science is Fiction: The Films of Jean Painlevé*. Cambridge: MIT Press, 2000.

Berry, Ian, ed. *Alloy of Love: Dario Robleto*. Saratoga Springs: Tang Teaching Museum and Art Gallery, 2008.

______. Opener 11: *Nina Katchadourian— All Forms of Attraction*. Saratoga Springs: Tang Teaching Museum and Art Gallery, 2006.

Bervin, Jen. *Nets*. Brooklyn: Ugly Duckling Presse, 2010.

Bervin, Jen, and Marta Werner. *Emily Dickinson: Gorgeous Nothings*. New York: New Directions Publishing/Christine Burgin, 2013.

Borchert, Till-Holger, and Joshua P. Waterman. *The Book of Miracles*. Cologne: Taschen, 2014.

Bradbury, Ray. *The Martian Chronicles*. New York: Doubleday, 1950.

______. *Something Wicked This Way Comes*. New York: Simon and Schuster, 1962.

Brady, Emily. *The Sublime in Modern Philosophy: Aesthetics, Ethics, and Nature*. Cambridge: Cambridge University Press, 2013.

Burda, Hubert, and Friedrich A. Kittler. *The Digital Wunderkammer: 10 Chapters on the Iconic Turn*. Munich: Wilhelm Fink, 2011.

Burke, Edmund. *A Philosophical Inquiry into the Ideas of the Sublime and Beautiful*. Edited by Adam Phillips. Oxford: Oxford University Press, 2009.

Bynum, Caroline Walker. *Metamorphosis & Identity*. New York: Zone Books, 2001.

Caillois, Roger. *The Edge of Surrealism: A Roger Caillois Reader*. Edited by Claudine Frank. Durham: Duke University Press, 2003.

Carroll, Noël. *The Philosophy of Horror or Paradoxes of the Heart*. New York: Routledge, 1990.

Carson, Anne. *Eros the Bittersweet*. Champaign: Dalkey Archive Press, 1998.

Carson, Rachel. *The Sense of Wonder*. New York: Harper Collins, 1998.

Castle, Terry. *The Female Thermometer: Eighteenth-Century Culture and the Invention of the Uncanny (Ideologies of Desire)*. Oxford: Oxford University Press, 1995.

Champion, Jean-Loup, ed. *The Perfect Medium: Photography and the Occult*. New Haven: Yale University Press, 2005.

Cobb, Edith. *The Ecology of Imagination in Childhood*. New York: Spring Publications, 1993.

Cook, James W., ed. *The Colossal P. T. Barnum Reader*. Urbana: University of Illinois Press, 2005.

Crary, Jonathan. *Techniques of the Observer: On Vision and Modernity in the Nineteenth Century*. Cambridge: MIT Press, 1990.

Crowther, Paul. *The Kantian Sublime: From Morality to Art*. Oxford: Clarendon Press, 1989.

Daston, Lorraine J. *Ravening Curiosity and Gawking Wonder in the Early Modern Study of Nature*. Berlin: Max-Planck-Institut für Wissenschafts-geschichte, 1994.

Daston, Lorraine J., and Katherine Park, eds. *Wonders and the Orders of Nature*. New York: Zone Books, 1998.

Descartes, René. *Passions of the Soul*. Translated by Stephen Voss. Cambridge: Hackett Publishing Company, 1989.

Dillon, Brian, and Marina Warner. *Curiosity: The Art and the Pleasure of Knowing*. London: Hayward Publishing, 2013.

Dixon, Deborah P., Harriet Hawkins, and Elizabeth R. Straughan. "Wonder-Full Geomorphology: Sublime Aesthetics and the Place of Art." *Progress In Physical Geography* 37, no. 2 (2013): pp. 227–47. *Academic Search Complete*. Web. December 6, 2013.

During, Simon. *Modern Enchantments*. Cambridge: Harvard University Press, 2002.

Ellis, Sharon. *Paintings*. New York: Greenberg Van Doren Gallery, 2011.

Evans, R. J. W., and Alexander Marr. *Curiosity and Wonder from the Renaissance to the Enlightenment*. London: Routledge, 2006.

Fisher, Philip. *The Vehement Passions*. Princeton: Princeton University Press, 2002.

_____. *Wonder, the Rainbow, and the Aesthetics of Rare Experiences*. Cambridge: Harvard University Press, 1998.

Francis, Richard, and Sophie Shaw, eds. *Negotiating Rapture: The Power of Art to Transform Lives*. Chicago: Museum of Contemporary Art, 1996.

Fred Tomaselli: Early Work or How I Became a Painter. New York: Grand Central Press, 2015.

Freud, Sigmund. *The Uncanny*. New York: Penguin, 2003.

Fuller, Robert C. *Wonder: From Emotion to Spirituality*. Chapel Hill: University of North Carolina Press, 2006.

Gamboni, Dario. *Potential Images: Ambiguity and Indeterminacy in Modern Art*. London: Reaktion Books, 2002.

Gardner, Daniel. *The Science of Fear*. New York: Plume, 2009.

Gausby, Christopher. *The Synoptic Collection*. New York: Christopher Gausby, 2003.

Gelder, Ken, ed. *The Horror Reader*. New York: Routledge, 2000.

Gilbert, Daniel. *Stumbling on Happiness*. New York: Alfred A. Knopf, 2006.

Glassie, John. *A Man of Misconceptions: The Life of an Eccentric in the Age of Change*. New York: Riverhead Books, 2013.

Graham, Gordon. *The Re-enchantment of the World: Art Versus Religion*. Oxford: Oxford University Press, 2010.

Grasso, Laurent. *The Black-Body Radiation*. Paris: Les Presses du Reel, 2009.

_____. *Soleil Double*. Paris: Editions Dilecta/ Galerie Perrotin, 2015.

_____. *Uraniborg*. Paris: FLAMMARION, 2012.

Greenblatt, Stephen. *Marvelous Possessions: The Wonder of the New World*. Chicago: University of Chicago Press, 1992.

_____. *The Swerve: How the World Became Modern*. New York: W. W. Norton and Company, 2012.

Gregg, Linda. *Things and Flesh*. Minneapolis: Graywolf Press, 1999.

Grunenberg, Christoph. *Gothic: Transmutations of Horror in Late-Twentieth-Century Art*. Cambridge: MIT Press, 1997.

Haan, Jason de. *Noghwhere Bodili is Everywhere Goostly*. Southern Alberta Art Gallery/Art Gallery of Nova Scotia/Kitchener-Waterloo Art Gallery, 2014.

Hainley, Bruce. *Tom Friedman*. New York: Phaidon Press, 2001.

Halberstam, Judith. *The Queer Art of Failure*. Durham: Duke University Press, 2011.

Harpham, Geoffrey Galt. *On the Grotesque: Strategies of Contradiction in Art and Literature*. Princeton: Princeton University Press, 1983.

Heaney, Seamus. *The Spirit Level*. New York: Farrar, Straus and Giroux, 1997.

Hoffmann, Roald, and Iain B. Whyte. *Beyond the Finite: The Sublime in Art and Science*. Oxford: Oxford University Press, 2011.

Holmes, Richard. *The Age of Wonder: How the Romantic Generation Discovered the Beauty and Terror of Science*. New York: Vintage, 2010.

Huyghe, Pierre, Emma Lavigne, and Amelia Barikin. *Pierre Huyghe*. Munich: Himer Verlag, 2015.

Irigaray, Luce. *An Ethics of Sexual Difference*. Translated by Carolyn Burke and Gillian C. Gill. Ithaca: Cornell University Press, 1993.

James, William. *The Varieties of Religious Experience*. New York: Basic Books, 2008.

Jamison, Kay Redfield. *Exuberance: The Passion for Life*. New York: Alfred A. Knopf, 2004.

Jones, Rachel. "On the Value of Not Knowing: Wonder, Beginning Again and Letting Be." In *On Not Knowing: How Artists Think*. Edited by Rebecca Fortnum and Elizabeth Fisher. London: Black Dog Publishing, 2013.

Kalba, Laura Anne. "Fireworks and Other Profane Illuminations: Color and the Experience of Wonder in Modern Visual Culture." *Modernism/Modernity* 19, no. 4 (2012): pp. 657–76. Art Abstracts (H.W. Wilson). Web. December 6, 2013.

Keen, Sam. *Apology for Wonder*. New York: Harper and Row, 1969.

Keller, Cory. *Brought to Light: Photography and the Invisible 1840–1900*. New Haven: Yale University Press, 2008.

Kelley, Mike. *The Uncanny*. Exhibition catalogue. Liverpool: Tate Liverpool, 2004.

Kenseth, Joy. *Age of the Marvelous*. Dartmouth: Hood Museum of Art, 1992.

Kristeva, Julia. *The Powers of Horror: An Essay on Abjection*. New York: Columbia University Press, 1982.

Kuhn, Thomas. *The Copernican Revolution*. Cambridge: Harvard University Press, 1957.

Lieberman, Archie, and Ray Bradbury. *The Mummies of Guanajuato*. New York: H. N. Abrams, 1978.

Light, Michael. *100 Suns: 1945–1962*. New York: Alfred A. Knopf, 2003.

Lightman, Alan. *A Sense of the Mysterious: Science and the Human Spirit*. New York: Random House, 2005.

Lochrie, Karma. "Sheer Wonder: Dreaming Utopia in the Middle Ages." *Journal of Medieval & Early Modern Studies* 36, no. 3 (2006): pp. 493–516.

Lucretius. *On the Nature of Things*. Translated by Martin Ferguson Smith. Indianapolis: Hackett Publishing, 1969.

Lynch, Jim. *The Highest Tide*. New York: Bloomsbury USA, 2006.

Maleuvre, Didier. *The Horizon: A History of Our Infinite Longing*. Berkeley: University of California Press, 2011.

Mauriès, Patrick. *Cabinets of Curiosity*. New York: Thames & Hudson, 2002.

Melville, Herman. *Moby-Dick*. 1851; reprint New York: Black and White Classics, 2014.

Nelson, Robert S. *Visuality Before and Beyond the Renaissance: Seeing as Others Saw*. Cambridge: Cambridge University Press, 2000.

Nicholas of Cusa. *De docta ignorantia* [On Learned Ignorance]. 1440, Book 1, Chapter 3: The Precise Truth is Incomprehensible. jasper-hopkins.info/DI-I-12-2000.pdf

Oliver, Demetrius. *Canicular*. Philadelphia: The Print Center, 2014.

Onians, R. B. *The Origins of European Thought: About the Body, the Mind, the Soul, the World, Time and Fate*. Cambridge: Cambridge University Press, 1988.

Pfeiffer, John E. *The Creative Explosion: An Inquiry into the Origins of Art and Religion*. Ithaca: Cornell University Press, 1985.

Plesch, Véronique. *Illuminating Words: The Artist's Books of Christopher Gausby*. Northampton: Smith College Museum of Art, 1999.

Potts, John. *Technologies of Magic: A Cultural Study of Ghosts, Machines and the Uncanny*. Sydney: Power Publications, 2006.

Quinn, Dennis. *Iris Exiled: A Synoptic History of Wonder*. Lanham: University Press of America, 2002.

Ray, Gene. *Terror and the Sublime in Art and Critical Theory: From Auschwitz to Hiroshima to September 11 and Beyond*. New York: Palgrave Macmillan, 2005.

Reynolds, David S. *Beneath the American Renaissance: The Subversive Imagination in the Age of Emerson and Melville*. Cambridge: Harvard University Press, 1989.

Ross, Stephen D. *The World as Aesthetic Phenomenon: The Image in Abundance, the Wonder of the Earth*. Binghamton: Global Academic Publishing, 2006.

Royle, Nicholas. *The Uncanny*. New York: Routledge, 2003.

Ruefle, Mary. *Madness, Rack, and Honey*. New York: Wave Books, 2012.

______. *Selected Poems*. New York: Wave Books, 2010.

______. *Trances of the Blast*. New York: Wave Books, 2013.

Sagan, Carl. *Contact*. New York: Simon and Schuster, 1985.

______. *Cosmos*. New York: Random House, 1980.

______. *The Demon-Haunted World: Science as a Candle in the Dark*. New York: Ballantine Books, 1997.

______. *Pale Blue Dot: A Vision of the Human Figure in Space*. New York: Ballantine Books, 1994.

Sagan, Carl, F. D. Drake, Ann Druyan, Timothy Ferris, Jon Lomberg, and Linda Salzman Sagan. *Murmurs of Earth: The Voyager Interstellar Record*. New York: Ballantine Books, 1979.

Sagmeister, Stefan. *The Happy Film Pitch Book*. Philadelphia: Institute of Contemporary Art, University of Pennsylvania, 2013.

______. *Things I Have Learned in My Life So Far*. Updated Edition, New York: Harry N. Abrams, 2013.

Schneider, Kirk J. *Rediscovery of Awe: Splendor, Mystery, and the Fluid Center of Life*. St. Paul: Paragon House, 2004.

Scott, A. O. "Above it All: A Cinematic History of Going Airborne." *The New York Times Magazine*, December 15, 2015.

Serres, Michel. *The Parasite*. Baltimore: Johns Hopkins University, 1982.

Shepard, Paul, and Daniel McKinley. *The Subversive Science: Essays Toward an Ecology of Man*. Boston: Houghton Mifflin, 1969.

Simons, Sarah. *No One May Ever Have the Same Knowledge Again: Letters to Mount Wilson Observatory, 1915–1935*. Los Angeles: The Museum of Jurassic Technology, 1993.

Solnit, Rebecca. *A Field Guide to Getting Lost*. New York: Penguin, 2005.

Spalding, Julian. *The Art of Wonder: A History of Seeing*. Munich: Prestel, 2005.

Spitz, Ellen Handler. *The Brightening Glance: Imagination and Childhood*. New York: Anchor, 2007.

Stafford, Barbara Maria. *Devices of Wonder: From the World in a Box to Images on a Screen*. Los Angeles: Getty Research Institute, 2001.

_____. *Visual Analogy: Consciousness as the Art of Connecting*. Cambridge: MIT Press, 1999.

Stewart, Susan. *Nonsense: Aspects of Intertextuality in Folklore and Literature*. Baltimore: Johns Hopkins University Press, 1978.

Sussman, Rachel. *The Oldest Living Things in the World* (with essays by Hans Ulrich Obrist and Carl Zimmer). Chicago: University of Chicago Press, 2014.

Swartz, Julianne, Racel Arauz, and Cassandra Coblentz. *How Deep is Your*. Lincoln: deCordova Sculpture Park and Museum, 2012.

Tippett, Krista. *Einstein's God: Conversations about Science and the Human Spirit*. New York: Penguin Books, 2010.

Todorov, Tzvetan. *The Fantastic: A Structural Approach to a Literary Genre*. Ithaca: Cornell University Press, 1975.

Vasalou, Sophia, ed. *Practices of Wonder: Cross Disciplinary Perspectives*. Eugene: Pickwick Publications, 2012.

Vicario, Gilbert, Dario Robleto, Naomi Oreskes, et al. *Survival Does Not Lie in the Heavens*. Des Moines: Des Moines Art Center, 2011.

Warner, Marina. *Phantasmagoria: Spirit Visions, Metaphors, and Media into the 21st Century*. Oxford: Oxford University Press, 2006.

Watson, Lyall. *Supernature*. Norwell: Anchor Press, 1973.

Weller, Sam. *Listen to the Echoes: The Ray Bradbury Interviews*. Chicago: Stop Smiling Books, 2010.

Wertheim, Christine, and Margaret Wertheim. *Crochet Coral Reef*. Los Angeles: Institute For Figuring, 2015.

Wertheim, Margaret. *A Field Guide to Hyperbolic Space: An Exploration of the Intersection of Higher Geometry and Feminine Handicraft*. Los Angeles: Institute For Figuring, 2011.

Weschler, Lawrence. *Compounding Visions: The Art of Trevor and Ryan Oakes*. New York: The National Museum of Mathematics, 2014.

_____. *Everything That Rises: A Book of Convergences*. San Francisco: McSweeney's Books, 2006.

_____. *Mr. Wilson's Cabinet of Wonder*. New York: Pantheon, 1995.

_____. *Seeing is Forgetting the Name of the Thing One Sees: Over Thirty Years of Conversations with Robert Irwin*. Berkeley: University of California Press, 2008.

Wiseman, Richard. *Quirkology: How We Discover the Big Truths in Small Things*. New York: Basic Books, 2008.

Wiseman, Richard, and Peter Lamont. *Magic in Theory: An Introduction to the Theoretical and Psychological Elements of Conjuring*. Hatfield: University of Hertfordshire Press, 2005.

Jonathan Allen (resides London, England) is an artist and writer whose work addresses the figuring of agency, the facticity of the image, and the various magics at play within secular modernity. He has had solo exhibitions at David Risley Gallery, London; Site Gallery, Sheffield, UK; recent group exhibitions and performances include *We are publication*, Institute of Contemporary Arts, London; *Outrageous Fortune*, Focal Point Gallery, Southend, UK; and *The Great Transformation*, Frankfurter Kunstverein, Frankfurt. His writing was featured recently in *Notes on The Magic of the State* (Beirut Gallery, Cairo, and Lisson Gallery, London, 2013), and *Truth is Concrete—A Handbook for artistic strategies in real politics* (Sternberg Press, 2014); and he was editor-author of *Lost Envoy—The Tarot Deck of Austin Osman Spare* (Strange Attractor Press, 2016). He is currently a curator at The Magic Circle Museum, London. jonathanallen.info

Jen Bervin (resides Brooklyn, NY) is a visual artist and writer whose works combine text and textiles with conceptual elements and a minimalist's eye for the poetic and essential. Exhibitions of her work include the upcoming *Strange Oscillations and Vibrations of Sympathy*, University Galleries, Illinois State University, Normal; *The Book Undone: 30 Years of Granary Books,* Columbia University, New York; *Stacks*, NYFA Gallery, Brooklyn, NY; *Pangrammar*, P!, New York; and */mit ðə detə/: Source Materials Visualized*, Center for Book Arts, New York. Bervin is the recipient of a Creative Capital grant, a Lucas Artist Residency at the Montalvo Arts Center, a Robert Rauschenberg Residency and is an artist in residence at the SETI Institute. jenbervin.com

Jason de Haan (resides Calgary, AB) creates sculptures, drawings, and videos that recognize potential in various unconventional systems, objects, and sets of conditions. Often incorporating non-human forces, temporal shifts, and unforeseen outcomes, de Haan seeks spaces where the invisible, serendipitous, and residual reveal their contingencies. Recent solo exhibitions include *Noghwhere Bodili is Everywhere Goostly*, Art Gallery of Nova Scotia, Canada; *The Wood and Wave Each Other Know* with Miruna Dragan, Museo de la Ciudad, Querétaro, Mexico; and *Free and Easy Wanderer*, Clint Roenisch Gallery, Toronto. De Haan is represented by Clint Roenisch Gallery, Toronto. jasondehaan.net

Tristan Duke (resides Los Angeles, CA) has a background in photography and holography and has long been interested in optics, visual perception, and optical illusion. Solo exhibitions include *Empty Forms*, Fest i Nova at Art Villa Garikula, Tbilisi, Georgia, and *A Series of Small Views from the Interstitial Observatory*, Velaslavasay Panorama, Los Angeles. In 2014, he created the first-ever hand-drawn holographic record for Jack White's solo album, *Lazaretto*. He is a founding member (along with Lauren Bon and Richard Nielsen) of the Optics Division of the Metabolic Studio. With the Optics Division he has exhibited at the DePaul Art Museum, Chicago; Los Angeles Contemporary Exhibitions (LACE); the Hammer Museum, Los Angeles; Les Rencontres d'Arles, France; The George Eastman Museum, Rochester, NY; and the Hirshhorn Museum and Sculpture Garden, Washington, DC. Duke founded Infinity Light Science in 2008 and is a fellow at The Museum of Jurassic Technology. infinitylightscience.com

Sharon Ellis (resides Yucca Valley, CA) is a painter who tends to follow in the tradition of Romanticism and Symbolism, envisioning pictorial reveries of nature, seen and imagined. Recent solo exhibitions include *Sharon Ellis*, Christopher Grimes Gallery, Santa Monica, CA, and *Sharon Ellis: New Paintings*, Greenberg Van Doren Gallery, New York. Her work has been included in group exhibitions at The Hammer Museum, the J. Paul Getty Museum, The Aldrich Contemporary Art Museum , and the Van Abbemuseum, among others. The Long Beach Museum of Art, CA, organized a ten-year survey of her work in 2002, which travelled to the Contemporary Arts Center, Cincinnati, and the San Jose Museum of Art. Ellis is represented by Christopher Grimes Gallery, Santa Monica.

Tom Friedman (resides Easthampton, MA) makes extraordinary works that explore perception, logic, and possibility. Recent solo exhibitions include *Looking Up*, Park Avenue, New York; *Tom Friedman: Untitled (Foundation)*, Mead Art Museum, Amherst College, MA; *Gravity*, Stephen Friedman Gallery, London; *Up in the Air*, Tel Aviv Museum of Art, Israel. Friedman's work has been exhibited at The Museum of Modern Art, New York; the Fondazione Prada, Milan; Magasin III Stockholm; the South London Gallery; and more. Friedman is represented by Luhring Augustine, New York and Stephen Friedman Gallery, London.

Christopher Gausby (resides New York City) is an artist, calligrapher, and writer who has reinvented the illuminated manuscript form to create book works meditating on philosophy and aesthetics. These works are in the collections of the New York Public Library and the Newberry Library, Chicago.

Hope Ginsberg (resides Richmond, VA) makes live work situated within or just at the edge of what can be considered everyday life. She uses a variety of strategies such as video, photographs, installation, and object making to represent these activities. Recent solo exhibitions include *Breathing on Land: Bay of Fundy*, Temple Contemporary, Philadelphia; *Land Dive Team*, The Complex(ity) Project Space, Narrowsburg, NY; Sponge HQ, Anderson Gallery, Richmond, VA; and *Hope Ginsburg*, CUE Art Foundation, New York. Her current *Breathing on Land* project began at the Robert Rauschenberg Residency in Captiva, FL. In 2016, she is participating in the Film/Video Studio Program residency at the Wexner Center for the Arts, Columbus, OH.

Laurent Grasso's (resides Paris, France/New York City) work is an exploration of the grey areas of ambiguity, mysteriousness, and wonder. He proposes temporal and geographical disjunctions in order to reveal the uncanny in the familiar. He is interested in strange phenomena situated at the border of science and magic, in the representation of catastrophes, and in the aesthetics of power. Grasso's work has been presented in numerous solo exhibitions: at the Hermès Foundation, Tokyo; Musée d'Art Contemporain de Montréal; Kunsthaus Baselland, Muttenz; Jeu de Paume, Paris; Bass Museum of Art, Miami; Hirshhorn Museum and Sculpture Garden, Washington, DC: Saint Louis Art Museum; Kunstverein Arnsberg; Palais de Tokyo and Centre Pompidou, Paris. He has also participated in many international contemporary art biennales, including Kochi, Gwangju, Manifesta, Sharjah, Moscow, and Busan. Additionally, he has created several installations in public spaces, most recently *Solar Wind* and *Nomiya* in Paris. A major monograph, *Soleil Double*, was published in 2016. His work is represented by Galerie Perrotin, Galerie Chez Valentin, Sean Kelly Gallery, and Edouard Malingue Gallery.

Pierre Huyghe (resides Paris, France) has been working with time-based situations and exploring the exhibition process since the 1990s. His works imply such diverse forms as living systems, objects, films, photographs, drawings, and music. In recent years, he has created self-generating systems, including living entities and artifacts, in which emergence and rhythm are indeterminate. Solo exhibitions include *Pierre Huyghe: The Roof Garden Commission*, The Metropolitan Museum of Art, New York; *Untilled (Liegender Frauenakt)*, The Museum of Modern Art, New York; *IN. BORDER. DEEP*, Hauser & Wirth, London; Pierre Huyghe, Los Angeles County Museum of Art; and *Pierre Huyghe*, Centre Pompidou, Paris. He has received many awards, including the Kurt Schwitters Prize (2015), the Roswitha Haftmann Prize (2013), the Smithsonian Museum's Contemporary Artist Award (2010), and the Hugo Boss Prize, Guggenheim Museum (2002).

The **Institute For Figuring** and **Margaret Wertheim** (Los Angeles, CA) engage in science and making, steeped in the belief that ideas presented in abstract terms can often be embodied in physical activities. Founded in 2003 by twin sisters Margaret and Christine Wertheim, the IFF develops exhibitions and programs for museums, galleries, and colleges internationally. The Institute's *Crochet Coral Reef* has been shown at the Hayward Gallery in London, Science Gallery in Dublin, and the Smithsonian's Natural Museum of Natural History, Washington DC. theiff.org

Nina Katchadourian (resides Brooklyn, NY) is an interdisciplinary artist whose work includes video, performance, sound, sculpture, photography, and public projects. Her video *Accent Elimination* was included at the 2015 Venice Biennale in the Armenian pavilion, which won the Golden Lion for Best National Participation. Katchadourian's work has been included in group exhibitions at the Serpentine Gallery, Turner Contemporary, de Appel, Palais de Tokyo, Istanbul Museum of Modern Art, Turku Art Museum, Museum of Contemporary Art San Diego, ICA Philadelphia, Brooklyn Museum, Artists Space, SculptureCenter, and MoMA PS1. In March 2017, a solo survey of her work opens at the Blanton Museum in Austin, TX, with an accompanying monograph. Katchadourian is an associate professor at NYU Gallatin. She is represented by Catharine Clark Gallery. ninakatchadourian.com

Michael Light (resides San Francisco, CA) is a photographer focused on the environment and its relationship to contemporary American culture. Recent solo exhibitions include *Some Dry Space*, James Danziger Gallery, New York; *Private Frontiers*, Hosfelt Gallery, San Francisco; *Two Sublimes, Idaho*, Craig Krull Gallery, Santa Monica; and

Some Dry Space: An Inhabited West, Blue Sky Gallery, Portland. Recent group exhibitions include *California and the West*, SFMOMA, San Francisco; *Too Much: Utter Beauty and Measureless Time*, Contemporary Jewish Museum, San Francisco; *They Used to Call it the Moon*, BALTIC Centre for Contemporary Art, Gateshead, UK; *Overdrive: Los Angeles Constructs the Future*, J. Paul Getty Museum, Los Angeles; and *Road Trip: Photography of the American West*, LACMA/Musée des Beaux Arts de Bordeaux, France. His work is in the collections of the San Francisco Museum of Modern Art, the Los Angeles County Museum of Art, the Getty Research Institute, New York Public Library, the Hasselblad Center, Sweden, and the Victoria & Albert Museum, London, among others. michaellight.net

Charles Lindsay (resides Preston Hollow, NY) is a multidisciplinary artist interested in technology, ecosystems, semiotics, and esoteric forms of humor. Projects include *FIELD WORK*, at MASS MoCA and Human Condition Headquarters, New York; *CODE HUMPBACK*, The Bolinas Museum, CA; *CARBON*, The Center for Photography, Woodstock, NY, and ISEA2012, New Mexico; *NEAR(ER)*, Rythms + Visions, USC, Los Angeles; and *UPSTREAM: Fly Fishing in the American West*, The Dennos Museum Center and the Boise Art Museum. Lindsay is the SETI Institute's artist in residence program director, a Guggenheim Fellow, and a recipient of the Robert Rauschenberg Residency. charleslindsay.com

Megan and Murray McMillan (reside Providence, RI) have been collaborating since 2002. They make interdisciplinary projects that incorporate video, installation, performance, and photography. Solo exhibitions include *In What Distant Sky*, Qbox Gallery, Athens, Greece; *The Coal Bin Project Launch*, WaterFire Art Center, *When We Didn't Touch the Ground*, Cohen Gallery, Brown University, and *The Remains of Something Whole*, Pell Chafee Performance Center, all Providence. Group exhibitions include *Cove: Visual Arts on Georges Island*, Georges Island, MA; *Nuit Blanche: The Night Circus*, Toronto; Ikono On Air Festival, Berlin; *Between Music and Art*, Berlin; *Locally Made*, RISD Museum, Providence; and *Character Study*, deCordova Museum and Sculpture Park, Lincoln, MA. They are represented by Qbox Gallery, Athens.meganandmurraymcmillan.com

Ryan and Trevor Oakes (reside New York City) are twin brothers who have been engaged in a conversation about the nuances of vision since they were children. They explored their mutual fascination with vision throughout grade school and during college at Cooper Union's School of Art in New York City. Since graduating in 2004, they've continued their dialogue with jointly built artworks addressing human vision, light, perception, and the experience of space and depth. The Oakeses have artwork in the permanent collections of The Field Museum and the Spertus Museum, Chicago; the Getty Research Institute, Los Angeles; The Museum of Modern Art, New York; New York Public Library; and the North Dakota Museum of Art, Grand Forks.

Demetrius Oliver (resides New York City) creates site-specific installations using photography, sculpture, and video to record the act of sidereal observation itself. His work draws on a variety of disparate intellectual interests related to interpreting phenomena, including American Transcendentalism, music of the spheres, and cosmology. Recent solo exhibitions include *Canicular*, Print Center, Philadelphia; *Azimuth*, Inman Gallery, Houston; *Orrery*, D'Amelio Terras, New York; *Penumbra*, Light Work, Syracuse, NY. Group exhibitions include *Works of Paper II*, Acme, Los Angeles; *Affinity Atlas*, Wellin Museum of Art, Hamilton, NY; *Bearden Project*, Studio Museum in Harlem, New York; *In Context*, Roberts & Tilton, Culver City, CA; *Sculpted, Etched and Cut: Metal Works from the Permanent Collection*, Studio Museum in Harlem; and *Collected. Reflections on the Permanent Collection*, Studio Museum in Harlem. demetriusoliver.com

Véréna Paravel and Lucien Castaing-Taylor (reside Cambridge, MA) are anthropologists and artists working at the Sensory Ethnography Lab at Harvard University. Their work is in the permanent collection of New York's Museum of Modern Art and the British Museum, has been exhibited at the Tate Modern, Centre Pompidou, MoMA, Whitney Museum of American Art, Berlin Kunsthalle, PS1, Whitechapel Gallery, and London's Institute of Contemporary Arts, and has formed the subject of symposia at the Smithsonian Institution, the Musée du quai Branly, and the British Museum. Their 2012 film *Leviathan* was lauded by critics and won numerous awards.

Dario Robleto (resides Houston, TX) is an artist whose multifaceted practice links careful research with romantic earnestness and conceptual precision with unorthodox fabrication. Recent solo exhibitions include *Setlists for a Setting Sun*, Baltimore Museum of Art, and *The Boundary of Life is Quietly Crossed*, The Menil Collection, Houston. In 2013, he served as the California College of the Arts Viola Frey Distinguished Visiting Professor, Oakland, CA. He has been a research fellow and resident at institutions such as Rice University and the Smithsonian Museum of American History. He is currently serving as an artist in residence in Neuroaesthetics at the University of Houston's Cullen College of Engineering and at the SETI Institute in Mountain View, CA. He was recently appointed as the 2016 Texas State Artist Laureate. dariorobleto.com

Rachel Sussman's (resides Brooklyn, NY) decade-long transdisciplinary project, *The Oldest Living Things in the World*, combines art, science, and philosophy into a traveling exhibition and *New York Times* bestselling book. She is a Guggenheim, NYFA, and MacDowell Colony Fellow, and a TED speaker. Her exhibitions include the MoCS, Staatiche Kunsthalle Baden Baden, the National Museum of Women in the Arts, Lianzhou Photo Festival, Berlin Botanical Museum, Kunstverein Hannover, New York University, the University of Pennsylvania, and the George Eastman Museum. In 2014, she began new work exploring deep time and deep space with the support of the LACMA Lab, working with SpaceX, NASA, and CERN. She is a 2016–17 SETI Institute artist in residence. rachelsussman.com

Julianne Swartz (resides Kingston, NY) works with sound, kinetics, and a range of lo-tech materials to make sculpture, installations, and photographs. Solo exhibitions include *How Deep is Your*, Indianapolis Museum of Art; *Terrain*, curated by Jacqueline Grandjean, Oude Kerke, Amsterdam; *Gravity*, Josee Bienvenu Gallery, New York; Miracle Report, Arizona State University Art Museum, Tempe; *The Sound of Light*, The Jewish Museum, New York. Group exhibitions include *When You Cut Into the Present, the Future Leaks Out*, Bronx Borough Courthouse, NY; *More Love*, Ackland Art Museum, Chapel Hill, NC; and *Good Night*, The Israel Museum, Jerusalem. julianneswartz.com

Chris Taylor (resides Providence, RI) began close-copying readymade objects in glass over twenty years ago. These objects combine his interests in subversion, irony, and humor with beauty, elegance, and a reverence for the tradition of glassmaking. Taylor's work transforms the daily conventional experience with things into a sculptural and performative art interaction. Particularly examining glass tradition and conventions, Taylor's projects have included learning to blow glass upside down. He also meticulously reproduced a sixteenth-century Venetian goblet, whose technique was lost for over five hundred years, and then planted it next to the original in the collections room cabinet at The Metropolitan Museum of Art, New York. Solo exhibitions include *Small Craft Advisory*, Real Art Ways, Hartford, CT; *Salad Days*, Artists Space, New York; and *The Truth About Brown Eggs*, Artspace, New Haven, CT.

Fred Tomaselli (resides New York City) draws upon art historical sources and Eastern and Western decorative traditions to create works that explode with mesmerizing patterns through the layering of resin, pharmaceuticals, and organic materials. Recent solo exhibitions include *Keep Looking: Fred Tomaselli's Birds*, Toledo Museum of Art, OH; *Fred Tomaselli: The Early Works or How I Became a Painter*, Begovich Gallery, California State University, Fullerton, traveled to the James Cohan Gallery, New York; *Fred Tomaselli: The Times*, University of Michigan Museum of Art, Ann Arbor, traveled to the Orange County Museum of Art, Newport Beach, CA; *FOCUS: Fred Tomaselli*, Modern Art Museum of Fort Worth, TX. Group exhibitions include *Night Begins the Day: Rethinking Space, Time, and Beauty*, Contemporary Jewish Museum, San Francisco; and *The Singing and the Silence: Birds in Contemporary Art*, Smithsonian American Art Museum, Washington, DC. Tomaselli is represented by James Cohan Gallery, New York.

Denise Markonish is the curator at MASS MoCA, where her exhibitions include *Jim Shaw: Entertaining Doubts*; *Teresita Fernández: As Above So Below* (catalogue); *Oh, Canada*, the largest survey of contemporary Canadian art (catalogue: MIT Press); *Nari Ward: Sub Mirage Lignum* (catalogue); *Iñigo Manglano-Ovalle: Gravity is a force to be reckoned with* (catalogue: D.A.P); *These Days: Elegies for Modern Times*; and *Badlands: New Horizons in Landscape* (catalogue: MIT Press). Markonish also co-edited with Susan Cross the book *Sol LeWitt: 100 Views* (Yale University Press). She has taught at Williams College and the Rhode Island School of Design and is the head of the advisory committee for the SETI Institute's artist in residence program. Markonish is currently working on projects with Nick Cave, Elizabeth King, Tanja Hollander, Sarah Oppenheimer, and Anya Gallaccio.

Sean Foley is an artist based in Columbus, OH. His solo exhibitions include *Rubes, Scuttlebutt & Loggerheads*, Irvine Contemporary, Washington, DC; *Phantasmagoria*, Center for Maine Contemporary Art, Rockport; and Allston Skirt Gallery, Boston; group shows include *The Biennial Exhibition*, Portland Museum of Art, ME; *Big Bang: Abstraction in the 21st Century*, deCordova Museum and Sculpture Park, Lincoln, MA; Academy of Arts and Letters, New York; a two-person show with Michael Oatman at the Mary Ryan Gallery, New York; and *Cryptozoology*, Bates College Museum of Art, Lewiston, ME. Foley has held residencies at the Rauschenberg Foundation; Kohler Arts/ Industry; and Headlands Center for the Arts. He has taught at the Maine College of Art and The Ohio State University, and is currently a professor at the College of the Atlantic, Bar Harbor, ME.

Steven Holmes is the curator of The Cartin Collection, Hartford, CT. From 2009 to 2012, he was adjunct curator at the Bass Museum of Art, Miami, where he curated *The Endless Renaissance* and *Human Rites*, and was director of visual arts at Real Art Ways in Hartford from 2000 to 2005. He has curated projects for Palais de Tokyo, Paris; Kunste- Werke Institute for Contemporary Art, Berlin; Sperone Westwater; New York; the Museo del Arte de Puerto Rico; and *1001 Chairs for Ai Wei Wei* with Creative Time. Holmes is a graduate of Harvard Divinity School.

Kay Redfield Jamison is perhaps this country's most famous writer about manic-depressive (bipolar) illness. Her books and articles not only help patients; they have raised society's consciousness. Her public appearances inform Americans about their millions of fellow citizens who suffer mood disorders. Her work and life chip away at the stigma of mental illness. Jamison is currently a Professor of Psychiatry at Johns Hopkins School of Medicine; she has written several works, including *An Unquiet Mind*, her memoir about her own battles with bipolar disorder.

Maria Popova is a reader and a writer; she writes about what she reads on *Brain Pickings* (brainpickings.org), which is included in the Library of Congress archive of culturally valuable materials. She has also written for *The New York Times*, *Wired UK*, and *The Atlantic*, among others, and is an MIT Futures of Entertainment Fellow. Popova is on Twitter as @brainpicker.

Stefan Sagmeister is a designer who blends typography and imagery in striking, fresh, ambitious, and unsettling ways. Having influenced the culture of design over the past decade, he is perhaps best known for his album covers for Talking Heads, Lou Reed, OK Go, and The Rolling Stones, to name only a few, as well as innovative campaigns for companies such as Levi's that have entered the public consciousness. In 2012, Sagmeister created his first museum exhibition in the United States, *The Happy Show*, at the ICA in Philadelphia and LA MoCA's Pacific Design Center.

Barbara Maria Stafford is William B. Ogden Distinguished Service Professor, Emeritus, at the University of Chicago. Her writing continues to examine the history and theory of imaging and visualization modalities from the early modern to the digital era. Her books interconnect the arts, sciences, and optical technologies. Since *Visual Analogy* (1999), then *Echo Objects* (2007), and *A Field Guide to A New Metafield* (2012), she has increasingly focused on analyzing the intersection of the neurosciences with the visual arts. Earlier volumes explored similar relations between geography/geology/ mineralogy (featured in *Voyage into Substance*); and anatomy and the life sciences (*Body Criticism*). She also writes historically grounded manifestos on the vital significance of the visual and sensory arts to general education as well as to society at large (*Artful Science; Good Looking*).

Jill Tarter is an astronomer and the holder of the Bernard M. Oliver chair for SETI at the SETI Institute in Mountain View, CA. She is one of the few researchers to have devoted her career to hunting for signs of sentient beings elsewhere. She was the Project Scientist for NASA's SETI efforts and then for the privately funded version, Phoenix Project, a decade-long SETI scrutiny of about 750 nearby star systems, using telescopes in Australia, West Virginia, Georgia, the UK, and Puerto Rico. Tarter led SETI Institute's efforts to build and operate the Allen Telescope Array, a massive new instrument that will eventually comprise 350 antennas. In retirement, she continues to raise funding to make it so. Jodie Foster's character in the film *Contact* was inspired by Tarter's research.

Robin Ince is an English comedian and writer. He is best known for presenting, with physicist Brian Cox, the BBC Radio 4 podcast, *The Infinite Monkey Cage*, which has won numerous science, comedy, and broadcasting awards. He has written and presented documentaries on Schrödinger's Cat, general relativity, Bertrand Russell, melancholy, and many other subjects. He is the author of *Bad Book Club*, the screenwriter of *Razzle Dazzle*, which opened the New York Children's Film Festival, and is editor of the horror anthology series, *Dead Funny*.

Sam Green is a New York-based documentary filmmaker. His most recent projects are the "live documentaries" *The Measure of All Things* (2014), *The Love Song of R. Buckminster Fuller* (with Yo La Tengo, 2012), and *Utopia in Four Movements* (2010). In all of these works, Green is the narrator for the film while musicians perform a live soundtrack. His 2004 feature-length film, *The Weather Underground*, was nominated for an Academy Award, included in the Whitney Biennial, and has been screened widely around the world. He has received grants from the Creative Capital, Rockefeller, and Guggenheim Foundations, as well as the National Endowment for the Arts. samgreen.to

Lawrence Weschler, a staff writer at *The New Yorker* for twenty years (1981–2001), where he shuttled between political tragedies and cultural comedies, is the author of over a dozen books, including *Seeing is Forgetting the Name of the Thing One Sees* (on artist Robert Irwin, 1982/2008); *Mr. Wilson's Cabinet of Wonder* (on Los Angeles's Museum of Jurassic Technology, 1995); *Vermeer in Bosnia* (2004); and *Everything that Rises; A Book of Convergences* (winner of the National Book Critics Circle Award for Criticism in 2007). He has taught widely, including at Princeton, Sarah Lawrence, Columbia, UC Santa Cruz, and NYU. Weschler

is director emeritus of the New York Institute for the Humanities at NYU (which he led from 2001 through 2014) and is also the artistic director emeritus of the Chicago Humanities Festival.

Mary Ruefle is a poet, essayist, and erasure artist. She has published ten books of poetry, two books of prose, and a comic book. Her most recent books are *Trance of the Blast* and *Madness, Rack, and Honey: Collected Lectures*. Ruefle is the recipient of numerous awards, including an Award in Literature from the American Academy of Arts and Letters, a Guggenheim fellowship, a National Endowment for the Arts fellowship, and a Whiting Award. She lives in Bennington, VT.

Thank you to Joe Thompson and the entire staff at MASS MoCA, especially Richard Criddle, Derek Parker, Tim Walker, Megan Tamas, Nicholas Tamas, Debora Coombs Criddle, Nina Ruelle, Jason Reppert, Dave Tatro, Joe Bordeau and the buildings and grounds crew, along with Nick Langner, Caitlin Tucker-Melvin, Brad Dilger, and Larry Smallwood. Thanks to Meghan Robertson for always hosting artists so conscientiously, to Paulette Wein and Mariah Tarvainen for help in proofreading and graphic design, and to Allie Foradas, without whose diligent and enthusiastic work this book and exhibition would not have happened—she always seemed to keep multiple trains on track, even as derailment threatened.

Everything we do at MASS MoCA is accomplished with the help of great interns. *Explode Every Day* was five years in the making, and the following interns provided invaluable assistance: Caitlin Link, Athena Knisley, Margo Cohen Ristorucci, Calley Morrison, and Thomas Huston. A special thank you to Katie Bullock, studio assistant, intern, student, and most importantly a friend—she was there at the start of this project and her wide-eyed wonder has been a continual source of inspiration to the very end.

Thank you to Mary DelMonico and her team at Prestel for supporting the vision for this book, and to Jane Calverley for her eagle-eyed and sensitive copy editing. Special thanks to Brett Yasko for his incredible graphic design—he added a new layer of wonder to the texts and images within this book, creating moments of surprise and discovery even for someone who was there every step of the way.

The following individuals and institutions helped make these artists' works a reality: Creative Capital (for support of Jen Bervin and Véréna Paravel and Lucien Castaing-Taylor); The Robert Rauschenberg Residency (special thanks to Matt Hall and Carrell Courtright for support of Hope Ginsburg and Charles Lindsay, and to Ann Brady for the time and quiet in which to write); RISD Glass is an ongoing collaborator in wonder (thanks to Rachel Berwick and Jocelyne Prince for working with Demetrius Oliver); the SETI Institute (especially Bill Diamond, Jill Tarter, and Laurance Doyle) and NASA Ames Research Center (Glenn Bougos) have supported Charles Lindsay, Dario Robleto, Rachel Sussman, and Jen Bervin; Roomful of Teeth and Bob Bielecki helped to make Julianne Swartz's new sound work possible; Nate Russell for help with Jason de Hann; Institute For Figuring's origami works were folded by Christina Simmons, Jacob

Dotson, and Margaret Wertheim, with business card design by Cindi Kusuda and Margaret Wertheim; and Hans and Kate Morris and Lauren Bon/The Metabolic Studio provided great hosting in San Francisco and Los Angeles.

Additionally, Hope Ginsburg's project was made possible by support from Temple Contemporary (Robert Blackson, Sarah Biemiller), VCUarts Department of Photography (Sasha Waters Freyer, Jon-Phillip Sheridan), VCUarts Art Foundation Program (Elissa Armstrong, Christine Costello), the Film and Video Studio Program at the Wexner Center for the Arts (Bill Horrigan, Jennifer Lang and Mike Olenick), Janice Wright Cheney, Sophia Bartholomew, COJO Diving (Connie Bishop and Joe George), and The Dive Shop, Richmond, Virginia (Jim McNeal). Charles Lindsay's work was made possible with the help of Adam Harvey, Wayne Campbell, Jennifer Gately, RCA Morse Code engineers Richard Dillman and Steve Hawes, Mark Farris, Steven Brower, Jack Kalish, Steen Sorensen, and the Human Condition Labs (Peter Raymond, Sergey Vikhlyanstev, Ryan Dobbins, Sanniti Pimpley, and Laura Schwamb).

The following galleries and artist studios have been extremely helpful: Justin Kemp and Matt Lenke at Tom Friedman's studio, Stacie Martinez at Christopher Grimes Gallery, Camille and Pauline at Laurent Grasso's studio, Jennifer Cohen and Ann Stenne at Pierre Huyghe's studio, Christina Simmons and Anna Mayer at Institute For Figuring, Clint Roenisch Gallery, Sean Kelly Gallery, Galerie Perrotin, Catharine Clark Gallery, Inman Gallery, James Cohan Gallery, Marian Goodman Gallery, Esther Schipper, and Hosfelt Gallery. And thank you to the lenders: The New York Public Library's Spencer Collection, Newberry Public Library, Chicago, Robert and Anne Conn, Tom Peters, Bronya and Andrew Galef, and James Keith Brown and Eric Diefenbach.

This book and exhibition would not exist without the amazing artists and writers featured within. Thank you for filling the world with wonder and taking to heart what it means to present that to an audience. It is a great honor that you took this challenge so seriously and provided personal and vulnerable responses to share with our viewers and readers. A special thank you goes to Lawrence Weschler—not only did he introduce us to many of the included artists and provide a great and insightful interview, but his very being, his continual quest to see the world through wide eyes, was the ultimate inspiration for both this exhibition and book. We can only hope that, when he receives this volume, he will say to those around him, in his enthusiastic way, "You're going to want to see this" or "Is that cool or what!?!"—both Weschler seals of approval!

This exhibition is supported by the National Endowment for the Arts, the Artist's Resource Trust of the Berkshire Taconic Community Foundation, the Horace W. Goldsmith Foundation, the Barr Foundation, the Massachusetts Cultural Council, and Debbie Landau.

Sean Foley would like to thank The Columbus Museum of Art; Laura Lisbon and Sergio Soave at The Ohio State University; Nancy Andrews, Jodi Baker, Catherine Clinger, Dru Colbert, Darron Collins, Jay Friedlander, Sarah Hall, Ken Hill, Isabel Mancinelli, and Karen Waldron at College of the Atlantic. Thanks also to Katie Bullock, Wilmont M. Schwind and Arlene Palmer Schwind, Linda and Richard Meyers, Julia and Eric Hinten, and Molly and Lloyd LaBadie, Christina Bussmann, Mark Dion, Casey Foley, Pat Foley, Alison Hildreth, Bill Horrigan, Ellen Lesperance, Matt Majesky, Angela Meleca, Perry Mostov, Lawrence Needleman, George Smith, Chris Thompson, and Peter Zaferidies.

Foley extends special thanks for the support of his family: his mother Susan E. Foley, his wife Cindy Meyers Foley, and his children, Emmett and Adeline, who are constant sources of wonder. Lastly, he wishes to thank his father, T. Michael Foley, and dedicate this book to him, "You sacrificed so much so that I might live comfortably in wonder. I miss you."

Denise Markonish adds, "I would like to thank Robert Szulkin, with whom I wish I could have shared this book, and who made me the thinker that I am today, and D, the wonder tether that holds this project together, for which I will always feel grateful and inspired."

All images courtesy of the artist unless noted below

cover: Lakehurst, NJ, inspecting prototype of Echo II communications satellite, 1963; image courtesy of a private collection (AP wire image)

endpapers: Young and Old Stars Found in Andromeda's Halo, Hubble Space Telescope, 2002–3; image courtesy of NASA, ESA, and T.M. Brown (STScl)

pp. 14–15, 18, 132: photos by Nooshig Varjabedian

p. 27: photo by Denise Markonish

p. 33: public domain

p. 35: Newberry Public Library, Chicago, IL

p. 36: private collection, New York

p. 53: Creative Commons, Wellcome Library, London

p. 56: photo by Scott Lindgren

p. 64: this work is in the public domain in the United States because it is a work prepared by an officer or employee of the United States Government as part of that person's official duties under the terms of Title 17, Chapter 1, Section 105 of the US Code

p. 65: photo by Robert Wedemeyer

pp. 73, 78, 80: photos by Sean Foley

p. 75: Henri-Cartier Bresson/Magnum Photos

pp. 22–23, 94–98, 102–103, 104 (bottom), 110 (left), 124–125, 154, 168–171, 228–230, 252–253, 264–265, 268, 276–277, 278 (top), 279–280: photos by Tony Luong

pp. 118–122: photos by Joshua White/jwpictures.com

p. 126: photo by Camron Allan

p. 128: top photo by Margaret Wertheim; middle and bottom photos by Christina Simons; all © Institute For Figuring

pp. 140–141: private collection, New York

pp. 156, 157, 160: photos by Jason Wyche; ©Laurent Grasso/ADAGP

p. 167: photo ©Paul Williams and a photogenic world, 2011–2016, aphotogenicworld.wordpress.com

p. 184: courtesy of The Estate of Birgir Andrésson & i8 Gallery, Reykjavik (fig. 1); photo by dronepicr on Flickr (fig. 2)

p. 185: Jason Gallicchio, South Pole Telescope, Winterover, 2013

pp. 201–209: photos by Sam Green

p. 210, 214: video stills and photos by Charlotte Lagarde

pp. 222–225: photos by Eric Swanson

pp. 240–244: photos by Scott Lindgren

p. 270: photo by Guillaume Ziccarelli

p. 271: photo by Hyla Skopitz, The Photograph Studio, The Metropolitan Museum of Art

pp. 272–274: photos by Andrea Rossetti

The publisher has made every effort to trace the photographers and copyright holders, and we apologize in advance for any unintentional omission, and would be pleased to insert the appropriate acknowledgment in any subsequent edition.

Published on the occasion of *Explode Every Day:
An Inquiry into the Phenomena of Wonder*
Curated by Denise Markonish with Sean Foley
May 28, 2016–April 2, 2017

MASS MoCA
1040 MASS MoCA Way
North Adams, MA 01247
413.662.2111
massmoca.org

Funding is generously provided by the National
Endowment for the Arts, the Artist's Resource Trust
of the Berkshire Taconic Community Foundation,
the Horace W. Goldsmith Foundation, the Barr
Foundation, the Massachusetts Cultural Council,
and Debbie Landau.

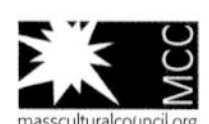

Published by MASS MoCA
and DelMonico Books • Prestel

DelMonico Books, an imprint of Prestel Publishing,
a member of Verlagsgruppe Random House GmbH

Prestel Verlag
Neumarkter Strasse 28
81673 Munich

Prestel Publishing Ltd.
14-17 Wells Street
London W1T 3PD

Prestel Publishing
900 Broadway, Suite 603
New York, NY 10003

prestel.com

Editor: Denise Markonish
Copy editing: L. Jane Calverley
Proofreading: Paulette Wein
Production coordinator: Luke Chase,
    DelMonico Books • Prestel
Design: Brett Yasko

Printed and bound in China

ISBN 978-3-7913-5565-8

Library of Congress Control Number:
2016908288